Judith;
Wage Peace!

Guys Like Me

Also by Michael A. Messner

Author

It's All for the Kids: Gender, Families, and Youth Sports
King of the Wild Suburb: A Memoir of Fathers, Sons and Guns
Out of Play: Critical Essays on Gender and Sport
Politics of Masculinities: Men in Movements
Power at Play: Sports and the Problem of Masculinity
Taking the Field: Women, Men, and Sports

Coauthor

No Slam Dunk: Gender, Sport, and the Unevenness of Social Change
Sex, Violence and Power in Sports: Rethinking Masculinity
*Some Men: Feminist Allies and the Movement
to End Violence against Women*

Editor

Sport, Gender and Sexuality: Critical Concepts in Sports Studies

Coeditor

Child's Play: Sport in Kids' Worlds
Gender Reckonings: New Social Theory and Research
Masculinities, Gender Relations, and Sport
Men's Lives
Paradoxes of Youth and Sport
Sport, Men, and the Gender Order: Critical Feminist Perspectives
Gender Through the Prism of Difference

Guys Like Me

Five Wars, Five Veterans for Peace

MICHAEL A. MESSNER

RUTGERS UNIVERSITY PRESS
NEW BRUNSWICK, CAMDEN, AND NEWARK,
NEW JERSEY, AND LONDON

Library of Congress Cataloging-in-Publication Data

Names: Messner, Michael A., author.
Title: Guys like me : five wars, five veterans for peace / Michael A. Messner.
Description: New Brunswick : Rutgers University Press, [2018] | Includes
    bibliographical references and index.
Identifiers: LCCN 2018012690| ISBN 9781978802810 (cloth) | ISBN 9781978802827 (pbk.)
Subjects: LCSH: Veterans—United States—Biography. | Veterans—United
    States—Attitudes. | Peace movements—United States.
Classification: LCC U52 .M48 2018 | DDC 303.6/6092273—dc23
    LC record available at https://lccn.loc.gov/2018012690

A British Cataloging-in-Publication record for this book is available from the British
Library.

www.rutgersuniversitypress.org

Manufactured in the United States of America

For all veterans of wars—past, present, and of all nations—who work for peace and justice in their communities and in the world

Contents

If peace begins with the individual, it is realized collectively with peace movements, for peace is not simply a matter of praying or hoping, although they, like dreaming, do not hurt. Instead, peace happens through confronting the war machine and taking over the industries that make it possible, which include the industries of memory. It is no surprise, then, that peace seems so much harder to achieve than war, which offers us an immediate profit.

—Viet Thanh Nguyen, Nothing Ever Dies

Prologue

My grandfather, Russell John Messner, became especially grumpy around Veterans Day.[1] I never understood why. In 1918, as a twenty-two-year-old working-class kid with an eighth-grade education, he was yanked out of the copper mines in the Upper Peninsula of Northern Michigan, handed a rifle, and sent for ten grueling months to the frozen tundra of northern Russia, where he fought with the U.S. Army's 301st Engineers. I knew Gramps didn't much like to talk about his World War I experiences, and I also knew that for several decades he'd been an active member of the Veterans of Foreign Wars (VFW). Every Memorial Day, he and Granny handed out VFW Buddy Poppies for small donations to support disabled and needy vets.[2] I would donate a dime and pin my Buddy Poppy on my T-shirt, putting on display the pride I felt for my grandfather, my father (a World War II veteran), and others who had served in times of war.

On the morning of Veterans Day in 1980, Gramps sat with his breakfast—a cup of watery coffee, a piece of burnt toast slathered with marmalade, and a single slice of cool liverwurst. A twenty-eight-year-old graduate student, I'd recently moved in with my grandparents in their Oakland, California, home. I tried to cut through Gramps's cranky mood by wishing him a happy Veterans Day. Huge Mistake. "*Veterans* Day!" he barked at me with the gravelly voice of a lifelong smoker. "It's not *Veterans*

Day! It's *Armistice* Day. Those gawd . . . damned . . . *politicians* . . . *changed* it to Veterans Day. And they keep getting us into more wars."

My grandfather was hyperventilating now, his liverwurst forgotten. "Buncha *crooks*! *They* don't fight the wars, ya know. *Guys like me* fight the wars. We called it the 'War to End All Wars,' and we *believed* it." He closed the conversation with a harrumph: "*Veterans* Day!"

The Armistice had been signed on the eleventh hour of the eleventh day of the eleventh month of 1918, but Private Messner was one of the unlucky doughboys who had to remain in northern Russia six months longer, as part of a counterrevolutionary U.S.-British force that tried—and failed—to defeat the Soviet Red Army. In the years following his return home, Armistice Day symbolized to Gramps not just the end of his war, but the end of all war, the dawning of a lasting peace. This was not an idle dream. In fact, a mass movement for peace had pressed the U.S. government, in 1928, to sign the Kellogg-Briand Pact, an international "Treaty for the Renunciation of War," sponsored by the United States and France and subsequently signed by most nations of the world.[3] When President Dwight D. Eisenhower signed the law changing the name of the holiday to Veterans Day, to include veterans of World War II, it was a slap in the face for my grandfather. Hope evaporated, replaced with the ugly reality that politicians would continue to find reasons to send American boys— "guys like me"—to fight and die in wars.[4]

When I was a little boy in the late 1950s and early 1960s, I would occasionally pry a story from Gramps about the Great War. But like many veterans of his generation, he was reluctant to talk about it. Mostly I had to read between the lines to get much information, and the artifacts he pulled out of his gun cabinet offered me tantalizing glimpses. A small scrap of paper, signed by a British officer, read: "Transport Officer: Please supply bearer with 3 sleighs for the purpose of moving material to burn Kitza 10:III:19." The sleighs, Gramps told me, were pulled by reindeer across snow and frozen lakes, and were loaded with canisters of gasoline that were used to burn down the Russian town of Kitza as the U.S. troops retreated.

Pvt. Russell J. Messner, 1918 (author)

Nearly breathless with excitement, I asked my grandfather, "Did you ever kill anyone in the war?" He snorted disapprovingly at the question, paused, and then told me a seemingly unrelated story: "We had no running water, and one night I woke up so thirsty. So I got up and drank from a puddle of rainwater in the middle of a dirt road. The next morning, in the daylight, I saw that the puddle had a big pile of horse manure in it." I wanted more, but I think he knew that I attached a false sense of glory and excitement to war—a common perspective for boys like me who cut our teeth watching John Wayne movies and playing fantasy war games with our friends on suburban lawns, spraying "Krauts" or "Japs" with imaginary bullets from plastic burp guns before heading inside for a pitcher of ice-cold cherry Kool-Aid prepared by Mom. There was nothing glorious about war for Gramps; war was freezing your ass off, drinking water with horseshit in it, and praying every day to escape the nightmare and get back home safely. The rest, I guess, was unspeakable, except in coded snapshots couched in dark humor.

When I was in college in the early 1970s, I became one of millions of people who opposed the American War in Vietnam.[5] I had learned not to talk about it with my father. A World War II veteran, still serving as a captain in the Naval Reserve, he had no patience for the antiwar movement: "There are some dirty jobs out there, and somebody has to do them," was his retort to anyone who opposed the war. I once hinted about my antiwar sentiments to Gramps, and he hit me with a big surprise: "Did you know the VFW was antiwar in the 1930s?" "No way," I stammered. As Europe was once again plunging into war, Gramps told me, his VFW and other veterans organizations were urging the United States to stay out of the conflict, to remain neutral. "Look at this," he said, as he pulled from his gun cabinet a single magazine page glued to a thin sheet of cardboard, its ragged edges obscuring some of the document's opening lines. It was a Memorial Day 1937 VFW position paper on war and peace. It presented evidence that the U.S. government had joined the fighting in World War I partly out of the pursuit of profit for rich industrialists. It declared, "The Veterans of Foreign Wars of the United States was the first veteran organization to

● PRIOR to 1929, ̶ ̶ ̶ ̶ ̶ ̶ ̶ ̶ ̶ ̶ ̶ ̶ ̶ was viewed by most Americans ̶ ̶ ̶ ̶ an impractical ideal being fostered by fanatics whose Utopian ambitions were beyond the comprehension of the average man. Then came the depression with its widespread sufferings, creating a bitterness that gave birth to a demand for deliverance from war and its penalties.

The old style pacifist, who demanded complete disarmament by the United States, and all other nations, as a means of ridding the earth of the scourge of war, was shoved out of the peace spotlight. He was supplanted by leaders in every walk of life, including many military figures, converted to the belief that peace can be achieved—at least for America—if certain sane and practical policies are adopted.

In 1934 this trend of thinking was stimulated by the results of a Senate investigation of the munitions industry, a probe which revealed startling evidence of graft, enormous profits and outrageous diplomatic connivance. The citizens of this country were shocked into a realization that war motives are not always inspired by pure patriotism and lofty ideals. For example, the message sent by Ambassador Walter Hines Page to President Wilson in March, 1917, is particularly to the point. It reads as follows:

QUOTE "If we should go to war with Germany all the money (gold from trans-Atlantic trade) would be kept in our country; trade would be continued and enlarged until war ends, and after the war Europe would continue to buy food from us, as well as an enormous supply of things to re-equip for peace industries. Perhaps our going to war is the only way we can maintain our pre-eminent trade position and avert a panic." End Quote

This blunt confession that profits played a dominant role in America's decision to participate in the World War has contributed greatly to the disillusionment of the American public on the subject of war in general. Moreover, Hitler, Mussolini and Stalin have proved the world was not made safe for democracy when the Armistice was signed in 1918. Europe's repudiation of its debts to America, the realignment of European powers in the struggle for supremacy, and the obvious lack of gratitude on the part of the Allies, have also convinced the American people that strict neutrality must be our only policy in the future.

The Veterans of Foreign ̶ ̶ ̶ ̶ ̶ ̶ ̶ ̶ ̶ ̶ ̶ United States was the first veteran organization to incorporate a militant demand for neutrality in its national program. The goal of "Peace-for-America," through the adoption of various proposed legislative measures, has become one of the chief objectives of the V.F.W. Happily this organization has been joined by other groups. Today public sentiment in favor of a mandatory neutrality policy is at its peak.

The approach of Memorial Day, 1937, finds Congress contemplating legislation designed to guard against conditions that might otherwise force the United States to become involved in a war between other foreign powers. But today, the menace of indecision, and unending harangue, threatens to thwart the objectives of such legislation if public interest is permitted to wane. The biggest stumbling block with which we are confronted today is the grave danger the gradual return of prosperity to America may act as an anesthetic. Good times, like a dose of ether, can easily make the people forget the tremendous costs of the last war and the privations of the resultant economic upheaval.

The danger of inaction can be offset only if the citizens of this country will continue to impress members of Congress with demands for favorable action without further delay. Letters and resolutions, urging early adoption of neutrality legislation, will force Congress to act. Every member of the Veterans of Foreign Wars of the United States, as well as all patriotic, clear-thinking citizens, is duty bound to help promote a deluge of communications that will convince Congress the public demand for continued peace stands unchanged.

As veterans, we have observed each Memorial Day, since 1918, with a solemn pledge that the sacrifices of our hero dead were not made in vain. Our opportunity to further the cause of neutrality for the United States gives us a chance to endow Memorial Day, in the future, with a new significance. If we, both as veterans and as citizens, can contribute in any way toward early enactment of neutrality legislation that will protect our boys and girls of tomorrow against the depravity of war in the future, our pledges will be adequately fulfilled and our promises will prove to be something more than fancy phrases inspired by emotional ceremonies and oratorical bombast.

VFW "Peace for America" statement for Memorial Day 1937 (author)

pressure the U.S. Congress to stick to the VFW platform of 'Peace for America.'" World War I veterans were urged to lead the country in making "a solemn pledge that the sacrifices of our hero dead were not made in vain." My grandfather's penciled edits remained on the page from the day he read the statement aloud at a Memorial Day VFW meeting.

The history of World War II that I'd learned in school and seen in the movies was of a country fully united against fascism, with the exception perhaps of a handful of unpatriotic anarchists who were swept aside and thrown in jail. No one mentioned that one of the most patriotic organizations in the nation—the VFW—had actively opposed U.S. entry into the war. Nor had anyone taught me that during the run-up to World War II, in the words of historian John Bodnar, "Pacifism and isolationism—so strange to Americans today—actually commanded considerable support in the 1930s and were tied to the public memory of the last war."[6] The fact that my grandfather had saved this mounted page declaring his organization's commitment to peace and neutrality shows how deep his feelings were. And it wasn't only politics and personal betrayal underlying Gramps's antiwar stance; this was a deeply personal matter as well. With a teenaged son (my dad) at home, he told me years later, he prayed that his country would not once again go to war.

World War I, I began to learn, like subsequent wars, incubated a generation of veterans committed to preventing such future horrors for their sons. From working-class army combat veterans like my grandfather to retired generals like Smedley Butler—who wrote and delivered public speeches arguing that "war is a racket," benefiting only the economic interests of ruling class industrialists—World War I veterans spoke out to prevent future wars,[7] and veterans of subsequent wars continue speaking out today.

This book is a response to a question that has poked at me for years: How is it that peace advocacy among military veterans, past and current, is so little known? I decided to conduct life history interviews with a small number of veterans who became lifelong advocates for peace, gathering the full picture of each interviewee's life to convey, hopefully, what it's like to *be* him or her. What did they experience, and how did they change, before and after enduring the hell of war? I've included one man from each major war stretching from World War II, through the Korean War, the American War in Vietnam, the Gulf War, and the recent ongoing wars in Iraq and Afghanistan. I introduce readers to Ernie "Indio" Sanchez, a World War II Army veteran—wounded with shrapnel and perhaps even more deeply with shame for the scores of Germans he killed—and his late-life turn to peace advocacy; Wilson "Woody" Powell, Air Force veteran of the Korean War who rose to national leadership in Veterans for Peace (VFP) and distinguished himself as a model for reconciliation with former enemies; Gregory Ross, Navy veteran of the War in Vietnam, poet, and peace activist; Army veteran of the Gulf War Daniel Craig, who continues to convert his anger over having killed people for what he now sees as lies to spiritual healing and peace activism; and Jonathan Hutto Sr., Navy veteran of the Iraq War whose antiwar work is but a piece of his broader commitment to opposing racism and promoting social justice in his community and his nation.

In writing this book, I sought to make these veterans' stories more publicly visible and to better understand how these individuals eventually overcame "manly silence"—the all-too-common tendency for veterans to stuff inside and cordon off their memories of war, their silence robbing themselves of emotional and moral healing, just as it deprives future generations the opportunity to hear the voices of veterans passionately opposed to future wars and learn about the inglorious realities of war. I also wanted to grasp how war veterans, once they commit themselves to a project of public peace advocacy, strategize to collectively contest the ways that past wars are remembered. The stories these and other veterans told me, along with my participation in recent years with VFP, have impressed me with the many ways the organization contests taken-for-granted, normalized views of history. For instance, in 2016 and 2017, VFP members prepared for the fiftieth anniversary of the My Lai Massacre, when U.S. soldiers slaughtered 504 civilians in a Vietnamese hamlet, the majority of them women and children, by disseminating their stories about the 1968 atrocity. This VFP effort was intended to counter what they saw as the Pentagon's "sanitized" version of the horrendous massacre that, when revealed by journalist Seymour Hersh in the *New York Times*, helped turn U.S. public opinion against the war.[8]

So too, in late 2017, during the release of Ken Burns's highly acclaimed and well-publicized PBS documentary on the Vietnam War, the VFP was active nationally and in local chapters presenting public panels and distributing *Full Disclosure*, an impressive twenty-eight-page document that billed itself as revealing "truth about America's War in Vietnam." For the VFP, this contest of memory and meanings of a war fought a half century ago is not simply about setting the record straight. The stakes are far higher than that. *Full Disclosure* is an effort to present an "alternative to the Department of Defense's efforts to sanitize and mythologize the U.S. role in the war, which legitimizes further unnecessary and destructive wars."[9]

The United States' defeat in Vietnam continues to be the quintessential terrain of contested memories and meanings. But it's not the only war about which veterans contest the dominant narrative. There have been six U.S. presidents since my grandfather's death in early 1981—Presidents Ronald Reagan, George H. W. Bush, Bill Clinton, George W. Bush, Barack Obama, and Donald Trump—and each has in one way or another committed U.S. military forces to overt or covert wars around the world. Most recently, when Trump ran for president in 2016 on a platform of "rebuilding" the American military, he promised that if elected he would defeat the Islamic State of Iraq and Syria (ISIS) "so fast it will make your head spin." As I write this prologue a year after Trump's inauguration as forty-fifth president of the United States, ISIS still stands, and Donald Trump has spun heads with his request for massive increases in the military budget— already larger than those of the five next-largest powers in the world combined; ordering the dropping in Afghanistan of the largest nonnuclear bomb ever deployed in warfare; enthusiastically continuing active drone warfare; and threatening Venezuela with military attack and North Korea with "fire and fury the likes of which the world has never seen."

Trump's predecessor, Barack Obama, was not nearly as bombastic, but during his eight years in office, the forty-fourth president did little to earn the Nobel Peace Prize that was bestowed upon him as he took office, apparently as a hopeful down payment on his bringing peace to the Middle East. Obama slowed the wars in Iraq and Afghanistan, partly by shifting from "boots on the ground" to drone warfare—a strategy that allows the

United States to target individuals and groups deemed "terrorists" and in the process killing many civilians mistakenly identified by the eyes in the sky as enemy combatants or who just happened to be in the wrong place at the wrong time. A major domestic outcome of the shift to drone warfare has been that far fewer American lives are put at risk, which allows the United States to wage wars that are less visible to the public, defusing antiwar sentiment.

Were he alive today, Gramps would surely express righteous indignation that American leaders continue to send the young to fight and die in wars throughout the world. He did live to see the final nail in the coffin of the hope for a "war to end all wars" when Congress renamed Armistice Day in 1954 as Veterans Day, an explicit acknowledgment that the United States had fought two more wars since World War I, including the just-completed stalemate in Korea. Still, I like to imagine my grandfather smiling had he lived to witness what I've seen the past two years on November 11 in Santa Fe: In the New Mexico state capital's annual Veterans Day Parade a lively contingent of VFP marching with a large banner that reads, "Observe Armistice Day, Wage Peace!"

The stories I share in this book begin in the mid-twentieth century with the run-up to World War II, stretching through subsequent wars up to the present. Each chapter focuses on an individual who fought in one of these wars. No one can, of course, represent the diversity of experiences of the millions of individuals who served, nor can one person's story represent the thousands of veterans from each war who became advocates for peace. But instead of being struck by the differences among this small group of men I got to know so intimately, I was impressed with what linked them. All the veterans struggled during the years and decades following their wars to come to grips with what had been done to them, and with what they had done to others. Eventually each veteran's story coalesced through his having embraced a life project that included varying combinations of personal healing, service to others, peace activism, and reconciliation with former enemies.

Veterans Day Parade, Santa Fe, NM, November 11, 2016 (author)

The individual veterans' stories I tell in this book are not simply inter-woven thematically. Most of them are members of an intergenerational organization, VFP, a central tenet of which is that the wars of the past century are not a series of discrete interruptions of an otherwise normal peacetime, but interconnected and institutionalized strategies of a govern-ment joined at the hip with industry to maintain a position of American economic and political dominance. The costs of this ongoing strategy of domination are paid for by the generations of soldiers sent to fight and die—"guys like me," as my grandfather put it—and by the citizens, often civilians, of the nations the United States bombs, invades, and occupies.

These veterans' stories reveal not just a shared critical perspective on the roots and consequences of war, but also overlapping narratives that stretch through and across from one war to the next: As Ernie Sanchez was mowing down German soldiers with his Browning Automatic Rifle in Ger-many, young Woody Powell was scanning the California skies for Japanese bombers and dreaming he would one day have a chance to fight in a war;

as Korean War vet Powell was self-medicating with alcohol in the late 1960s, the big guns on Gregory Ross's ship were roaring 24/7 as they bombarded the coast of Vietnam; as veteran Ross was writing poetry, caring for others, and engaging in peace activism to seek personal absolution and recovery from guilt and depression, young Daniel Craig was in a tiny northern New Mexico town dreaming of military glory and honor; as Craig's artillery unit rolled into Iraq with Operation Desert Storm, young Jonathan Hutto was learning his first lessons about racial justice in his home town of Atlanta; as Hutto watched jet fighters roar from his aircraft carrier to bomb targets in Iraq, World War II vet Sanchez awoke to long-slumbering symptoms of post-traumatic stress disorder, and Powell, Craig, and Ross leaped into the swelling antiwar activities of VFP.

The stories I tell of veterans of different wars and generations illuminate what sociologist C. Wright Mills identified as the interrelationship between individuals and society, between biography and history.[10] As young draftees and recruits sent off to wars they barely understood, these men's lives illustrate the ways historical events and powerful institutions buffet individual people about like ping-pong balls in a lottery machine; the lucky ones getting to come home alive, albeit emotionally battered and often physically wounded. But these veterans' stories also reveal another dimension of the relationship between biography and history: when individuals gather with others, develop a critical understanding of their youthful roles in wars, they learn to see themselves not simply as objects manipulated by an all-powerful system, but as individuals with critical stories to tell. And in the process, they become active subjects, veterans for peace who embrace and exercise their responsibilities as citizens to make and rewrite history.

War is a racket. It always has been. It is possibly the oldest, easily the most profitable, surely the most vicious. It is the only one international in scope. It is the only one in which the profits are reckoned in dollars and the losses in lives.

—Brig. Gen. Smedley D. Butler, *War Is a Racket*

-⫸⫷◆⫸⫷-

CHAPTER 1

Projects of Peace

If I step outside the door of my home in South Pasadena at just the right time on New Year's Day, I stand a chance of witnessing the tail end of a B-2 stealth bomber's flyover of the nearby Rose Bowl. A neighbor who viewed this spectacle gushed to me that the low-flying bomber was "just the coolest thing ever." I agreed that seeing the bat-like stealth bomber so close up was awe-inspiring, but wondered aloud why we need to start a football game by celebrating a $2 billion machine that has dropped bombs on Kosovo, Afghanistan, Iraq, and Libya. When I suggested that the flyover, to me, was yet another troubling instance of the militarization of everyday life, my neighbor replied that, well, perhaps it was thanks to such sophisticated war machines that we are now enjoying a long period of peace. I reminded him that we are still fighting a war in Afghanistan, that we have troops still in Iraq, and that even this past fall, four U.S. Special Forces soldiers died in battle in Niger. It may feel like peace to many of us at home, but for U.S. troops, and for people on the receiving end of U.S. bombs, drone missile strikes, and extended ground occupations, it must feel like permanent war.

War Is Both Everywhere and Nowhere

The fact that my neighbor and I talked past one another should come as no surprise. For most Americans today, war is both everywhere and nowhere. On the one hand, it seems omnipresent. Politicians continually raise fears among the citizenry, insisting that we pony up huge proportions of our nation's financial and human capital to fight a borderless and apparently endless "Global War on Terror." We're inundated with war imagery—an unending stream of films and TV shows depicting past and current wars,[1] pageantry like the Rose Bowl flyover, and celebrations of the military in sports programming exploit sports to recruit the next generation of soldiers.[2] The result, according to social scientist Adam Rugg, is "a diffused military presence" in everyday life.[3]

Following the American invasions of Afghanistan and Iraq in 2001 and 2003, U.S. wars in the Middle East have continued to rage, spilling over national borders and introducing new and troubling questions about modern warfare. Though scaled back since the initial invasions, these wars continue. Through fiscal year 2018, the financial cost of our "Post-9/11 Wars" has surpassed $1.8 trillion, and Brown University's Costs of War Project puts that number at $5.6 trillion, taking into account interest on borrowed money to pay for these wars and estimates of "future obligations" in caring for medical needs of veterans.[4] The human toll has been even costlier. By mid-2016, 6,860 U.S. military personnel had been killed in the Global War on Terror, and more than 52,000 had been wounded.[5] Most of these have been young men. Through the end of 2014, 391,759 military veterans had been treated in Veterans Affairs (VA) facilities for "potential or provisional Post Traumatic Stress Disorder (PTSD)" following their return from Afghanistan or Iraq.[6] It's difficult to accurately measure the carnage inflicted on the populations of Iraq, Afghanistan, and Pakistan, but the Costs of War Project estimates that between 2001 and 2016 more than 109,000 "opposition fighters" and over 200,000 civilians have been directly killed, and 800,000 more "have died as an indirect result of the wars."[7]

Military conscription was halted in the United States in 1973, a direct legacy of the mass movement that helped to end the war in Vietnam. With no draft in place, the military shifted to an all-volunteer force that required intensifying recruitment strategies, especially in times of escalating wars. During the Iraq and Afghanistan Wars, the volunteer military faced dire personnel shortages that led to multiple redeployments, placing huge burdens on military personnel and their families.[8] Two years into the Iraq War, U.S. military desertions were on the rise, and "recruiters were consistently failing to meet monthly enlistment quotas, despite deep penetration into high schools, sponsorship of NASCAR and other sporting events, and a \$3-billion Pentagon recruitment budget."[9] In response, the military stepped up recruitment ads on TV and in movie theatres, and launched direct recruitment efforts in American high schools and community colleges.[10] The American high school, faced with increased recruiting efforts and opposition from parents and others, became, in education scholar William Ayers's words, "a battlefield for hearts and minds."[11]

Since 9/11 the military seems omnipresent and a state of war permanent, while paradoxically, the vast majority of Americans feel untouched by it all. Disconnected from the wars, we go about our daily lives as though we're living in a period of extended peace. For most of us, war is nowhere. How is this Orwellian situation tolerable, or even possible? Following America's defeat in Vietnam, the government has engaged in a carefully controlled, public-relations framing of news of all wars and invasions, containing contrary views that could emerge from critical investigative reporting.[12] Examples include "embedding" reporters with U.S. troops during the invasion of Iraq and prohibiting the news media from filming or photographing flag-draped coffins being unloaded from military transport planes.

Another reason most people experience these omnipresent wars as "nowhere" lies in the shifting nature of warfare. Today, the military can deploy new technologies to minimize the number of U.S. casualties while maximizing the carnage of those designated as terrorists, enemies, or targets. The normalization of drone strikes—escalated by President Barack Obama and expanded by President Donald Trump—is the epitome of this "out of sight, out of mind" warfare. As the United States deploys drone strikes, war becomes "unilateral . . . a kind of permanent, low-level military action that threatens to erase the boundary between war and peace and . . . makes it easier for the United States to engage in casualty-free, and therefore debate-free, intervention while further militarizing the relationship between the US and the Muslim world," according to anthropologist Hugh Gusterson.[13]

Another reason for the electorate's distance from current wars is the vast divide between civilians and the military. Only half of 1 percent of the population is in the military, the lowest rate since between the world wars. *Los Angeles Times* reporters David Zucchino and David Cloud also note that Congress today has the lowest rate of military service in history, and four successive presidents have never served on active duty.[14] As many as 80 percent of those in the military come from families in which a parent or a sibling is also in the military. Military personnel often live behind the gates of installations or in surrounding communities. This segregation is so pronounced that nearly half of the 1.3 million active-duty service members in the United States are concentrated in five states: California, Virginia, Texas, North Carolina, and Georgia. In short, Zucchino and Cloud conclude, the U.S. military is becoming a separate and isolated warrior class. With no draft in place, large proportions of the population, especially those from the privileged classes, are increasingly insulated from the experience and realities of military service and war.

Veterans are symbolically made visible through "Support the Troops" celebrations and political oratory, but the voices of actual veterans who have fought our wars are mostly under the radar. And even less audible are the voices of vets who advocate for peace. I wrote this book because I believe it's more important than ever for us to listen to the voices of veterans for peace, those who have been there and recovered sufficiently (no easy task) to inform us how traumatically devastating and morally compromising it is to be an instrument of America's military-industrial geopolitics. This book highlights the life stories of five veterans whose experiences spanned five wars: World War II, the Korean War, the war in Vietnam, the Gulf War, and the recent and continuing wars in the Middle East. Why is this legacy of peace advocacy by military veterans so little known?

MANLY SILENCE

Part of the reason many Americans do not know the true costs of war, I believe, is due to a phenomenon I've come to call "manly silence," like my grandfather's reluctance to talk about his World War I experiences or about his opposition to future wars. Every war births a new generation of veterans who live out their lives with the trauma of combat embedded their bodies and minds, but many remain silent about their experiences. That was certainly my father's modus operandi after World War II, and even my grandfather's predominant way of dealing with his experiences in World War I.

How do we understand so many men's silence about what they endured, not only that of the millions of combatants of the two world wars, but also that of combat veterans today? Although women fight shoulder to shoulder with men today, and perhaps this phenomenon of manly silence will slowly change, the military is still a place governed by rigid and narrow conceptions of masculinity, a key aspect of which is keeping a stiff upper lip. One common refrain among war veterans is that it makes no sense to talk of such things because only someone who was there can truly understand their experience. Only veterans who endured the same traumas, witnessed similar horrors, or committed comparable acts of brutality are worth opening to. Otherwise silence, often accompanied by self-medication and other efforts at dissociating oneself from these traumas, prevails.

The foundation for this kind of emotional fortification rests on narrow definitions of masculinity, often internalized at an early age and then enforced and celebrated in masculinist institutions like the military. But rigid masculinity is not confined to the military; it's more general. Research by psychologist Joseph Schwab and his colleagues showed that men routinely respond to stressful life experiences by avoiding emotional disclosure that they fear might make them appear vulnerable.[15] Silence, the researchers concluded, is the logical outcome of internalized rules of masculinity: a real man is admired and rewarded for staying strong and stoic during times of adversity.

Who benefits from this manly silence? Certainly institutions like the military that instill and then rely on men's private endurance of pain, fear, and trauma. But individual men (and women) rarely benefit from such taciturnity. Trying to live up to this narrow ideal of masculinity comes with severe costs for men's physical health, emotional well-being, and relationships.[16] Researchers and medical practitioners have compiled long lists of the costs men pay for adhering to narrow definitions of masculinity: undiagnosed depression;[17] alcoholism, heart disease, and risk-taking that translate into shorter lifespans;[18] fear of emotional self-disclosure and suppressed access to empathy, resulting in barriers to intimacy.[19]

A 2015 study of 1.3 million veterans who served during the Iraq and Afghanistan Wars showed suicide rates twice that of nonveterans.[20] The *New York Times* reported in 2009 escalating rates of rape, sexual assault, domestic violence, and homicide committed by men who had returned from multiple deployments to the war in Iraq.[21] PTSD impedes—often severely, and sometimes for the rest of one's life—veterans' reentry into civilian life, and thus their development of healthy, productive, and happy postwar and postmilitary lives. A combat veteran of the Vietnam War told me, "PTSD? It don't ever go away." For the men I interviewed, PTSD was a lifelong challenge that—after in some cases years of denial, struggle, alcoholism, and medical care—eventually served as an impetus to do something healthy, positive, and peaceful with their lives.

During World War I, military leaders and medical experts were concerned with the growing problem of "shell shock" among troops subjected to the horrors of trench warfare. Little understood at the time was the emotional impact of modern warfare's growing efficiency—with machine guns, volleys of artillery fire, or strafing from low-flying planes—in maiming and massacring hundreds, even thousands in a very short time. Leo Braudy argues that by World War I, technological war had "obliterated" the ways wars traditionally elevated and celebrated a chivalrous ideal of heroic warrior masculinity. Eclipsed by the realities of modern warfare in the first decades of the twentieth century, these outmoded ideals were still widely held, including the belief that "war . . . would affirm national vitality and individual honor . . . and rescue the nation from moral decay."[22]

The belief that fighting a war would build manly citizens plagued men's already terrible experiences on the battlefield. Grunts like my grandfather experienced no glorious affirmation of their manhood; they were exposed instead to terror, vulnerability, and disillusion. For many, this experience of modern warfare manifested as a suite of crippling somatic symptoms that came to be called shell shock, viewed at the time, as described by George L. Mosse, as a kind of "enfeebled manhood": "Shattered nerves and lack of will-power were the enemies of settled society and because men so afflicted were thought to be effeminate, they endangered the clear distinction between genders which was generally regarded as an essential cement of society. . . . The shock of war could only cripple those who were of a weak disposition, fearful and, above all, weak of will. . . . War was the supreme test of manliness, and those who were the victims of shell-shock had failed this test."[23]

During World War II, attitudes began to shift. General Dwight D. Eisenhower expressed dismay with General George Patton's denigration and abuse of soldiers suffering from "battle neurosis" as malingering cowards. Mosse explains that in 1943, General Omar Bradley issued an order that "breakdown in combat be regarded as exhaustion, which helped to put to rest the idea that only those men who were mentally weak, 'the unmanly men,' collapsed under stress in combat."[24] Relabeling such breakdowns as "combat fatigue" shifted blame away from individuals and began to shed light on the conditions that created the symptoms.

During the Vietnam War, the cluster of physical and emotional symptoms brought on by the trauma of war was given a medical label: PTSD.
A 2003 study by the National Center for PTSD concluded that twenty to
twenty-five years after the end of the war, "a large majority of Vietnam
Veterans struggled with chronic PTSD symptoms, with four out of five
reporting recent symptoms."[25] The most common symptoms the study
pointed to were alcohol abuse and dependence, generalized anxiety disorder, and antisocial personality disorder. Vietnam vets who had served
"in war zones suffered at much higher levels than Vietnam-era vets who
didn't." What caused these high rates of PTSD? A common view is that
the sustained levels of fear that men in battle normally experience create
lasting psychological fears that impact one for years, perhaps the rest of
one's life. Others point to physical wounds as causing PTSD.

MORAL INJURY

In his riveting book *On Killing*, Dave Grossman surveys research on PTSD
to argue that the most powerful cause of the disorder is the guilt, shame,
and denial that follow the "burden of killing" other human beings in war.
Grossman points out that a fundamental problem of military leaders
throughout history has involved training and motivating soldiers to overcome "a simple demonstrable fact that there is within most men an
intense resistance to killing their fellow man. A resistance so strong that,
in many circumstances, soldiers on the battlefield will die before they can
overcome it."[26] During World War II, Grossman points out, military
leaders were dismayed by their troops' frequent "failure to fire": 80 to
85 percent of riflemen "did not fire their weapon at an exposed enemy."
Many who did fire missed their targets purposefully. Military trainers in
future wars transformed training regimes in ways that dramatically
increased the "fire rate." In Vietnam, U.S. soldiers with an opportunity to
fire their weapon at an enemy soldier did so 95 percent of the time. If, as

Grossman argues, knowledge of killing one or more other human beings contributes the most potent psychological fuel for PTSD, it should come as no surprise the huge numbers of veterans who came home from the Vietnam War suffering from symptoms of PTSD. Absent the group absolution that returnees from previous wars received from victory parades and other postwar celebrations, Vietnam veterans more often experienced their guilt as a private, individual burden.

This focus on the internalized shame one carries from having killed others led professionals who work with veterans to focus their interventions on what they began to call "moral injury." Clinical psychologist Brett Litz and his colleagues argue that the broad symptom profile of PTSD results from internalized fear reaction to threat; moral injury, on the other hand, results from negative emotions about oneself, one's own character, grounded in shame, remorse, and self-condemnation over what one has done to others.[27] Moral injury results when one's self-image as a good person is undermined by the knowledge of having killed other people, when one's moral compass has been irredeemably transgressed. Several of the men I interviewed expressed this kind of shame and remorse—both for individual acts they committed and for the shared collective responsibility for killing enemy soldiers and civilians in what they came to believe were unjust wars.

Moral injuries have plagued recent veterans who have returned from the wars in the Middle East. Modern technological warfare often increases the distance between the killer and the killed, thus theoretically lessening the shame the killer might feel. But Hugh Gusterson, in his fascinating analysis of drone warfare, observes that an Air Force pilot sitting in a trailer in Nevada, directing a drone strike at a distant target in the Middle East is separated geographically from his or her target by thousands of miles. However, Gusterson argues, unlike the bomber pilot who never sees his target close-up, the drone pilot is required to engage in an extended, magnified surveillance of the target site, creating a kind of "intimacy" with those on the ground. And following a drone missile strike, the pilot must again carefully surveil the now-smoking site to be sure the intended target is dead (and to order a second strike if not). In this "after" view, the pilot will also witness the civilian bystanders—the "collateral damage"—who were also killed or maimed by the strike. Gusterson asserts that the shame that drone pilots experience from their distant kills is a form of moral injury.[28] The powerful 2016 documentary film *National Bird* focuses on the experiences of a handful of former drone operators, illuminating the deep moral injuries they carry and also the reasons why, as veterans, they became whistleblowers and antiwar activists.

GENDER AND PEACE

Some war veterans break through the limits of stoic masculinity, alcoholism, drug abuse, and destructive silences to become vocal advocates for peace. How does a man accomplish this pivot from forgetting to remembering, from crippling constraint to positive action, from being a cog in a massive war machine to taking on a project of history-making through peace advocacy? For one thing, a shift toward peace advocacy involves adopting a critical, oppositional political perspective. A study by social scientist David Flores revealed that the narratives of Iraq War-vets-turned-peace-activists were "conversion stories" of political resistance to the stories they had been told about the reasons for the U.S. invasion of Iraq. In my interviews, I also heard politically resistant narratives. Also fundamental to most of these men's transformations to peace advocacy were the ways they faced the moral and therapeutic challenge of coming to grips with deeply embodied emotional trauma, including guilt, shame, and fear.

A second foundational aspect of taking on a life project as an advocate for peace involves confronting previously learned, widely accepted, and celebrated definitions of masculinity. In focusing this book on war and men, I understand that I risk rendering invisible women's experiences of war and the military. As the feminist scholar Cynthia Enloe has shown, the militarization of everyday life in the United States and throughout the world has dire consequences for civilian women's lives. Women also have a long history of serving in the military—traditionally as nurses and medics, and increasingly today in the center of combat zones. And women have been and continue to be a driving force in U.S. and international peace movements.[29]

Though they are a numerical minority in organizations like Veterans for Peace (VFP) and Iraq Veterans Against the War (IVAW), women veterans are assuming increasingly visible leadership roles in these organizations and in public debates about gender and war. Consider, for instance, the two women former drone operators-turned activists who are featured in *National Bird*, and the brave women veterans who appear in *The Invisible War*, the powerful 2012 documentary that illuminates widespread sexual harassment and sexual assault in the military. I interviewed Army veteran and IVAW member Wendy Barranco, who fended off sexual harassment and assault while serving in a combat zone in Iraq. Barranco, who had moved at age four from Mexico to Los Angeles with her mother, recalls how Army recruiters "roamed the halls" of her Los Angeles high school in 2003 as the United States was ramping up its war in Iraq: "I mean they were everywhere." The teenaged Barranco had to fight off a drunken sexual advance from her married and considerably older recruiter. Still, she decided to enlist, and part of the reason, she recalls, "was patriotism for September 11, after it happened," and her desire "to give something back to this country that gave my family and I so much."

Trained as a medic, Barranco found herself deployed in 2005 to Iraq, where the nineteen-year-old private spent nine months working in the hospital operating room (OR) in the hot combat zone of Tikrit. Barranco found "a sense of purpose and personal fulfillment" in the OR, saving lives of wounded U.S. soldiers and local Iraqis, occasionally while wearing "a flack vest" to protect against "incoming mortar rounds." She learned soon that dealing with such "heavy trauma" meant that her "feelings were going to have to be put aside. The moment that you let fear or sadness or anything like that in, your job becomes compromised. I put it away."

However, Barranco had not counted on having to fend off continual sexual harassment from the lead doctor in the OR. For "the entire fucking nine months," she recalled, "I not only had to do my job, but I had to watch my own back with this guy. That's an added layer of I'm already in a fucking war zone. I'm already having to do my job. Now I have to deal with your ass too, and I can't do anything about it. It's not—it is not fun." Nor had Barranco expected to have to scratch, wrestle, and knee in the groin a colleague who attempted to rape her in her sleeping quarters. A woman sergeant who knew of the assault told Barranco to "keep my mouth shut. Keep my head down. Don't do anything. Don't cause trouble for the unit."

Following Barranco's return to civilian life in the summer of 2006, the trauma she had "compartmentalized" while in Iraq "started really coming out. I felt used by the military. I felt like a rag that had just been used to clean up a mess and just discarded." Barranco discovered the fledgling IVAW, soon assuming a leadership role in the Los Angeles chapter and helping to organize counterrecruitment education and antiwar forums. She related her story of sexual harassment at a high-profile national IVAW event, Winter Soldier: Iraq and Afghanistan, and her account was included in a 2008 book of the same name.[30] Wendy Barranco's activism illustrates how the growing role of younger women in veterans' peace organizations steers these organizations to meld peace activism with feminist actions to confront issues like sexual harassment, sexual assault, and domestic violence that disproportionately impact women military personnel, veterans, and their families.[31]

As always, when gender becomes more visible in an organization—in this case, through women's activism within the ranks and as veterans—we are invited to ask new and critical questions about men's experiences. This book tells a story of five men—"guys like me"—who fought in wars and became advocates for peace. It is a story that, like much of my previous work, asks questions about men and masculinity that would not have occurred to me had it not been for the influences of feminist scholarship and women's activism. Since men, masculinity, and militarism are so often seen to be in close (and mythically heroic) correspondence, the war-veteran-as-peace-advocate may be viewed as an oxymoron. This is precisely what interests me. The veterans for peace I interviewed experienced political and moral awakenings, to be sure. But their ability to translate these political and moral commitments into public advocacy for peace was predicated on a fundamental shift in each man's understanding and embodiment of what it means to be a man.[32]

None of the men who appear in this book experienced what I would call a feminist transformation, though Gregory Ross, veteran of the American war in Vietnam, did join a pro-feminist men's antiviolence group in the late 1970s. But their stories reveal how in joining the military and deploying to war, each had been sold a "manhood package" that was intended to make nonreflexive warriors of them, and that ultimately proved to be self-destructive. The parameters of this manhood package are likely to be especially alluring to very young men who, when they first deploy to war zones, are barely old enough to drink alcohol legally; are still immersed in cultural images of male heroism in warfare from film, TV, and video games; and have had limited experience with sex. Deployed to wars in distant locales, these young men learn quickly that there is little room for elevated conceptions of individual heroism in war. But they also learn that when on leave—in places like Japan, the Philippines, Vietnam, and Korea—the fear and loathing they experience in war zones can be temporarily numbed through ready access to commodified recreation in the form of booze and sex workers. With several decades to reflect on this, Korean War vet Woody Powell referred to inexpensive sex with local prostitutes as part of the spoils of being "part of a conquering army."

An important element of the transformations the five men profiled in this book experienced involves rejecting the manhood package they were sold as young men. This means accepting, talking about, and sharing one's emotional vulnerabilities with others. It means, in many cases, learning to respect women as colleagues and allies in collective efforts for justice. It means rejecting pop culture military heroes and finding flesh-and-blood heroes, women and men in one's own life, who have inspired their commitments to progressive activism. It also means coming to grips with one's own memory of war and with the ways we as a society remember and misremember our wars.

Contesting the Industry of Memory

On a scorching July day, I stood on the street corner with a handful of Santa Fe VFP members at their weekly vigil, wearing my green VFP T-shirt, the back of which is emblazoned with an antiwar quote from Dwight D. Eisenhower, the World War II Army general who became the thirty-fourth president of the United States:

> I HATE WAR
> as only a soldier who has lived it can,
> as only one who has seen its *brutality*,
> its *futility*, its *stupidity*.

I stood next to a combat veteran of the war in Vietnam who pointed his VFP banner toward passing cars as he quipped about my shirt, "Do you think maybe Eisenhower said that while he was crushing veterans at Anacostia?" He was referring to Eisenhower's role, along with other future World War II heroes Douglas MacArthur and George Patton, in violently suppressing the "Bonus Army" of more than 20,000 U.S. World War I veterans who descended on Washington, DC, during the nadir of the Great Depression to demand the bonuses they'd been promised. During the spring and summer of 1932, much of the Bonus Army camped on Anacostia Flats across the Potomac River from the Capitol. When President

Herbert Hoover ordered the Army to evict them, troops under the command of General MacArthur, his aide Major Eisenhower, and Major Patton attacked with tear gas and set Bonus Army huts on fire. In the words of historian Howard Zinn, "The whole encampment was ablaze." Two veterans were shot to death, a baby died, an eight-year-old boy was blinded, and "a thousand veterans were injured by gas."[33]

My fellow protestor's sally about the Eisenhower quote on my T-shirt was more than a sarcastic one-liner that called into question the depth of the former general's antiwar commitments. It was emblematic of the way activist members of VFP pride themselves in being students of history. Knowing history is a key component of peace activism, as antiwar veterans' groups continually find themselves responding to the government's purposeful revisionism that distorts what actually happened to create ideological framings that justify current and future wars. Collective memory of wars, in other words, is a contested terrain of stories, symbols, and meanings upon which antiwar veterans insist on speaking *their* truth. For antiwar veterans, this is a continuous uphill battle.

History, it's often said, is written by the victors. This truism normally points to the reality that following wars, the nation that emerges victorious has the power to impose its version of the "truth" as to who caused the war, who should be punished for atrocities or war crimes, who should pay reparations, and who should be honored as heroes. But consider this question: Who, following a war, gets to impose their "truth," not simply *between* nations formerly at war, but also *within* a nation? Most often, it is powerful political leaders, aligned with the nation's economic elite and supported by the owners of mass media, whose version of history gets adopted as official truth, becomes required reading in textbooks, and crystallizes as national mythology. In *Nothing Ever Dies*, Viet Thanh Nguyen argues that a powerful "memory industry" inundates citizens with official versions of the truth about past wars. "By far the most powerful of its kind, the American industry of memory is on par with the American arms industry."[34] The military itself is part of this industry of memory. Top military brass—who after all not only survived past wars, but were also promoted up the ranks and commended for their wartime service—become purveyors of the official truth, as they induct, train, and lead the next generations of soldiers into the next wars.

In *A People's History of the United States*, Howard Zinn offers dozens of counterstories that challenge the official versions of history. It takes tremendous effort and chutzpah to assert these or any unsanctioned versions of history. My grandfather's frustrated outburst on a long-past Veterans Day was a moment of private resistance against what he saw as the official hijacking of Armistice Day. General Smedley Butler's antiwar rants in the 1930s challenged the official story on the causes and consequences of World War I, reframing it as a story of collusion of heads of state to send American boys off to slaughter in support of wealthy industrialists' greed.[35]

The meaning of the Vietnam War continues to be fiercely contested. As I was writing this book, activists in VFP were organizing on several fronts to challenge the communal memory of this war, as several fifty-year anniversaries of major events in the war approached.[36] Veterans organized to support Vietnamese efforts to rebuild the My Lai memorial at the site of the infamous 1968 massacre.[37] For months, I tracked the dialogues of veterans in anticipation of how they would respond to the Ken Burns documentary on the war in Vietnam. Members of the VFP Vietnam: Full Disclosure group expressed dismay that Burns adopted a neutral view of the war, promoting a narrative of false equivalences: that all sides entered into the war with good intentions, all made mistakes, and the war was tragic for everyone concerned.[38] These veterans—many had been active in the GI resistance during that war, later joining veterans' antiwar organizations—saw it not as an unfortunate "mistake" made by well-meaning people, but as a normal manifestation of U.S. foreign policy that deploys military power to impose "U.S. interests" in far reaches of the world, one that was launched and justified on a foundation of lies from U.S. leaders. In *Hell No*, written shortly before his death in 2017, antiwar activist Tom Hayden added his voice to this battle of memory to "put a stop to false and sanitized history" of the war. "We need to resist the military occupation of our minds," he wrote. "The war makers seek to win on the battlefield of memory what they lost in the battlefields of war."[39]

When the United States withdrew from Vietnam in 1973, more than 58,000 U.S. soldiers were dead, and in excess of 3 million Vietnamese, Laotian, and Cambodian soldiers and civilians are estimated to have been killed during the conflict. In the United States, a vibrant and sometimes militant antiwar movement had succeeded in helping end the war. But the battle to frame the meanings of the war had begun long before. President Richard Nixon, Vice President Spiro Agnew, and their political allies had worked to drive a strategic wedge between the rapidly growing antiwar movement and the so-called silent majority of Americans upon whom Nixon relied for pro-war support. A key prong in Nixon's strategy was to charge that antiwar protesters were engaging in unpatriotic acts that disrespected and endangered the troops in the field. The increasingly visible role played by GI war resisters and returning war veterans within the antiwar movement, as we'll see in chapter 4 through the story of Gregory Ross, made the Nixon administration's story an increasingly tough sell with the general public.

By the time the war ended, the impact of years of disastrous carnage, the well-documented revelations that the government had lied about both the reasons for and the execution of the war,[40] and the political and cultural changes instigated by the antiwar movement combined to dramatically shift public opinion toward a skeptical, even oppositional stance toward government claims about the necessity of new military interventions abroad. The public adopted a cautious, noninterventionist view: The war in Vietnam, it was widely believed, was ill-advised, and perhaps it was a mistake to think the United States could continue to be the world's policeman. And many held more critical views, seeing the American war in Vietnam not so much as a "mistake," but rather, as revealing the ugly side of the normal values and practices of U.S. foreign policy: an assumption that our military can and should control the destinies of distant nations through brute force and violence; the reality that the U.S. military, rather than being a force for democracy abroad, was a tool of imperial domination.

By the late 1970s and early 1980s, these noninterventionist and critical views of U.S. foreign policy were being hotly contested. President Ronald Reagan bemoaned Americans' reluctance to support foreign interventions as resulting from what he dubbed "the Vietnam Syndrome," a crippling national timidity that translated into weakness and vulnerability. Reagan contributed to a largely successful effort to reframe the story of the Vietnam War, blaming the U.S. defeat not on bad policy, but on the ways that the antiwar movement and weak-willed politicians forced the military to fight "with one hand tied behind its back." A key part of this reframing involved disseminating a story that became a widely accepted myth: that returning Vietnam veterans were routinely spat upon by antiwar protesters. In his book *The Spitting Image*, sociologist and Vietnam War veteran Jerry Lembcke traces the rise of the story of the spat-upon veteran as "the grounding image for a larger narrative of betrayal [that] told a story of how those who were disloyal to the nation's interests 'sold out' or 'stabbed in the back' our military."[41] His research with veterans and his analysis of mass media coverage concluded that the image of the spat-upon veteran had little if any basis in fact. Rather, most actual incidents he uncovered of veterans being verbally abused, egged, and publicly insulted were stories of antiwar veterans being attacked by pro-war demonstrators; Lembcke had experienced this form of abuse himself. Indeed, a 1975 study found that 75 percent of Vietnam War veterans were opposed to the war,[42] organizations like Vietnam Veterans Against the War (VVAW) had been for years a highly visible force in massive public antiwar demonstrations,[43] and media-savvy veterans staged powerfully symbolic events like the April 1971 discarding of war medals and ribbons by more than 800 Vietnam veterans on the steps of the U.S. Capitol building.[44]

However, Lembcke shows, as a widely accepted "perfecting myth"[45] the image of the spat-upon Vietnam Veteran helped to radically reconfigure the collective memory of the Vietnam War. It was not just politicians who promulgated this story. Hollywood played a key role as well. Nineteen-seventies films like *Coming Home* and *Tracks*, according to Lembcke, "created an American mindset receptive to suggestions that veterans were actually spat upon."[46] By the 1980s, popular culture seemed fully on board with the goal of countering the "post-Vietnam" mistreatment of Vietnam veterans and the peace movement's supposed feminization of America. Hollywood urged American men to muscle up through popular 1980s films like *The Terminator* (1984) and *Commando* (1985), both starring Arnold Schwarzenegger, and three films (1982, 1985, 1988) celebrating the heroic exploits of Vietnam War veteran John Rambo, played by Sylvester Stallone, who returns to Vietnam with a vengeance, muscles flexing and guns blazing, to rescue U.S. prisoners of war who had been forgotten and left to die by weak-kneed bureaucrats at home.

Rambo, John Matrix in *Commando*, the Terminator, and other rock-hard, men-as-weapon, men-as-machine images filled the nation's screens in the 1980s, a cultural moment that media studies scholar Susan Jeffords calls a "remasculinization of America," when the idea of real men as decisive, strong and courageous arose from the confusion and humiliation of the U.S. defeat in Vietnam and against the challenges of feminism and gay liberation.[47] The major common theme in these films is the Vietnam veteran—or prisoner of war/soldier missing in action—as abandoned and victimized by his own government, American protestors, and the women's movement—all of which are portrayed as feminizing forces that shamed and humiliated American men. Two factors were central to the symbolic remasculinization that followed: First, these film heroes of the 1980s were rugged individuals, who stoically and rigidly stood up against the bureaucrats who were undermining American power and pride with their indecision and softness. Second, hard, muscular male bodies accessorized with massive weapons were the major symbolic expression of this remasculinization. These men wasted few words and preferred to express themselves through explosive and decisively violent actions.

Jeffords argues that the male body-as-weapon serves as the ultimate spectacle and locus of masculine regeneration in post-Vietnam-era films of the 1980s. There is a common moment in many of these films: the male hero is seemingly destroyed in an explosion of flames, and as his enemies laugh, he miraculously rises (in slow motion) from under water, firing his weapon and destroying the enemy. Drawing from Klaus Theweleit's analysis of the "soldier-men" of Nazi Germany,[48] Jeffords argues that this moment symbolizes a "purification through fire and rebirth through immersion in water."[49] In this historical moment, the Terminator's most famous sentence, "I'll be back," perhaps best articulated this remasculinized American man: "back" from the cultural feminization of the 1960s and 1970s, and "back" from the national humiliation of the lost war in Vietnam.

Following Ronald Reagan, subsequent U.S. presidents built support for and defused dissent against new U.S. military interventions by exploiting the myth of the abused Vietnam veteran, and promoting a remasculinized image of America. During the 1990–1991 Operation Desert Storm— popularly known as the Gulf War—President George H. W. Bush defused possible dissent and mobilized support for the war in two ways. First, media access to coverage of the war was far more controlled and restricted by the Pentagon, compared with reporters' more open access to the war in Vietnam. And second, the Bush administration carefully orchestrated a "support the troops" campaign at home, invoking the supposedly shameful way that Vietnam veterans had been treated, and by promoting "Operation Yellow Ribbon," a visible campaign to build symbolic support at home for the troops in the field. Lembcke recounts that when some parents objected to what they saw as the propagandistic goals of "Operation Eagle," the campaign to build support for the troops in public schools, "the press and grassroots conservatives construed their objections as anti-soldier."[50] In equating any antiwar sentiment with *antitroops* sentiment, the government had succeeded in framing its war effort in a way that defused antiwar mobilizations. Over a decade later his son would renew his father's war against Iraq—with disastrous results—but for the moment President George H. W. Bush concluded his 1991 speech to the American Legislative Council on a note of triumph for a remasculinized America: "It's a proud day for America. And, by God, we've kicked the Vietnam Syndrome once and for all."[51]

Battles over the interpretations of past wars are not just academic. The stakes over whose "truth" will prevail are high: What we believe to be true of past wars powerfully influences whether we'll support, express skepticism, or actively oppose efforts to wage current and future wars. Winning public acceptance of the American war in Vietnam continues to be foundational to strategies developed by neoconservatives attempting to muster public support for U.S. interventions in the Middle East, just as collective amnesia about the early 1950s Korean War contributes to public confusion about the saber rattling between President Trump and North Korea. At the same time, counternarratives of the America war in Vietnam have been crucial to antiwar movements' ongoing resistance to current and future wars. The words we use to describe the past matter. Today, members of VFP insist on adopting the name used by the people of Vietnam for this war, "the American War in Vietnam."

Although it's a recent and still ongoing war, the meanings of the Iraq War are also highly contested. Leaders that drew us into this war like former vice president Dick Cheney still stubbornly claim that the war was right and good, while a central tenet of the conventional frame for the Iraq War was that it was a "mistake," based on false information. Many Democratic Party leaders who voted in favor of the U.S. invasion of Iraq (including then senator Hillary Clinton) now chide the second Bush administration for having misled the nation and Congress, thrusting the United States into a years-long disastrous war that has cost billions of dollars and wasted

many lives, while yielding no discernable gains, either for the people of
Iraq or for the long-term security of the United States (although it seems
the fossil fuel industry has profited). "If only we had known" that Iraq
actually had no weapons of mass destruction, many of these leaders now
lament. But many people did know in advance, including U.N. weapons
inspectors, and 12 million people worldwide who demonstrated in opposition to the invasion.

Now, in the collective memory, the Iraq War is commonly seen as an
unfortunate "mistake" rather than as a routine operation of U.S. foreign
policy. "All wars are fought twice," Viet Thanh Nguyen asserts, "the first time
on the battlefield, the second time in memory."[52] The effort to frame the
collective memory of past wars is an ongoing battle. There is the industry
of memory attempting to impose its official storyline, and there are veterans grappling with the trauma, guilt, fear, pain, and anguish embedded in
their bodies and minds.

Memory, Bodies, and Identities

The veterans I interviewed for this book viewed their public opposition to
war as an act of moral necessity and patriotism. They also viewed it as a
necessity for healing; for many of these men, public antiwar activism
is coupled with deeply personal efforts to heal their own emotional wounds,
sustain sobriety, help other veterans, and engage in community activism
to stop interpersonal violence and address poverty and homelessness. Veterans' peace advocacy is often coupled with therapeutic healing, and with
social justice activism in the community and in the world. It is at once an
effort to heal the self, to connect with others in peaceful ways, and to say
yes to peace in the world.

As I spoke with these men, I became fascinated with the question of
how their past experiences with war and their current commitments to
peace and healing have become salient aspects of their identities. I've come

to understand individual identity not through a layered "onion" image that imagines a core self, fixed during infancy and childhood, continuing throughout life to assert conscious and unconscious influence on a person, even as more life experiences are layered upon the core. Rather, I've come to understand identity as a never completed, always developing tapestry. As a person ages, experiences the ups and downs of interpersonal relationships, moves through a historically shifting array of institutions (families, schools, mass media, military, twelve-step programs, social movement organizations, churches, workplaces), new fabrics are sewn in and the tapestry of one's identity shifts its shape and textures. Previous experiences don't disappear; they remain as threads that are woven and rewoven into the tapestry, seeming to disappear at times, later reemerging and attaining new meaning.

Extending this image, I see a man's wartime experience as a thread in the larger, always-growing tapestry of his life. Like all threads, it can be woven and rewoven, shifting in importance, salience, and meaning as he moves in and out of different contexts, as his sense of self in the world shifts and his values change or ossify. But the wartime thread is extraordinary, often among the most salient of threads in a man's life, even if, as when I interviewed World War II veteran Ernie "Indio" Sanchez, it constitutes less than 2 percent of the entire tapestry of his life. Nor is the wartime thread made of soft cloth that easily blends in; rather, it is more akin to a copper wire, shining at times, tarnishing with time, but always carrying the possibility—all it takes is the right precipitating event—to trigger visceral bodily reactions grounded in past trauma. We will see this in Sanchez's story of PTSD triggered a half century after World War II; in Korean War veteran Woody Powell's awakening to action, facilitated by his newfound sobriety and sparked by the U.S. invasion of Iraq; and in Vietnam veteran Gregory Ross's description of his automatic recoiling, still today, when he hears crashing noises that conjure his embodied memory of the 24/7 booming of Navy artillery.

What became fascinating to me in talking with these men were the ways that deeply embedded memories of wartime trauma were, in some cases, "forgotten" for long periods of time. In *The Warriors*, the most profound book I've read on the psychology, emotions, and ethics of combat, philosopher and World War II veteran J. Glenn Gray wrote, "The effort to assimilate those intense war memories to the rest of my experience is difficult and even frightening. Why attempt it? Why not continue to forget? . . . I am afraid to forget. I fear that human creatures do not forget cleanly, as animals presumably do."[53] Indeed, some of the men I interviewed appear at times in their lives to have achieved some tentative life-stability in "forgetting" their wartime experience, but they would likely agree with Gray's conclusion that this forgetting is incomplete, that "what protrudes and does not fit in our pasts rises to haunt us and make us spiritually unwell in the present."

As I learned more about the experience of war, the workings of memory, PTSD, and moral injury, a veteran's ambivalence about remembering or forgetting became less puzzling to me. What I began to wonder about is how, and under what conditions, men consciously seek to transcend or to mobilize their wartime trauma. Once foregrounded, what do they do with memories of war? For the men I studied, how did the threads of memories of physical pain, fear, guilt, or shame, once ignited, get rewoven into efforts to heal the self and others, to advocate daily for peace, and to engage in collective action for social justice? A veteran's moment of engagement with a conscious life project of peace and justice advocacy begins to take shape when he seizes this thread, and commences a conscious—and often a painful and difficult—reweaving, often against the grain.

I have come to see that in making a public claim of peace advocacy and in connecting with others politically as peace activists, these veterans are enacting what existentialist philosophers Jean-Paul Sartre and Simone de Beauvoir called a "project of freedom."[54] At first glance, asserting a language of human freedom to describe these men's experiences may seem questionable. It seems common sense to understand a soldier in a combat situation existing in a situation where "freedom" is almost nonexistent. Indeed, I listened to stories of men drafted into the military, thrust into dangerous, frightening, and appalling situations not of their choosing, positioned in the lower rungs of chains of command that ordered them what to do and when to do it, and confronted with situations that one can only hope to survive, not to control. Few situations in life—incarceration, perhaps—seem more the antithesis of freedom than war. But for the existentialists, freedom is not defined as unfettered choice and action. Put another way, human freedom is not *prevented* by the existence of limits and constraints—what Sartre called "facticity" and de Beauvoir called "contingency"—instead, it is only, in Sartre's words, an individual's "going beyond a situation" and pushing against constraining facticity and contingencies through which a person can assert a project of individual freedom. This "going beyond," for Sartre, is not simply a negation of a given situation one may find intolerable; it is simultaneously a positive, forward-looking project that "opens onto the 'nonexistent,' to what *has not yet been.*"[55] As I witness a small group of VFP members struggling to keep their antiwar banners aloft on a gusty street corner as hundreds of cars drive past, left and right, most of the drivers paying no apparent attention to war and peace issues, these activists' collective project is illuminated for me by Sartre's description of human freedom. Through their actions they are "transcending the given" of a world of violence, war, and injustice, and they are also imagining and acting together to move the world "toward the field of possibles."[56]

How does a veteran get to this point of joining with others to attempt to transcend the given and push toward a different "field of possibles"? Following his wartime experience, a veteran may feel his range of possible choices and actions expanding—or at least the moment-to-moment constraints around him becoming less evident than they were during combat. But the situation of the war veteran is likely still to be one of difficult—emotional, health-related, relational, financial—contingencies. The conscious forging of an existential project involves seeing beyond the limits of current contingencies, and acting to create a different future. The stories I tell in subsequent chapters illuminate four intertwining themes, expressed in different ways by each individual veteran.

> *Self-healing.* The men I interviewed confronted their own moral injury or PTSD variously, through individual and group therapy, through spiritual healing practices like meditation, acupuncture or yoga, through twelve-step recovery programs, or through creative writing.
>
> *Service to others.* Some of vets I interviewed found their way into helping professions—working with homeless people, serving veterans in recovery, providing health or community support for the poor.
>
> *Political activism.* All of the men I interviewed engaged in peace advocacy, engaging individuals in their everyday lives about war and peace issues, often wearing VFP buttons or clothing to create conversations. Most of these men also engaged with VFP and other veterans' organizations, building coalitions to work for peace and justice and to contest the industry of memory.
>
> *Reconciliation.* Reflecting the observation of Viet Thanh Nguyen that in remembering past wars Americans too often "remember our own" dead but fail to remember our fallen enemies or civilian casualties as full human beings, veterans for peace insist on talking about former enemies, including people they killed, as fully human, and some of the veterans engage in organized transnational projects to build human connections with former "enemies."

I have found the life history interview to be an ideal way to understand individual lives as "projects," at once constrained by war and other violent and unjust social processes, while also expressing transcendent creativity, stubborn political resistance, and hopeful ideals of freedom. I spent many hours, in multiple sittings, collecting the life histories of the veterans who are featured in this book. To be sure, such a small number of life history interviews cannot illuminate what developmental psychologist Daniel Levinson described as predictable stages of development in the "seasons of a man's life."[57] Instead, as sociologist Raewyn Connell has shown, a "theorized life history" offers a window into individual agency and the social processes of embodiment and memory. Life history studies, Connell emphasizes, are useful not only for uncovering psychological dynamics, or even simply for understanding how the social world constrains actions; they also illuminate how individuals' choices and actions in turn shape the world. In Connell's words, a life history interview reveals "the making of social life through time. It is literally history."[58]

In *Guys Like Me*, I draw from life history interviews with five men who fought in five wars to better understand these men's lives from the inside, and to illuminate contemporary history. Each chapter foregrounds the voice of one man, supplemented with my own secondary research, to illuminate the personal experience of war and its aftermath, and to better understand the ways in which individuals take on a project of peace advocacy. In chapter 2 we meet World War II Army combat veteran Ernie "Indio" Sanchez, who confronted his wartime deeds fifty years after his war, following a traumatic bout with PTSD. Chapter 3 tells the story of Wilson "Woody" Powell, an Air Force veteran of the Korean War who eventually became an activist and leader in VFP. Vietnam Navy veteran and VFP member Gregory Ross is the focus in chapter 4. Chapter 5 chronicles the experiences of Daniel Craig, an Army veteran of the Gulf War. Chapter 6 centers on the life of Navy veteran Jonathan Hutto, an Iraq War veteran active in VFP.

There is a necessary intimacy in getting inside one man's life story. But rather than viewing the five stories in this book as discrete tales of separate individuals and separate wars, I seek to show the ways in which these men's biographies, and their wars, are overlapping and interconnected parts of an ongoing social history.[59] These men's actions as peace advocates too are interconnected. When individual projects of healing, service to others, reconciliation with former enemies, and peace activism are joined in an organization like VFP, the result is a collective project of veterans and allies aiming to make history.

The effort to assimilate those intense war memories to the rest of my experience is difficult and even frightening. Why attempt it? Why not continue to forget? I fear that human creatures do not forget cleanly, as animals presumably do. What protrudes and does not fit in our pasts rises to haunt us and make us spiritually unwell in the present.

—J. Glenn Gray, *The Warriors*

We go out there to win the war and kill people. I don't know why they're patting us on the back. I really didn't, I thought, "What was wrong with humanity here? Why are they doing that? They really shouldn't celebrate." Because the reason we have a soldier is to go kill people—huh? Isn't that true?

—Ernie Sanchez

CHAPTER 2

—«‹•›»—

There Is No "Good War"

ERNIE "INDIO" SANCHEZ, WORLD WAR II

As the U.S. military pounded the overmatched Iraqi forces with twenty-one days of "shock and awe," the pyrotechnics of the 2003 U.S. invasion were televised through a mass media that had jumped on the pro-war bandwagon. Ernie Sanchez—then a seventy-eight-year-old retiree—sat in his Los Angeles home absorbing the sights and sounds of the aerial bombings of Baghdad, and something unexpected bubbled up inside him. "I was sitting right there where you are, looking at TV, and all of a sudden I see the war, and I start shaking. I said, 'What?' And I started getting scared. I says, 'What the hell?' And I get up, I says, 'I don't know what's wrong.' So I ran to my room and I started sobbing in my room, and I'm shaking, and my son came: 'What's the matter, Dad?' 'I don't know, I don't know!' I was crying."

Sanchez's son took him to a doctor, and then to a VA psychiatrist who seemed to recognize what was going on. "She says, 'Were you in combat?' I says, 'Yeah, I was in combat.' She wrote a note and said, 'Here you take that to the VA.' And I went to the VA and a psychiatrist saw me and said, 'Yeah, you have PTSD.' 'How do you know?' I says. 'Well we know the symptoms—you were in combat?' I says, 'Yeah.' And they gave me sedation . . . and I start relaxing. And I said, 'What the hell is Post Traumatic Stress Disorder?' [*laughs*]. I didn't know what the hell that was!" Sanchez was puzzled by the diagnosis, and confounded at the sudden onset

31

of his bodily symptoms. "What the hell" was with this sudden and uncontrollable trembling and weeping? After all, it had been fifty-eight years since he had fought in World War II.

Unlike today's apparently permanent conflicts, each major war of the first half of the twentieth century seemed to have had an end. The guns finally fell quiet on November 11, 1918, Armistice Day. The artillery ceased on May 8, 1945, Victory in Europe Day, and the bombs no longer fell after September 2, 1945, Victory over Japan (VJ) Day. When the killing and dying finally stopped, an exhausted nation celebrated and then moved on to what was optimistically called "postwar life." But a war never really ends, especially for the warrior. This is certainly the case for Ernie Sanchez. For nearly six decades following World War II, Sanchez did his best to forget his war, pouring his time, heart, and soul into building a family and strategizing his next move up the civil engineering career ladder.

But over the years, a jagged scrap of shrapnel lodged near his spine delivered unexpected reminders of suffering during those long days in the Hürtgen Forest, as German artillery rained on nineteen-year-old Ernie Sanchez and the advancing U.S. 4th Infantry Division. He never forgot how the shelling left him and his comrades "shaking in our boots . . . scared shitless." Nor could he jettison the guilt he felt about nearly shooting himself in the leg, a moment when the prospect of a self-inflicted wound seemed like a rational exit strategy from the horrors of the war zone. More than anything, Sanchez could never shed the moral burden of having mowed down with his Browning Automatic Rifle (BAR) between fifty and a hundred German soldiers, killing "these sons, brothers, people who were loved." When Sanchez thought about it, even that VE Day date was laughable. On May 8, 1945, folks at home may be been celebrating the formal surrender of the Germans, but Sanchez and his BAR were still at work the following day, and again on the next: "They wouldn't give up, and us Americans went up there and had to *kill Germans after the war*. What a shame. Oh, the shame."

All of this—the bone-chilling fear, the guilt, the moral shame—hid out in Ernie Sanchez's body for the remaining seven decades of his life, ambushing him when he least expected it, jabbing him like that piece of shrapnel lodged near his spine. He could never make it go away, not entirely. Eventually he learned that talking about it—testifying to anyone who would listen to his stories of the stupidity of war, the burdens of having fought and killed, and the hope of peace—was the best salve for his wounds. This sort of talk didn't come easily for Sanchez, as it involved bumping up against the stoic manly silence that so many war veterans internalize. The emotional vulnerability exposed by such talk of fear, regret, and a hope for peace also ran counter to the youthful toughness he had successfully embodied in the streets and jails of prewar Los Angeles.

-◄◄◄◆►►►-

When I arrived at Ernie Sanchez's Los Angeles home for our first interview, he was eighty-eight-years old, with five grown children and several grandkids. His wife Dora had died five years earlier, and he apologized that the house didn't look as tidy as it had when Dora was alive. "She did everything," he said. "She was the perfect woman, the perfect wife." The place looked clean and neat to me.

Sanchez welcomed me to sit at his kitchen table, on which he had set a Tupperware container with two large baggies of his war decorations and his medals (though he'd given away his Purple Heart years earlier), an annotated map of the European war area that he used to guide me through his combat ordeals in 1944 and 1945, and a 1980 newsletter that featured his accomplishments as a civil engineer with the City of Los Angeles.

As we sat down, Sanchez pointed to a scatter of books on his dining room table, and a lined pad on which he'd jotted down a list of words he intended to look up in the dictionary. He was an avid reader, he told me, and was always working to expand his vocabulary "'cause I have to keep my brain active." As I took a couple of photos, Sanchez mentioned somewhat apologetically that in recent years his smile had become "crooked," the result of a bout with Bell's palsy. During the many hours I spent with Ernie Sanchez, I came to think of his asymmetrical smile and deeply lined face as the most visible indicators of the joys and burdens he carried in his body.

Sanchez's long life cut across a large swath of history as he moved in and through social contexts that were changing, sometimes dramatically. His story offers a window into embodied manhood, not as a fixed or ever-completed product, but as an ongoing project, always temporally embedded with skills, postures, and strategies that change over the course of a life. Across time and place, Sanchez absorbed and displayed what social scientist Pierre Bourdieu called *habitus*—embodied dispositions and skills that were appropriate to the *fields*—the institutional contexts—in which he found himself.[1] It took him a while in each new situation to learn to adapt, and at first he often employed a modus operandi that had worked previously but was counterproductive in the new field. Over his nearly ninety nears, Sanchez had navigated bumpy roads that were shaped by the indignities of poverty and racism, the physical and emotional violence of incarceration and war, and the challenges of work and family, but he always found a way through.

When I first asked Sanchez if he was willing to do a life history interview with me, he didn't hesitate: "I like to talk," he said. Indeed he did. Sanchez was a gifted storyteller who punctuated his tales with a wry sense of humor, the occasional burst of outraged anger, and the modulated whisper of a man who has seen and done unspeakable things.

Becoming Indio

Ernie Sanchez was born in 1925 and raised in the Boyle Heights neighborhood of Los Angeles, not far from where I interviewed him at his home more than eighty years later. Sanchez didn't recall anyone in his immediate family having had military experience, but he was proud to tell the tale of how his family came to the United States from Mexico. His grandmother had been a *soldadera* traveling with and providing food and medical attention for Pancho Villa's army during the Mexican Revolution. Eventually, she had to hightail it out of Mexico with her brother, a *fusilador*, whose job as an officer was to take captured federal troops, "put 'em against the wall and give the command to kill 'em." Sanchez explained: "Carranza, the General of Mexico was eliminating Zapata and Pancho Villa, and Pancho Villa was running away. Any officers they would get, they would kill 'em. So at that time, my grandmother brought her brother to the United States before they would get killed. So that's how we come to the United States, to live here."

Sanchez's grandmother landed first in the tiny mining town of Washington, Arizona, and later moved to Los Angeles. Eventually, she birthed "nine children, all different fathers [*laughs*]; my father was number one." His father endeavored to instill a work ethic in his son, but the streets of Los Angeles were Sanchez's primary manhood instructor. His earliest brush with the law was at age eight or nine, when police busted him for stealing bikes, and he was sent to Valyermo Camp, a place in the desert "for little hoods" that aimed to make youngsters "straighten out and be nice kids." In 1938 or 1939, at the age of thirteen or fourteen, he moved with his family nearby to Temple and Figueroa, then "the narcotics center of LA, the prostitute center of LA." There, he "started hanging around with the Califa Gang," a group of Mexican American boys who "ruled Temple Street." He was especially drawn to Califa leader J.J. Morales, who invited Sanchez into the gang. The six or seven members of Califa were a tightly knit group: they hung out, sometimes engaging in petty theft, underage drinking, or smoking marijuana. Each boy had a gang nickname. At the center of the gang were J.J. and his brother, dubbed Reindeer due to his ability to run and jump "like a deer." Other gang members' names also referenced obvious aspects of a boy's anatomy:

We had a guy named Snow White, because he was blacker than I was [*laughs*]. And we had a guy named Largo, tall guy, you know. We had another guy named Cabezon. He had a big head. We all had nicknames. We'd look at him, "Oh yeah, he's got a big head: *Cabezon!*" Or look at me [*touching a finger to his dark brown face*]: "Indio!" You know, because I looked like an Indian. And that's the way we identified ourselves. Even now, when I see somebody, I hear "Hey Indio!" They remember me as Indio from Califa and the thing is, in that environment, you were noted by your reputation, you had to have a reputation. And J.J., he had already gone to Juvenile [correctional facility]. By the way, I went to Juvenile a few times too [*laughs*].

Sanchez earned his reputation by learning to fight, displaying courage and physical toughness. This had started at home: "My father, you know, he had his ways and you had to obey him, there were no ifs or buts about it. And he never wanted me to come home crying that somebody beat me up. I had to go out there, and I learned how to box." Physical toughness was crucial within the gang too, where in-group loyalty and a show-no-fear willingness to fight "determined the hierarchy, you know, and who got the girls." Sanchez also learned from J.J. that the best way to avoid having to fight someone outside the gang is to display an intimidating willingness to fight: "I learned how to be a boxer because I didn't want nobody to jump me. And if they did jump me, they knew they had somebody that knew how to fight. And J.J. told me, 'You look the guy straight in his eyes [like] you're gonna fight him. If he shows—[when] you see the little fear in him, you got it made.'"

Sanchez's youth was punctuated by brushes with the law, expulsions from schools, and short stints in jail. He was kicked out of eighth grade for running what adult gangs might call a protection racket: "We didn't consider ourselves hoods, [but in] junior high we had a deal where there were a lot of Asians, foreigners, and they had to be taken care of 'cause they didn't know their way around too well. So we had to protect them, you know, they'd give us a dime or a quarter or something to protect them. Because other guys would just try to beat them up and take their money away from them, but if they would just tell them, 'Indio's my friend,' they'll leave them alone. And sure enough, they did, because you know how bad Mexicans were at that time [*laughs*]."

Trading on cultural fears of Mexicans to extort weaker kids in a racialized street hierarchy made sense within the tough and limited range of opportunities the Califa boys saw around them. "Filipinos were little anyway, you know—we'd ask for donations or else [*laughs*]. God how could I have done such stupid things like that, you know? And I look back now, jeez, I didn't know any better. I wanted to be successful in life and I knew I was gonna be successful because my aim was to become a pimp. I didn't know what a CEO [was], a doctor, or a lawyer, or a business—there were no such things like that around my environment. Yeah, I saw pimps. Who had the best car? Who had the best suit? Who had the diamond rings, and who had the girls?"

A few years later, still in his teens and small in physical stature—his sinewy 5'9" frame barely tipped the scales at 130 pounds—Sanchez used this same intimidating street toughness to his benefit when he was sent to jail.

> I don't know what I did, they must have put me in jail for two or three days, you know, Juvenile. They give you the clothes, they give you the bed sheets and [tell you,] "You gonna bunk there," you know. So I look at the cells, and I [think], "I think I can take this guy." So I tell the guy, "Get out of here, I'm taking over your bunk." He looks at me, and I look at him, and he says, "Okay" [*laughs*]. "Okay." Because we're gonna slug it out, and I knew I didn't wanna fight that guy, you know. I'd get hurt too; when a guy fights back you're gonna get hurt. But they knew my reputation already and he says, "Sure, you might beat Indio up, but you know you're gonna get hit some hard punches too."

Sanchez's tough guy habitus clearly helped him thrive in the street and survive in jails, mostly because it was an embodied bluff of manly toughness that secured respect and safety in social fields made up almost entirely of young men of color from poor and working-class backgrounds. In jail, Sanchez won respect and relative safety with his street name and reputation, and with his ability to intimidate by showing a willingness to use his fists.

However, the tough guy street habitus backfired on Sanchez in public schools, co-ed institutions governed by adults who upheld middle-class values and standards. This illustrates a common finding in research on poor boys of color: embodiments and displays of toughness that benefit boys in the street are commonly read as "trouble" and punished by school-teachers and administrators.[2] While some boys learn to "code-shift," deploying less threatening masculinity displays in schools, others maintain the tough veneer that upholds their reputations and relative safety in the street. This commonly leads, as it did for Sanchez, to being suspended or expelled from school and delivered to the criminal justice system. It began with a few "little difficulties" in high school that the teachers "mostly tolerated," until an incident precipitated his expulsion. "Reindeer, myself, another two guys were walking down the hallway and there's a beautiful little girl in front of us, she had a real nice-looking ass, you know. So Reindeer, he goes and gooses her. And she turned around and *hits me*—slap! And I see stars and I hit her back and I knock her down. And I says, 'What the hell did I do?' It was a reaction, you know? And she's bleeding from her mouth and nose. That's when they sent me to Fort Hills, a special school for boys."

At Fort Hills, Sanchez got into a few more scrapes: it was "nothing but ruffians there, you know, there were lot of blacks, 'cause they come from different areas." From there, he was sent to Belmont High School. "I didn't like the way they ran Belmont, [so] they kicked me out and sent me to Lincoln. I went to Lincoln for another two months. And I didn't like the way they were running Lincoln, so they kicked me—so I quit. I quit."

At the age of sixteen, Sanchez was done with school, and school was apparently done with him. He had been "running around with Largo and Blackie," whose mother was offered a job in Northern California. Sanchez

Ernie "Indio" Sanchez, ca. 1943 (Ernie Sanchez)

accepted an invitation to move with them to the Bay Area, where he took a job at a mill, "throwing coals into burners" and earning 58 cents an hour—"that was good money!" They lived in a three-room apartment nestled behind a bar: Blackie's mom and a man occupied one room, three prostitutes shared a second room, and Sanchez roomed with Blackie.

The United States declared war on Japan following the December 7, 1941, attack on Pearl Harbor. Ernie Sanchez knew about the war, but it was mostly background music to his young life in California. He recalls being aware that a Japanese American kid in his high school was sent away with his family "to a concentration camp," but mostly, he said, "I wasn't really thinking about it. In 1941 I was still in school, you know. I was too young; I was only sixteen then." By 1943, with the United States now fully engaged in both the Pacific and European theaters of the war, Sanchez was approaching the age of eighteen. "My mother sent me a letter: 'You better come home because you have to sign up for the draft.' So I said, 'Well I gotta go.'"

THEY ACCEPTED ME AS WHITE

A few months after his eighteenth birthday, Ernie Sanchez became one of the many Mexican Americans and other Hispanics who joined or were drafted into the U.S. Armed Forces.[3] He was inducted at Forth MacArthur in nearby San Pedro, California, and was soon off for sixteen weeks of basic training at Camp Roberts. Like many young military draftees before and after him, Sanchez encountered people and places very differ- ent from his thus far limited experiences. At the outset of World War II, the U.S. military was still racially segregated for blacks, but other men of color were integrated, at least to a degree. At home in Los Angeles San- chez's dark brown skin had marked him as a second-class citizen, but in the military he found that "I was white [*laughs*]. They accepted me as white." While it is true that Mexican Americans were formally "integrated" in the Army, many of them experienced racial discrimination in the ser- vice, and they were mostly sorted into the lower ranks of the service, thus placing them disproportionately on the front lines of combat, in harm's way.[4] Sanchez would experience the reality of this in due time, however he did not see combat until after his nineteenth birthday, something he described as one of the "lucky breaks" of his life: "I thank God for having Franklin D. Roosevelt as the president. . . . He said, 'We're getting too many of our young men [killed], too young to be going to the front lines, from

Pvt. Ernie Sanchez, ca. 1944 (Ernie Sanchez)

now on, we're not gonna send anybody else to the front lines till they're nineteen.' I was already on my way, and they pulled me back, and I stayed in North Carolina."

There, Sanchez discovered a black-white racial regime radically different from what he'd known in Los Angeles. He saw segregated drinking fountains and restaurants, and "blacks having to get out of the sidewalk to let the white woman pass. I was flabbergasted, I didn't know anything like that, you know, I'm from LA!" In North Carolina, Sanchez explored both worlds, befriending blacks who introduced him to jazz clubs—"I was the whitest person there"—and meeting white girls from Duke and Wake Forest, "co-eds who'd come and entertain us before we'd go overseas to be killed." In North Carolina, Sanchez was astonished to be treated— especially by the white college women—either as some kind of welcome exotic, or as an honorary white person.

> Oh god, these girls! Man, they were all nice. And to top it off, some of the girls wanted to dance with me! Because I was different than most of the guys, you know. And I'd dance with them, and they'd ask me, "Where are you from?" I was Hawaiian, I was Filipino, I was [*laughs*], I was Jewish, I was Mexican, and I came from Hollywood! "You know all the movie stars?" "Yeah!" I was so sophisticated! I was way different than the rest of the people there, you know. And I said, "What a beautiful world this is!" I liked that; I enjoyed it. And there was no prejudice against Mexicans, they didn't know Mexicans, they didn't have any over there, so I was strange. But the girls, they were inquisitive, you know, they wanted to know. And I could kinda dance pretty good too, you know.

SCARED SHITLESS

The dancing abruptly ended when Ernie Sanchez was shipped out following his nineteenth birthday. D-Day had already happened in Europe, and the Allies had begun their bloody push though German-occupied France. Sanchez landed in Le Havre, France, and was immediately put on a train, loaded into a truck, and delivered to the front lines. At this point in the interview, Sanchez pulled out his annotated map of the Allied push and placed his index finger on a spot between Belgium and Germany, the Hürtgen Forest, where he had joined the 4th Infantry Division. Sanchez had always thought of himself as brave, and as "a good poker player" who could read and take advantage of "how other people reacted." His tough guy bluffing had served him well in jail and on the streets, but these skills were worthless in the Hürtgen Forest: "That's part of being a soldier, you know, you gotta be brave. Shit [laughs sarcastically], we were brave: shaking in our boots!" The carnage was immediate and dramatic. "In two-and-a-half weeks, they had to pull out the 4th and 28th Infantry Divisions, because they were decimated. In two-and-a-half weeks, that Division lost 9,500 men, either killed or wounded. Two-and-a-half *weeks* I'm talking about. In this war we're having [now] in Iraq, we haven't killed 6,000 people yet. How many years we've been over there?"

Sanchez grew pensive as he described the slaughter in the Hürtgen Forest. His voice softened, the lines on his face deepening as he squinted, perhaps trying to see the map more clearly, perhaps entertaining unwelcome memories in his mind's eye. A half century later, Sanchez lamented, he still could not understand the logic of the bloody battle in which he was wounded. "That's one of the dumbest battles we had because the Germans were in trenches there. They had bunkers and tanks and everything else. I don't know what the hell we were doing, they could have gone around it, but Eisenhower wanted to take that place over. So he sent the 4th Infantry Division and the 28th Infantry to get annihilated. That was one of the stupidest battles we had."

The "stupid" battle nearly cost Sanchez his life. "A person in the Hürtgen Forest was only supposed to last, average, seventeen days, either killed or wounded. I was lucky, I lasted about a month and a half, but I was wounded [laughs]." A shard of shrapnel from an artillery explosion had lodged a quarter inch from his spine. When the medic at the field hospital told him, "We can't do nothing for you here," Sanchez thought, "I'm dead." But what the medic meant was that they had to send him to a hospital in Paris. "Oh yeah?" [laughs]. Thank you, Lord! I'm going to the hospital in Paris!" This turned out to be a huge stroke of luck. While Sanchez was hospitalized in Paris, from December 1944 through early 1945 the Germans mounted the major counterattack that was the Battle of the Bulge. "Thank God I wasn't there," Sanchez said. It was the bloodiest battle of

Ernie Sanchez lamenting "one of the stupidest battles we had," the Battle of Hürtgen Forest, in which he was wounded (author)

World War II for the U.S. military, with estimates of 19,246 Americans killed, 62,489 wounded, and 26,612 captured and missing.

Returned to the front lines, Sanchez found himself in bitter combat. His faltering courage, it seemed, was shared by a good number of his comrades. "I never saw so many cowards in my life. One time we were attacking, and all of a sudden, because we were in mostly the forest, I saw all these trees moving and I saw Americans and they're running, they're throwing their helmets and their guns and their packs away so they could run faster. And I said, 'What the hell?' They said, 'Counterattack! Counterattack!' The Germans were counterattacking. Shit, I took off my helmet and threw my gear and I run with 'em. I'm not gonna be brave and stay there and fight it out with the Germans, would you?"

Sanchez had playfully turned the tables of the interview on me, so I replied with a chuckle, "No," to which he responded with a friendly ribbing: "Huh? You coward, you lousy coward! What the hell's the matter with you? And back in the States I thought we were all brave. And I wondered, 'Am I in the right army?' Goddamn Americans are running scared shitless."

Sanchez's fears escalated, his body eventually betraying him with an uncontrollable trembling that anticipated his symptoms nearly sixty years later. In a dugout trench during an artillery attack with his "foxhole buddy" Jose Simone Eragon, "a big husky dago from New Jersey," Sanchez could take no more. "Artillery, it's incoming, and I come out shaking, *Jesus* that was close!' Then we get another barrage of artillery, and I'm shaking, *'Goddamn*, that was close! *Jesus!*' I'm like this [*shows his shaking hand*]. You know, that was it. I reached for my rifle, this is the second time around, I'm gonna shoot my leg. I says, 'Bullshit! I'd rather—at least I'll live and I might have a wounded leg for a while, but that'll heal, it'll get me out of the front lines.' Isn't that smart? Huh? I'm dying every goddamn minute on the front lines. I'm the biggest coward."

Instead, his buddy Eragon covered their foxhole with tree limbs, partially shielding them from the artillery fallout: "That's what I was afraid

[of] because I had gotten shrapnel already, and I didn't wanna get it again, this time it might hit my head or kill me." Eragon talked Sanchez out of the self-inflicted wound. And as the war wound down Sanchez began to hope he might get out of it alive. But the horrors were not over, not quite yet. He witnessed Jews newly liberated from German concentration camps: "I saw these guys laying around, sitting around with striped suits, black and white stripes on them; they were *skeletons*." And there was the cleanup duty, hauling away the bodies of dead comrades, dirty work that "was part of the war, I mean somebody's gotta do it." A final indignity for Sanchez was participating in the killing of German soldiers after the war was officially over. "Believe it or not, the war ended and there was Germans up in the hills. We had to kill them, they wouldn't give up, and us Americans went up there and had to kill Germans after the war. What a shame. Oh, the shame."

What Was Wrong with Humanity Here?

Ernie Sanchez discovered the tough guy posturing that had benefited him in the street was useless when the artillery began to rain down. Here, the enemy was not proximal, not so easily stared down with aggressive bravado; instead, the faceless German army was firing bullets and lobbing artillery from afar—"from the trees." In jail, Sanchez had successfully confronted challenges by deploying his embodied street habitus; the challenges he faced in war evoked feelings of fear and vulnerability, eventually manifesting in uncontrollable shaking and crying. Sanchez responded to his fears with what he later described as acts of "cowardice"—running away from a battle; even once considering escaping death with a self-inflicted wound. Amplifying his fears and loss of control was the moral injury—"Oh, the shame!"—that was blossoming inside him for the men he killed.

Sanchez not only survived the war, his country decorated him with the Combat Infantry Badge, the Good Conduct Medal, a Purple Heart, and three Battle Stars. He had killed scores of Germans, but at the time he managed for the most part to deny or repress that knowledge. I asked him if, after the war, he considered himself to be a hero. He bristled at the question. His words revealed a muddle of confusion and ambivalence about what he had done and how he would remember it.

> When I had come out of the service, I didn't know I had killed all those people. I didn't know that. But unconsciously, back in here [*pointing to the back of his head*], I think I had an inkling. Near Sacramento, we got discharged. It took me a week to get to LA because coming down, we stopped in a town, everybody wanted to buy me drinks and [treated me] like a hero, you know, the war was over. And—I felt uneasy because I used to say, "Why are these people buying these things for me after killing all these—you know, that's nothing to be proud of." I felt a little guilty but I didn't really know that I had killed—but I thought, "We go out there to win the war and kill people. I don't know why they're patting us on the back." I really didn't, I thought, "What was wrong with humanity here? Why are they doing that? They really shouldn't celebrate." Because the reason we have a soldier is to go kill people—huh? Isn't that true?

Thirty years later, combat veterans would return from Vietnam with similar physical wounds and moral injuries, but their sentiments could be given meaning and focus through a vibrant antiwar movement that included thousands of antiwar veterans. After World War I, mainstream veterans' organizations galvanized in an effort to once and for all put an end to war. When Sanchez returned from his war, he found no such group, no organization, no social movement that might help him make sense— much less act upon—his doubts and emotional turmoil. It's not that there was unanimity in public or in veterans' opinions about the meanings of World War II. In *The "Good War" in American Memory*, historian John Bodnar illustrates the many ways that American opinion during that war was "marked by fractures and fissures," including some 40,000 men who registered as conscientious objectors.[5] In the years following World War II, popular novels by veterans—notably Joseph Heller's *Catch-22* and James Jones's *The Thin Red Line*—highlighted the inherent irrationality and insanity of war.[6] And in his many books and essays, veteran-turned-historian Paul Fussell chronicled the scorn, resentment, and sense of victimhood felt by many veterans of the war.[7] This postwar sentiment among veterans was given form by the American Veterans Committee (AVC), which in the immediate postwar years promoted racial justice and a program of "Peace, Jobs and Freedom." However, Bodnar observed, the postwar political climate of "militarization and anticommunism" generated a narrow "traditionalist remembrance" of World War II, buttressed by the powerful and conservative American Legion, whose nationalist and pro-military voice eclipsed that of the more liberal and internationalist AVC, whose ranks were ultimately thinned as a result of the Red Scare.[8] Individual veterans' sentiments of regret, ambivalence, or dissent were largely submerged or silenced in the increasingly repressive 1950s political context.

It was within this growing Cold War ideological consensus about the meanings of "the Good War," and its manifestation in a national strategy of "containment" of communism in Korea that Ernie Sanchez returned to civilian life. In the years following the war, he found a nation proud of its victory and people prepared to buy him a drink and then to move on with life. He also landed in a momentarily sluggish postwar economy that seemed to have few places for brown-skinned men like Sanchez, no matter how many war commendations they'd earned overseas.

CLIMBING THE LADDER

Following the war, Ernie Sanchez returned to Los Angeles, eventually marrying Dora and laboring through an upwardly mobile trajectory of jobs with the Civil Service. But things were not smooth. While Sanchez may have been treated as "white" in the military, at home, racism against

Mexicans was still in full force. "I got discharged. I had been wounded; I was disabled . . . I didn't know prejudice was that bad here in California. I start hanging out with my ruffians, I start getting in trouble again. And I went to jail up in Fresno. We had stolen cars, were selling the parts . . . I saw guys who had been in jail all their lives, and I says to God, 'I don't want to live like this.' So I got out of prison. I learned. I says, 'I gotta find me a right way to live, I'm gonna come back and I want to do something—quote—'legitimate.'"

His exposure to hardened prison lifers may have scared Sanchez straight, but his commitment to "a right way to live" also came from his devotion to his wife Dora and his growing family: Ernie Jr. was born in 1948, followed by two more sons, David in 1951 and Mike in 1958, and eventually two daughters, Laurie and Vianca in 1960 and 1964, respectively. And part of Sanchez's commitment to a settled life on the straight and narrow came from a deeply rooted work ethic he'd learned as a boy during the Great Depression, largely from his father "who had no education." "As a kid I loved my father, because, during the Depression, he would always have jobs: he was a laborer; he knew carpentry, cement work, construction. My father never gave me a present [when] we were small for Christmas. He told me, 'Go out and work,' you know. When I was eight, nine years old I started shining shoes. I started selling papers. And the summer when I was in school, I'd knock on doors and sell fruit. [From] the vendor, I would get a penny or two for the pail."

Following the war, Sanchez found employment sanding cars in an auto painting business, but it was tough and unhealthy work. An adviser at the VA told him, "The GI [Bill] will pay for your school," and this started what for Sanchez would become a string of educational stints, learning partic-ular skills that allowed him to move through a succession of progressively higher-paying jobs.

Sanchez became a mechanic, "but they weren't giving jobs to Mexicans as mechanics." So around 1953, he continued his education, taking his Gen-eral Educational Development (GED), generally considered a high school diploma equivalency, and eventually earning an Associate's degree from a community college. He passed a test and was hired by the City of Los Angeles as a surveyor.

The rapidly expanding postwar Civil Service Sanchez encountered was an almost entirely white and male occupational niche that didn't begin to desegregate until subsequent decades. "I looked and all you see is white guys in there; *where are the Mexicans?*" During his professional ascent, he frequently found himself the only, or one of the very few, Mexicans in his field. When he earned a promotion as a civil engineering draftsman, "They were all white in there, all of them. 'Look at the Mexican,' 'Oh yeah, he's the janitor.' And I was up there, brown like this, and all the whites over there, they didn't talk to me very well. Because at that time, they were trained not to talk to blacks, to Mexicans—they're dogs."

Sanchez allayed his white colleagues' racist fears by being a nice guy, for instance delivering a cup of coffee daily to his immediate supervisor, who was initially wary of him: "I was a Mexican, he knows I'm gonna poison him, right?" He also set about proving himself through determined hard work: "The white guys began to kind of like me; I was getting to be part of them." Sanchez took more tests and became a civil engineer. His crowning achievement was supervising the laying of the Los Angeles International Airport runways.

As Sanchez moved up during the 1960s and 1970s, the Civil Service was becoming a more highly credentialized field, increasingly made up of people with bachelor's, master's and doctoral degrees. Though he had muted his former tough guy persona to be accepted by his white colleagues, Sanchez believed his street education gave him an edge. He was good at his work because he had learned his craft through experience in the field, "using all five senses," whereas the guys with degrees had learned in the classroom using "only two senses."

See, I was a *vato* ["homeboy"]. I come from Temple Street! The District Engineer would come and ask me questions regarding construction, and he's the District Engineer! The highest—he's got a PhD, and he's asking me! "You did it, Ernie, I mean I learned it in school, but I didn't learn it as intricate as you do," he says, "I didn't know you could compact the dirt the way you did it." You know I told you about building the international airport? And this guy didn't know, and he wanted to know the consistency of asphalt. And that's how I got promoted, that's why I surpassed all the people that had an education.

Sanchez's strategies for achieving middle-class mobility and respectability within a mostly white and increasingly college-educated occupational field drew on some of the skills he had incorporated in the street. But he also consciously shifted away from the intimidating *vato* masculinity displays in order to avoid triggering his white colleagues' racist fears— or at least to mitigate the tendency for others to mistake him for the janitor. Instead, Sanchez embodied a middle-class masculine habitus that was less threatening to college-educated white men, and thus more conducive to upward mobility in his occupational field.

In his years working for the City, Sanchez's appearance morphed. "I had to wear my tie and my suit," he said. As his dark hair began to gray, his weight topped 180 and his once youthful wiry body took on a roundness that bespoke the comforts of middle age and middle class. Appearances aside, Sanchez never completely abandoned his *vato* identity; he saw his roots on Temple Street as source of practical knowledge that fueled his career success. Still, he became a firm believer in the middle-class ideology of individual meritocratic success.

There are two kinds of people in this world: people that are entitled and people that are empowered. In a way that's why I don't like the Mexicans that come from Mexico, because what they want is, "You know what, I'm here in the United States, I deserve food stamps, I deserve government to pay for my rent," you know. And they're entitled to it, and "my children should go to school for nothing." I'm talking about all the foreigners that come, you know, they sneak into the United States.

I believe in justice, I believe in [*laughs ironically*]—I learned it the hard
way, I believe in lawful ways. Not when I was a kid, I didn't believe in it
[*laughs again*].

Sanchez's narrative of success might, on the surface, suggest that
he somehow "exchanged" his youthful *vato* habitus for a middle-aged,
middle-class, and more "white" masculine habitus. This would be a sim-
plistic conclusion. It's more accurate to say that Sanchez strategically
navigated his white colleagues' racist fears, as well as his own lack of a
formal college education, in the process developing hybrid displays of
masculinity. On the one hand, he learned the performative aspects of the
professional-class masculinity that dominated his occupation: "I had to
speak the way they were speaking." On the other hand, he selectively drew
from some of the skills and pride of the youthful *vato*—including "using
all five senses" in his work. In this sense, Sanchez's experiences anticipated
those of current young Latino men's "reformed gang masculinity,"[9] and
perhaps even more so today's black male professionals who strategically
navigate their positions as "partial tokens" in predominantly white
occupations.[10]

Sanchez's hard work paid off, and he thrived in the workplace: by the
time he was in his forties, "I was a supervisor and I was already a million-
aire." But his between-two-worlds hybridity, his "outsider-within" status,
to adopt the sociologist Patricia Hill Collins's term, also created strains
and tensions in each of the worlds he straddled.[11] When Sanchez donned
his suit for work, he recalled, "I felt great," but he also feared that "I looked
like I was a farce, like I didn't belong there." When he would get together
with friends from his youth, especially his pals from Califa who "were all
blue-collar workers," he said, "I felt like a traitor. I didn't really belong that
much with my gang."

How did Sanchez attempt to bridge the chasm between the world of his
youth and the world he had moved to? He expressed unbridled pride in
how far he'd come from his youth in the *barrio*, his words distancing him

Ernie Sanchez dressed for middle-class success, ca. 1980 (Ernie Sanchez)

from those who still live in that place, such as the many recent Mexican or Central American immigrants who populate Los Angeles. His primary narrative in creating this distance is his celebration of the meritocratic, pull-yourself-up-by-the-bootstraps story of individual success. But Sanchez's self-made-man story is not just ideological talk; at its center is the deep desire of a man of lower-class origin to earn public respect by accumulating what social scientists Richard Sennett and Jonathan Cobb called "badges of ability . . . that restore a psychological deprivation that the class structure has effected."[12] Sanchez's story is also the narrative of an embodied middle-class habitus through which he distanced himself from the physically threatening and legally transgressive dimensions of his youthful street habitus, and with which he navigated the continuing challenges posed by his colleagues' responses to his dark brown skin in a field dominated by whites.

Like many self-made men, Ernie Sanchez described clearly the ways in which the social structures of racism and class severely constrained his educational and occupational options—"my aim was to become a pimp"—and took pride in the successful strategies he employed to overcome those constraints. On the other hand, he spoke little of the ways in which a shifting postwar social context may have *enabled* his upward mobility. Mostly missing from his narrative was acknowledgment of the GI Bill of Rights' dramatic expansion of educational opportunities for veterans. The historian Lizabeth Cohen has shown that Servicemen's Readjustment Act of 1944, more commonly known as the GI Bill, was a hugely important motor for upward mobility for World War II veterans, granting them access to education and health benefits as well as low-cost mortgages.[13] Nor did Sanchez acknowledge benefiting from the postwar economic boom that included a meteoric expansion of public sector jobs, including Civil Service occupations, as well as the Civil Rights, Chicano, and "Brown Power" movements that began to open doors for Latinos from the 1950s through the mid-1970s, right when Sanchez was breaking into all-white occupational niches.[14]

By the time he retired in 1982, Sanchez proudly pointed out, "I had 250 to 300 men working under my jurisdiction . . . people with college degrees." For him, it was a symbol of his success that he was able to retire at age fifty-seven with a secure pension and an impressive accumulation of income-generating properties. When I would see Sanchez, he would frequently deliver a friendly ribbing, asking me, now past sixty, "Why the hell are you still working?"

RETURN OF THE REPRESSED

Following his retirement, Ernie Sanchez kept busy. He traveled with Dora—to Albuquerque to visit relatives, vacationing numerous times in Hawaii and in Cancún, where they owned a timeshare. He took up photography, he read, he got his real estate license and mirrored the successful investment property ventures of his brother, about whom he proudly boasted, "He's a multimillionaire." But eventually, Sanchez's wartime chickens came home to roost. "You know, when I worked for the City, I was going to school, I was going to college, and my mind was so darn busy, I was trying to educate my children and all that. But once I retired, my children were gone, I didn't have to supervise 250 men, and I was looking at TV—it came back to me."

When he was diagnosed with PTSD at the VA in 2003, Sanchez came to realize that for years "I pushed it all away" as he built his career and raised his family. In therapy, he dredged up memories he hadn't allowed himself to acknowledge consciously. I could feel the back-and-forth tug between denial and revelation in Sanchez's pained descriptions.

> When I didn't have all these other things I had to think about, they came back to me and then I found out. God, the psychiatrist told me that I killed between fifty and 100 Germans. But I didn't shoot to kill. I shoot to keep the guys down from shooting back. My job was to shoot right in front of the trench so dust and rocks and everything was right overhead so the Germans [are] not gonna stick out their heads to shoot back. That was my job, to keep them down, and keep 'em from fighting back. That was my mentality. I wasn't killing anybody. And that's what I was saying all these years. But the goddamn Iraq War reminded me what a dirty SOB I was.

The story Sanchez told himself—that he was firing his BAR just to "keep 'em down," not to kill German soldiers—is a twist on a common pattern in warfare, referred to by Dave Grossman in his book *On Killing* as a "conspiracy to miss . . . firing over the enemy's head." Sanchez's story that he had aimed not at men, but at the dirt in front of them seems to have held up as emotional insulation for much of his life. But like all insulation, it eventually wore thin and the truth began to leak through. The resulting avalanche of pain that Sanchez confronted in therapy—"that I had killed between fifty and 100 Germans"—crushed him under what Grossman called "the burden of killing."[15]

I wondered if Sanchez still felt guilty, after years of therapy and reflection. "Yeah in a way, I still do. But it's done, you know what I mean? I feel—I did it and I'm more aware of it. That's why I don't feel as bad, because guiltiness, if you try to stash it away somewhere, it grinds at you. But this way if you kind of let it out, at least look at it: you screwed up, you did it, you killed all these sons, brothers, people that were loved by everybody and you didn't even know 'em and you go and kill 'em? What kind of a person are you to go kill complete strangers, when they belong to their fathers, their brothers, you know?"

While many Americans have come to see the war in Vietnam and the current U.S. wars in the Middle East as "mistakes," many celebrate World War II as "the Good War." When I mentioned this to Sanchez, he bristled in response and lectured me: "There is no 'good war.' Any war is no good. I don't care what war it is. It's not good. I hate war more than anybody else, you know. I saw children in pieces—not dead—but pieces. I saw women, old men in pieces. How would you like to go over there, be a hero, doing that? Huh? And then one time we attacked somewhere and, goddamn, these kids are eleven, twelve, thirteen years old in uniform! And we're shooting them? And we're shooting them? What kind of an SOB are you to be shooting children? Huh?"

It was only in the final ten years or so of his life—after being jolted awake when "the goddamn Iraq War reminded me what a dirty SOB I was"—that Sanchez began to openly express these visceral antiwar sentiments. In the immediate postwar years, it was not uncommon for World War II veterans to feel ambivalence and regret about the war, feelings that too often found no legitimate space for expression in the context of anti-communism and militarism. Many vets, as a result, turned their emotional injuries inward for years, just as Ernie Sanchez had, and adopted a stoic silence about the war as they went about their daily work and family lives. There are costs to be paid for sublimating wartime trauma. Several historians have documented that the transition to civilian life may seemed to have been smooth for most World War II veterans, but there is ample evidence that as a group they suffered from higher rates of divorce, depression, anxiety, and alcoholism than non-vets.[16]

Sanchez's narrative of upward mobility is a triumphant story of individual control over his environment, but his body continued to speak a parallel story of vulnerability and deeply embedded fears and shame. His description of feeling like "a farce" to his white, professional-class peers and like "a traitor" to his childhood friends speaks to the unresolvable tensions and hidden injuries to dignity that are built in to the sort of hybrid manhood that he had strategically constructed. And his delayed PTSD chronicles a remanifestation of out-of-control bodily symptoms that for more than half a century he had sublimated into work and occupational strivings. The onset of delayed PTSD symptoms has been described by some researchers with an old Freudian term, the "return of the repressed," a resurfacing of trauma that had been partially and temporarily contained through psychological defense mechanisms, but had lingered as embedded "body memories," available to be triggered by subsequent experiences.[17] When Sanchez was finally diagnosed with PTSD—a clinical term that did not even exist in the post–World War II years—he received helpful talk therapy and medication from the VA.

Some clinicians argue that the PTSD diagnosis is too limited, focusing as it does on memories and trauma from having been harmed in circumstances beyond one's control.[18] It overlooks, they say, the moral injury a person has to live with having harmed or killed others. Brett T. Litz and his colleagues argue that clinicians who work with combat vets need to attend more "to the impact of events with moral and ethical implications," especially killing other people. "Moral injury," they conclude, "involves an act of transgression that creates dissonance and conflict because it violates assumptions and beliefs about right and wrong and personal goodness."[19] The common result, they argue, is deep anxiety and shame, such as Ernie Sanchez's shaking hands, and his self-condemnation as "a dirty SOB."

In Sanchez's view, for several decades he had been too busy working to confront his internalized anxiety and shame—"my mind was so darn busy"; "I pushed it all away"—he could not afford to feel himself to be so out of control, at least not until his work was done, his kids all grown up. The stoic silence he maintained over most his adult life about his wartime deeds was consistent with the ascendant John Wayne-style, grin-and-bear-it postwar views of American manhood. And the vehicle Sanchez deployed to maintain his emotional stoicism—the role of hard-working, upwardly mobile male breadwinner—also reflected his era's dominant views of middle-class masculinity. And at times when that was not enough, Sanchez drank—sometimes a bit too much, he admitted, but never so much that it became a problem. Postretirement, he became more vulnerable to the trigger that was the televised war in Iraq. Uncontrollably shaking and weeping after a fifty-eight-year hiatus, he sought medical help and began to deal with the costs of having sublimated his wartime trauma.

For the last dozen years of his life, Sanchez advocated for peace, rarely missing an opportunity to engage other people, young or old, about the evils of war. Unlike the other veterans I interviewed, Sanchez's peace advocacy remained an entirely individual project. He never became a political activist, never joined antiwar marches or pro-peace organizations. He told me he'd never heard of VFP, and he didn't seem that interested. That Sanchez was more conservative than the leftist peace activists I've met in VFP makes sense in part because his war did not generate a substantial antiwar movement.

By the time Sanchez reawakened to his moral injury at age seventy-eight, the mode through which he had sublimated his wartime trauma—a decades-long project of achieving dignity through occupational success—was firmly embedded in a conservative, individualist ideology of upward mobility that was largely antithetical to a collective progressive position. As a result, Sanchez combined personal healing with a politics of everyday, face-to-face antiwar advocacy. Unlike the members of VFP who appear in this book, most of whom take a morally relative position, not against all wars, but against what they see as their nation's wars of aggression and imperial domination, Sanchez's antiwar stance was a morally absolute position against all wars: "There is no 'good war.'" He is nevertheless similar to other war veterans I interviewed in the ways that he was injured, both physically and morally, by his experience in war. And he also shares with many of these other vets a long stretch of postwar psychological denial, followed by an awakening that forced him to confront his memories. But while the VFP members I interviewed engaged in collective political action to contest U.S. foreign policy and militarism, Sanchez's personal healing was expressed through everyday peace advocacy with just about everyone he met. His car sported no antiwar bumper stickers, nor did he wear a peace symbol on his lapel, but Sanchez did wear his antiwar sentiments on his sleeve.

Sanchez's peace advocacy shared another element with the leftist VFP members who appear in this book: He spoke of the men he killed in wartime not as flat (two-dimensional) caricatures, as "Krauts" or "Gooks," or even as "enemies," but as "sons, brothers, people that were loved by everybody." Unlike Korean War vet Wilson "Woody" Powell who traveled to Korea and met and sought absolution from Korean survivors of that war, Sanchez never directly reconciled with German survivors or family members. But at the heart of his everyday peace advocacy is a narrative of reconciliation through which he renders the men he killed as full human beings, beloved family members. In the terminology of Viet Thanh

Nguyen, Sanchez takes on the fundamentally humanistic task of not only "remembering our own" fallen comrades, but also "remembering others." This rendering of former enemies as "round," Nguyen reminds us, is an "alternative ethics of remembering others" that is both necessary and radical, in the sense of getting to the root of a problem, if we are to have any hope of avoiding future wars.[20]

Ernie Sanchez's story illuminates the lived body as it moves through time and through changing and shifting social contexts. An individual's embodied disposition, we can see in his story, is never rigidly fixed; it is an ongoing project, constantly reconstructed over the course of a life. Aspects of a youthful masculine disposition (like Sanchez's tough guy *vato* habitus) might be joined with elements of a habitus absorbed in a new field—perhaps one shaped by a radically different regime of race and class relations—resulting in hybrid identity formations. Hybrid or otherwise, to the extent that a masculine habitus is developed in social fields that produce and reward the use of male bodies as instruments of violence and domination—be it in the street, warfare, or a profession—the institutions that produce and thrive on an emotionally contained and violent masculine habitus generate a wake of carnage ranging from the shock and awe of military bombardment to the tears and trembling hands of the wounded warrior. Sanchez's story also illustrates hopeful possibilities: that the meanings of one's past actions, including the trauma and shame that result, can be rewoven into a project of healing, reconciliation, and peace advocacy.

-«‹◆›»-

The last time I met with Ernie Sanchez at his home, he wasn't feeling well. Thin and coughing frequently, he was recovering from a two-month regimen of chemotherapy. I asked if he'd had a chance to look at a book I had gifted him a couple of months earlier, *A Legacy Greater Than Words*, by Maggie Rivas-Rodriguez and her colleagues, a collection of oral history-based stories of Latinos and Latinas who served during World War II.

Though an avid reader, Sanchez confessed that he hadn't looked at the book for the same reason he'd rarely watch a war movie: "It brings you back, you know?" He coughed hard, and after a short pause he flashed his crooked smile and uttered, "I'm getting old," before continuing with a story of how he was mentored by an experienced combat veteran when he first took up his BAR:

> When I was on the front line, the first thing the guy told me was, "You're gonna see the Germans over there; don't shoot at 'em."
>
> "Whadya mean?"
>
> "They're not attacking you."
>
> "Yeah, but they're our enemy."
>
> You know? You never see that in a movie. Why would I make up such a dumb story?

In late 2014, as Sanchez's health began to fail, his children urged him to move from his home to an assisted living facility. He begrudgingly visited one, his daughter Laurie later told me, and in no time at all he was sharing his views on war and peace with the elderly residents he met there. But Sanchez decided he would not find his final peace there. He moved into his daughter's home and announced he would stop eating. Within a few weeks, bedridden and weak, Sanchez lay in bed to say farewell to children and grandchildren, and to four surviving members of his Califa gang.

Ernie Sanchez's funeral on January 10, 2015, included short devotions from daughters Laurie, who prayed, "May we all be judged by the content of our character, not the color of our skin," and Vianca, who delivered the simple entreaty, "May all former gang members and war veterans with PTSD find peace." Perhaps sixty people showed up at the cemetery, under a steady rain. The priest spoke of Sanchez as a "hero," a moniker I guessed Sanchez would have scoffed at. Two U.S. marines played taps and folded an American flag, presenting it to the family. Later, at the lunch reception, Sanchez's son Michael approached me and pulled a sealed envelope from his breast pocket. "You know what this is?—It's shrapnel from my dad's body." Michael had asked the mortician to get this to him after the cremation. "My dad carried this shrapnel in his back for the rest of his life, after the war," he explained. "It caused him ongoing physical pain. But now that is over."

It is typical for an imperial people to have a short memory for its less pleasant imperial acts, but for those on the receiving end, memory can be long indeed.

—Chalmers Johnson, *Blowback*

I was an honorable person doing dishonorable things, I guess you could say. When I had the chance to examine what I was doing and get out of that condition that caused me to do that, then I was able to make the change and become a little more honorable.

—Wilson Powell

CHAPTER 3

-‹‹‹◆›››-

Being Honorable

WILSON "WOODY" POWELL, KOREAN WAR

"For Americans," historian Bruce Cumings observed, "Korea is both a forgotten war and a never-known war. The war began to disappear from
consciousness as soon as the fighting stabilized."[1] But for Ms. Hwang Jum
Soon, as for countless other Korean survivors, that war could never be forgotten. The terror of August 10, 1950, when U.S. soldiers attacked from
the ground and from the air, massacring eighty-three of the then-twenty-
two-year-old mother's kin and neighbors in the southern village of Kokan-
Ri, still burned in her memory. Grisly evidence of the atrocity was etched
in the multiple bullet wounds still scarring Hwang's arms, legs, and torso
half a century later, as she sat on a bench and spoke through an interpreter
with a visitor.

It was September of 2000, and Hwang Jum Soon was welcoming Wilson "Woody" Powell, an Air Force veteran of the U.S. war in Korea. This
was Powell's first time back since he departed Korea in 1953, immediately
following the signing of the truce that had established the 38th parallel as
the still-contested divide between North and South Korea. Following a
visit to China as a representative of VFP, Powell had arranged through the
American Friends Service Committee to connect in Seoul with Serapina
Cha, an "underground figure in the resistance movement in South Korea."
Together, the two "hopped on a train" and rolled south to the small village
of Kokan-Ri, where Cha had arranged a meeting with seventy-two-year-old

Hwang. Powell described the old woman as "all of four-foot two, stocky, dressed in a pink tunic and flowered pants, tiny feet in black, rubber-soled shoes. Her hair was close-cropped and her skin fine-wrinkled and reddened by outdoor living."[2] Hwang led Powell through a grove of trees, arriving at a shrine that had been built at the site of the 1950 massacre that she alone survived.

> I could see the results of the strafing across the floor of the shrine. Oh yeah, the bullet holes are still there—hundreds, perhaps thousands of them. Just about everybody was wiped out. And there were two groups of soldiers, two squads, I assume, coming from two different directions as she described it, and wiped them out. She was hit seven times by rifle fire. She had the scars all over her body. She passed out. She had a baby and when she woke up the baby was gone. She had hoped against hope that the GIs coming through had picked it up and it was still alive and that maybe someday she'd be reunited with her son.

Following their visit to the bullet-ridden shrine, the two sat on a concrete bench and spoke through an interpreter, and it is here that Powell issued his apology.

> She takes my hands in both of hers and looks me in the eyes. Through our interpreter, she tells us all that I am the first American soldier ever to come here since the day of the killing. She is very glad that an American veteran cares to come and learn from her. I can only say, "I am so sorry," how terribly sorry I was for what happened to her—that I felt some responsibility because I was part of that organization that did it. I am speaking for myself, of course, but I am also speaking for all other veterans who feel as I do; that we need to make amends wherever we can, and to let people know that wars have very personal, very harmful, consequences, are certainly avoidable and unnecessary.

Delivering that apology to Hwang Jum Soon was, Powell recalled, "very simple, and it felt very, very good." By the time of his return visit to Korea

Hwang Jum Soon (left) meets Wilson Powell at Kokan-Ri, South Korea,
September 2000 (Wilson Powell)

in 2000, Powell was fully aware that the Korean War had not only ended
in a stalemate—a war about which some U.S. veterans had complained
they'd been ordered "to die for a tie"—the war also left a lasting and hor-
rific impact on civilians like Hwang, the sole survivor of the massacre that
wiped out her village. Casualties in the three-year war were steep for the
major combatant forces—North Korean, South Korean, Chinese, and
American troops—but the carnage suffered by civilians was worse. "The
Korean War was an exceptionally bloody affair," historian John Tirman
observed, "and more than half the deaths, perhaps much more than half,
were civilians."[3] From an American vantage point, writing off the Korean
War as the "Forgotten War" was a central part of the problem, Woody
Powell had come to believe. It is in remembering, becoming accountable
for one's actions, and being prepared to "make amends" with former enemies and traumatized civilians that former soldiers like Powell might
begin to make peace with themselves and with the world.

Woody Powell's 2000 apology to Hwang Jum Soon in Kokan-Ri is a punctuated moment in his life story. It is also indicative of a larger pattern of reconciliation that had begun a few years earlier, when Powell befriended Zhou Ming-Fu, a Chinese veteran who had fought on the side of the North Koreans during the war. Similar to the other men I profile in this book, Powell's story fuses themes of personal healing, service to others, and peace activism. But his commitment to reconciliation with former "enemies" stands out as the salient thread in his weaving together a life project that he hopes will be "a little more honorable."

Using Viet Thanh Nguyen's terminology, I observed the ways that Powell's story teaches us how to experience "the Other" as "round," as fully human. "Without this mutual recognition," Nguyen writes, "a genuine reconciliation will be difficult to achieve."[4]

—《《◆》》—

While in the early stages of my research, I asked several members of VFP if they knew a Korean War veteran who would be a good fit for my book. Everyone I asked told me, "You have to talk with Woody Powell." I contacted Powell via email, and after some productive back-and-forth, he graciously agreed to do a life history interview. I flew to St. Louis, and spoke with him for the better part of two days at his home, where he lives with his wife Joan and their Chow mix, Merlin. I sat in a comfortable easy chair in their den, as Powell settled in on his couch, periodically rising to fetch an old photo or an article he wanted to share. Merlin lazed on the floor, not far from Powell's feet, eventually moseying out of the room. From time to time Joan offered coffee, and on one occasion handed Powell a scrapbook she thought might spur memories of his work with VFP.

Pushing eighty-four when I met him, Woody Powell sported a neatly trimmed beard, a thinning but striking shock of white hair, and wire-framed, aviator-style glasses. His khaki polo shirt with the VFP logo on the left breast was neatly tucked into brown shorts. Standing just shy of six-feet tall, his body is considerably thicker than the lanky rail-thin first class airman I see in the 1951 photos he showed me. He seems content with having slowed in recent years, his national and international work with VFP ebbing to a trickle. But he is still active locally, and is especially proud of his work as executive director of the Veterans Court Technology Clinic, a local nonprofit he helped to form in 2012 that provides veterans in recovery with computer and other skills, assisting them in accessing education and jobs. On the second day of our interview, the phone rang. After speaking briefly and hanging up, Powell beamed and told me, proudly, "That was a guy from the clinic, calling to tell me he just got a job." The day after my departure, he said, he'd be spending several hours writing grants to raise funds for the clinic.

Woody and Joan settled in St. Louis in late 1976, but for the previous twenty-five years he'd been a man in motion, shifting from job to job and place to place. In retrospect, Powell's starts and stops seem like a frantic pace of life transitions, from the East Coast to the West Coast and places in between, in the early years hitchhiking and later driving an assortment of cars and motorcycles. I was puzzled at first when he would interrupt his narrative with parenthetical asides about particular cars or motorcycles, but I came to see his infatuation as emblematic of a mid-twentieth-century cultural love affair with the individual autonomy and freedom of movement across our vast continent. Powell conveyed a whiff of nostalgia when he talked of cherished cars or motorcycles—the 1936 Chevy Coupe ("Cherry! It was beautiful"), or the used '48 Indian bike he bought and rebuilt. But Woody Powell is not stuck in the past. In the hours we spoke, he displayed the composed and easy style of a man who has made peace with his past, is comfortable where he has landed, and feels he has meaningful tasks ahead of him, though his pace has slowed.

A FATHER'S WAR

Born in June 1932 in Cambridge, Massachusetts, "during the middle of the Great Depression," the infant's naming remained briefly in limbo pending a tug-of-war between his father Wilson Marcy Powell III's desire to name his son after his best friend David, and the family patriarch Wilson Marcy Powell II's desire for the boy to carry on the patrilineal name. The family patriarch, who "was lord of a small manor" raising Merino sheep in upstate New York, eventually won out, and the baby was officially dubbed Wilson Marcy Powell IV. Wilson spent the first three years of his life in Cambridge as his father completed his PhD in physics at Harvard. Following two years at Connecticut College for Women, his father had a "brief little stay" at Swarthmore, before taking a faculty position at Kenyon College in Gambier, Ohio. Though the family would stay in Gambier for only a few short years, it was here, at age five, that young Wilson "really sort of began my childhood."

Wilson's parents "dabbled in Quakerism" during his childhood, but in retrospect he sees them as "pretty confused religiously." He remembers his mother, Fredrika, as "kind of a background figure" in his life. His father looms large in his memory, even though he "was mostly distant, very tied in to his work." The work, it turns out was a field of theoretical physics that, within a few years, would have awesome, practical implications for a nation at war. In 1940, his father's scientific successes won him a Guggenheim fellowship to the University of California, Berkeley, and the family moved for what they expected to be a yearlong stay.

Young Wilson loved his life from ages six to nine in Gambier. There were woods in the backyard. From a downed tree he created his own imaginary submarine. "I'd go out there alone and just play submarine." He roamed freely with groups of kids who "formed gangs," and "we had our little wars." When one kid shot Wilson in the rear end with an arrow, "it broke their arrow and after that, they called me 'Iron Pants.'" Just as with the arrow, that nickname didn't stick, but the next one did. "I had two front teeth that were widely separated, so they called me Woody Woody Woodchuck." Gambier, Powell recalls, was "really kind of an idyllic place. It was hard for me to leave there."

But in the summer of 1941, his father "obtained a 1939 Studebaker Commander, which was a pretty stellar automobile, [and] an old secondhand Hoover trailer. Maroon. It ended up filled with his equipment." The Powell family spent the summer in the Rockies, "my father on the top of Mt. Evans photographing cosmic rays in a home-built cloud chamber that cost him $28, the family in a log cabin at 10,000 feet, fishing and roaming the mountains."

From there, the Powells completed their cross-country drive to Berkeley. His father's experimental device in the Hoover trailer was "a cloud chamber with massive amounts of batteries." With that device, his father made "a new discovery to share with the world; he'd photographed a meson's [a subatomic particle] unmistakable trail. Unknown even to himself, he was qualifying to work on the most destructive scientific endeavor ever, in a war that had already begun."

A few months after the family's arrival in Berkeley, Powell recalls Sunday, December 7, 1941, as the day "my life changed": "On Monday morning, no sooner had I walked to school than I was sent home. That night, we draped newly purchased blackout curtains while we listened to news about the Japanese attack on Pearl Harbor. Everybody's imagination was fired. We thought bombers would arrive overhead at any moment." As the initial fear faded, Powell remembers the war years mostly being exciting, rather than as a scary time. He was, "you know, a kid," and he recalls being "just kind of excited" about the war, confident the United States would win quickly and that his family would return to Gambier.

I got very interested in the war during that time. I became an aircraft spotter; I studied the silhouettes of enemy and friendly aircraft so I could tell them apart and report the enemy planes. I built model Tomahawk and Spitfire fighter planes, battleships, and submarines. The most exciting Christmas present I received was a wooden M1 Garand rifle. I did my own version of a close-order drill, wearing a plastic helmet liner and sergeant stripes pinned to my sleeve. We subscribed to *Life* magazine. I avidly absorbed the chronicles of war that appeared every week. Comic books, radio shows, newspapers, dinner talk, movies— all were about the war.

At ages ten and eleven, Powell got into sports, but that source of joy was short lived. When he was thirteen, he badly crushed his hip playing football and was on crutches for a year and a half. During this time his parents temporarily broke up. His father seemed to be "gone forever" during the war years, working in the lab with J. Robert Oppenheimer, the lead scientist on the Manhattan Project and later dubbed "the father of the atomic bomb." "On his leaves home," Powell remembers, "he and my mother fought long-running battles, using the strategies of shame and silence." His mother suffered a nervous breakdown. Powell's younger brother and sister were placed in a boarding school in Oakland, and he was sent to live and work on an apricot farm near Sacramento. "We didn't even know why we were sent away." Powell recalls feeling "depressed," and for the first time in his life, seriously suicidal.

The United States imposed brutal exclamation points on the end of World War II by dropping atomic bombs on the Japanese cities of Hiroshima and Nagasaki. The initial blast and resulting firestorm on August 6, 1945, from the device nicknamed "Little Boy" immediately killed about 80,000 and injured another 70,000 people in Hiroshima, the vast majority of them civilians. Three days later, U.S. pilots dropped "Fat Man" on the city of Nagasaki, immediately killing about 40,000 and injuring another 60,000, nearly all of them civilians. In the ensuing years, though accurate numbers are hard to come by, tens of thousands more from these two cities died of the short-term or long-term effect of injuries, burns, and exposure to radiation.

VJ Day was celebrated in the United States on August 14, 1945. In Berkeley, this meant the Powell family would finally be reunited. His father returned home, but it soon became apparent that there would be no going back to the "idyllic" life Powell had known as a youngster in Gambier. "My father was gone all the time until they dropped the bomb and the war was over. After the war, he came home. He was very ill. He had boils on his neck and was bedridden for several weeks."

Powell's father would not talk much about it, but bits and pieces of the story of his role in building the bomb began to trickle out. The one time Powell asked his father about what he did during the war, the response was minimal. "I designed huge magnets, Woody. That's all. Just great big magnets."[5] While his father was ill in bed, however, colleagues would come by to visit, and Powell would hear the scientists talking about the bomb. "I overheard him say to one man, another physicist, 'They didn't have to drop it on all those people, did they? Did they?'"

His father stayed on as a physics professor at University of California, "working with [Ernest] Lawrence," who developed the cyclotron in Berkeley's famous radiation laboratory. Powell's parents resumed their connection with Quakerism for a time. His mother dabbled in Christian Science, while his father eventually "became active in the Vedanta Society, a Westernized version of Hinduism. I believe Robert Oppenheimer may have had something to do with his conversion, and somewhere in that ancient system of belief, they both found ways to mitigate guilt."[6] Despite this spiritual turn, his father fell deeper into drink in the postwar years. At home, Powell saw his father routinely imbibe from a jug of sherry, "just kind of zone out and he wasn't available." In 1955 his parents split up for good. His father, who would remarry in 1956, died of a stroke in 1974. In retrospect, Powell is convinced that "their marriage and my father's alcoholism could be considered casualties of the war."

For Powell's part, he does not recall thinking much in the postwar years about "what had happened at Hiroshima or Nagasaki." He was in high school and finally off crutches. He was thinking forward, "champing at the bit" to "have adventures." His years of itinerant work and travel commenced in his mid-teens. At fifteen, in the winter of 1947–1948, he was sent to a private school in Pennsylvania. In February, after just two weeks, he

ran away and hitchhiked back to California during one of the coldest
winters on record. When he was sixteen, he and a friend "hitchhiked
from California out to Ohio and back." By the time he was seventeen, he
was living alone in a rented room in Berkeley, attending high school and
taking jobs picking pears, assisting at a Boy Scouts Camp, "flipping pan-
cakes, eggs, and bacon at a great rate," cleaning cages in a pet store, and
working at a skating rink. On the night of his high school graduation, he
got drunk, and "the next day I hitchhiked out with a friend. Went down
to Santa Monica, and that's where I remember going down into Tijuana
and getting my cherry popped by a French whore. She was lovely. She was
very, very, very nice to me." He stayed in Los Angeles for a spell, found
work selling magazines door-to-door. He and some friends drove "a brand
new 1950 Ford" to Kansas City and "did a little selling there." The work
was unsatisfying, and as he approached the age of eighteen, Powell was
aware the United States was ramping up a war in Korea. He hoped to be a
part of it.

My War

In mid-1950, as the United States was committing to war in Korea, Woody
Powell realized he was finally just the right age. As a boy during World
War II, he had witnessed "my father's students going off to war," but
Powell was old enough only to watch from afar, participating as an "air-
plane spy": "I thought, well, they've got their war and this one was mine,
obviously. I turned eighteen on June 24, the day before the war started. So
I was ready to get into it." But it was not so easy for Powell to "get into it."
First, the Marine Corps rejected him. When their doctors saw the scar on
his hip from that old football injury, they told him, "We don't want you
because that's a disability. You could collapse it fighting." Undeterred,
Powell tried the Air Force, and when their doctor saw the scar, Powell told
him it was "Osgood-Schlatter disease." When the doctor left the room to
look up the disorder, Powell surreptitiously picked up the medical form

from his desk. "I checked off the box on the paper and went on and it never caught up to me. I passed myself in the physical." On August 6, 1950, Wilson Marcy Powell IV had signed on for a four-year stint with the Air Force, a division of the U.S. Armed Forces that had become independent from the Army less than three years earlier.

In Oakland, Powell boarded a train to San Antonio, and from there it was on to Sheppard Field in northern Texas, for basic training. The U.S. military had been downsizing since the end of World War II, and Powell arrived to a facility with inadequate mess halls, roach-ridden barracks, and leftover World War II clothing and equipment. "It was a real clusterfuck." Eventually, they assigned Powell to duty as an air policeman, which involved infantry training, learning jujitsu, and "how to defend yourself against the baton and how to use a baton. People would get their heads cracked and everything. I thought it was a bunch of shit. It was a real crock. It was what I was signed up for four freaking years."

Still, Powell was keen to join the fighting in Korea, and he recalls this desire initially being driven by his dream of "glory." Instead, he was assigned three months at Edwards Air Force Base, and then seventeen months working "a little AC&W, which is Aircraft Control and Warning, out in the Mojave Desert, about fifteen miles north and east of the borax mines at Boron." Powell was not happy to be here, so far removed from the action. He became "disturbed with the way things were being handled there," so here he engaged in perhaps his first publicly rebellious act, using a mimeograph machine to put out "a clandestine newspaper. I just wrote criticism of how the outfit was being run." The commanding officer "read me the riot act and talked about sedition and all kinds of terrible things that could happen to me," but eventually he placed Powell in charge of putting out the squadron newspaper. This and some side adventures—like driving his '36 Chevy to Los Angeles and befriending actress Debbie Reynolds—helped pass the time. Still, Powell's frustration was growing. "I wanted to get over there. I'm putting my name on every volunteer list that I can put it on, you know. I had to get over there, and

I'm being passed over and passed over and passed over. My eagerness to join the war had more to do with needing to do my part than glory, now. The glory notion was fast fading. I think it was the stories, the attitudes of the veterans I lived with that was getting to me. That, and the ingloriousness of day-to-day military bullshit. But I still wanted to get to Korea."

At the time, Woody Powell's knowledge of history and foreign affairs was limited. He had a somewhat shallow—and certainly not a critical— understanding of the roots or consequences of the war he was so eager to join. Americans eventually came to view the three-year armed conflict in Korea as the initial flash point of the Cold War between the United States and the Soviet Union. But the Korean War was also tethered to the war Powell's father had helped to end just five years earlier. The Japanese occupied Korea from 1910 through the end of World War II. When the United States defeated and occupied Japan in 1945, the United States and the Soviet Union agreed to a five-year bilateral trusteeship in Korea, and the United States imposed the 38th parallel as the dividing line between North and South. By early 1946, according to Bruce Cumings, "Korea [was] effectively divided [with] two regimes and two leaders": Kim Il Sung in the North, and Syngman Rhee, who had been installed by the United States in the South.[7] By the end of that year, several rebellions against the U.S. occupation had broken out in the South. In 1948 through 1949, the United States endorsed and supported Syngman Rhee's bloody counter-insurgency campaigns that killed approximately 100,000 Koreans, before what most people think of as "the war" began.

There is still disagreement about what precipitated the fighting, but it's clear that on June 24 and 25, 1950, combat between the North and the South exploded. The next six months would constitute what Cumings calls "the known and observed Korean War," a time of brutal ground and air combat marked by dramatic back-and-forth momentum swings. At the outset of combat, General Douglas MacArthur, the hero of the U.S. World War II victory in the Pacific, assured President Harry Truman and the

American people that the enemy would be quickly defeated: "I can handle it with one hand tied behind my back."[8] The general's overconfidence was fueled by his infamously imperial hubris. MacArthur's prediction of an easy victory, echoed in Washington, DC, and the U.S. media, was also supported by two widely accepted and wildly misguided American beliefs. The first, according to historian John Tirman, was Americans' "Oriental-ist" view of the "racial and moral inferiority of Koreans," who were widely seen as "gooks or coolies," as uncivilized "savages" who would easily be crushed by the mighty armed forces of a superior civilization.[9]

The U.S. political and military leadership was wrong in their second assumption as well: the belief that China wouldn't dare enter the war. Though Joseph Stalin, likely fearing the Americans' ability to strike with their then-superior nuclear arsenal, made clear that the Soviet Union would not devote troops in support of North Korea, Mao Tse Tung eventually committed Chinese troops. With a massive intervention of ground troops in late 1950 and early 1951, China stalled the U.S. and South Korean forces' surge and tipped the momentum back to the North. As Airman First Class Wilson Powell marked time in the Mojave Desert, Zhou Ming-Fu, the man who three decades later would become Powell's friend, was poised with the Chinese People's Volunteer troops to enter the battlefield from the North. In the book he later penned with Powell, Ming-Fu recalled, "The voice condemning U.S. imperialism was everywhere." In March 1951, Ming-Fu advanced with the Chinese infantry into Korea. Marching through cities that "had been destroyed by heavy bombs," double-timing it with a 30-kilogram pack and covering "no less than fifty kilometers a night," it took them twenty-four days to reach the front. "We would spend over 1,000 days and nights there that I would remember forever."[10]

Meanwhile, Woody Powell stewed in the desert. While visiting Los Angeles, he had gotten engaged with a young woman, Hope, "but then she went home and found another guy. I was devastated." During night duty five miles from the base, Powell considered killing himself with his .45, but when he saw a lovely desert sunrise, he relented: "Jesus, it was just so glorious. You know, I just thought, nah." Not long after that, he got the call.

On September 19, 1952, Powell and 6,000 other troops shipped out from San Francisco to Japan on the USNS *General Nelson M. Walker*. Traveling from Yokohama by train to Itazuke Air Base in southern Japan, Powell recalls, "We passed through Nagasaki. We could still see the A-bomb damage, though most had been cleaned up." I asked him what passed through his mind when he saw the destruction in Nagasaki, and he replied, "I thought about my father and wondered what he would have felt had he seen it firsthand. I had some idea already—deeply dismayed."

Powell recalls feeling "frustrated" at having to do a stint in Japan before being deployed to Korea. "By then the air over Korea was ours and enemy planes were rare. Most of the war had been fought already, and I still wasn't there. But I was having other adventures. I was discovering how it felt to be part of a conquering army. First of all, women were everywhere—available for the asking. I asked for what I wanted and received it as long as I could pay the modest fee."

Powell's description of his "adventures" with Japanese prostitutes as a sort of reward for being "part of a conquering army" reflects a political understanding that he did not yet have when he was a twenty-year-old first airman. At the time, as with many very young men sent to foreign wars, Powell's discovery that Japanese "women were everywhere—available for the asking" meshed with an all-too-common culture of military men's entitlement to women's bodies in conquered and occupied nations.[11]

By early December 1952, when Powell finally landed in Korea for his assignment at K-2, a major F-84 fighter bomber base near Taegu, most of the ground fighting had abated. On July 10, 1951, well before Powell's arrival, truce talks had begun. During his time in Korea, positional ground skirmishes persisted along the demilitarized zone and U.S. planes continued to take off and land from K-2 and other air bases, bombing targets in the North. As an air policeman, Powell's job was patrolling around the parked F-84 "Blowtorches" to prevent sabotage by guerillas. Night duty,

Airman First Class Wilson Powell, K-2 Air Force Base, Taegu, Korea, 1952 (Wilson Powell)

he recalls, "was icy cold. I had to just keep moving the whole night long." And it was scary too, "walking airplanes" by himself, with just his .45. "Just before I'd gotten here, Syngman Rhee had released 40,000 prisoners into the southern area, so we were bedeviled by the guerilla activity around that base and they were constantly sneaking in and sabotaging and draining fuel and stealing. We could see their campfires up in the hills at night. We'd go beyond the perimeter of the base and we'd take over these areas which were roughly 800 linear yards and patrol those areas. I'd get sniped at."

Powell learned that the base police were developing a brand new canine unit, "and I wanted to get into that." He was paired with a German

Shepherd, Bodo, who at first was too distrustful and fierce to approach safely. After some patient training and trust-building, Powell and Bodo bonded and became an inseparable and effective team. One night, they were patrolling the base perimeter near an ammunition dump they called the "rocket shed," when Bodo alerted Powell of "an incursion." Powell attempted to alert the base, but a mountain was blocking his radio signal. Alone in the dark with his dog and his .45 pistol, he found himself in "a firefight" with an unseen enemy. "It was a hold-them-off type of firefight. I just fired in their direction and they'd move and they'd fire back at me. Then I'm sure they moved because I don't think anybody hit anything but this went on for a long time. At least an hour before daylight. Going from tree to tree and firing. I'd always kept a whole bunch of ammunition with me. It was just me and the dog. It was very nervous work."

The Blowtorch fighter bombers that Powell and Bodo were protecting were flying daily sorties to the North, "each carrying two 500-pound bombs." Powell regularly witnessed "massive takeoffs. Seventy-six aircrafts were taking off at once," from their 10,000 foot strip. "Their mission was ground support for our forces at the front. They often carried napalm, which I had a firsthand experience with when a pod failed to toggle off until the plane was opposite my unit, flying over a riverbed. When the pod let go we were blasted by the fireball, but spared the jelly. I had a good idea of what it must have been like for enemy troops." In retrospect, Powell realizes that he "had no idea at the time I was there of the extent of the bombing." Much later, he learned that "we were bombing the shit out of that place and I didn't really understand how indiscriminate the bombing was. It was totally indiscriminate. Every crossroads. Every village, every city, every town. Every bridge. Every bit of infrastructure. Dams."

Bruce Cumings documents the extent and devastating impact of the massive U.S. carpet bombings of cities and villages in North Korea. In addition to raining "oceans of napalm" on North Korea, U.S. planes dropped 635,000 tons of bombs, more than dropped in the entire Pacific Theater in World War II. "At least 50 percent of eighteen of the North's twenty-two major cities were obliterated," Cumings writes, including 75 percent of the North Korean capital, Pyongyang.[12] Civilian casualties were massive. As peace talks dragged on, Cumings notes, "the United States also brandished the biggest weapon in its arsenal" with public atomic bomb tests in Nevada. President Dwight D. Eisenhower and the Joint Chiefs of Staff made public proclamations suggesting a possible use of nuclear arms in North Korea, and also against China.[13] "This atomic black-mail," in the words of Cumings, was "a way of getting a message to the enemy that it had better sign the armistice."[14]

Woody Powell may have remained ignorant of the impact of the daily comings and goings of the warplanes he guarded, but he witnessed local acts of barbarism close-up. As an air policeman, part of his job was to serve as liaison with the local Korean national police, whom he came to view as highly corrupt and untrustworthy. One night, he was on duty with the national police in a nearby small village. He observed a lieutenant, "a miserably vicious brutal person," interrogating an old woman, and "just beating the shit out of her." Powell had authority in that situation and told him to stop. "So very reluctantly he stopped and I said let her go and he let her go." Another time, however, Powell could not intervene in time to stop that same Korean police officer from committing what shocked Powell as "a casual homicide": "We came across one of his men asleep and he had me take the rifle out of the guy's hands and then he shot him. I was stunned. I didn't know how to react to that. I just did not know what to do. It was part and parcel of the brutality that was just all around us. And I had participated." Immersed in a context of fear and brutality, Powell laments, "I became an angry, violent person for a time. So did my dog, made paranoid by distrust training."

Harnessing that violent anger, Powell and Bodo became an effective team in interrogating prisoners of war. "I tortured people using my dog. I thought I was being humane but actually the dog was more terrifying to them than getting beat up. The kennels were narrow and deep and we'd put a prisoner in one of those kennels and lock the door on them and the dogs all around would sense his presence and they'd be pulling on their choke chains and making these horrible hacking noises to get at them. The Koreans had kind of an abnormal fear of dogs for some reason. And, after twenty-four hours of that, he'd just fold and we got out of them what we wanted. Yeah. We broke them with dogs."

During his months in Korea, Powell recalls mostly "drinking pretty normally," but he once went "on one monumental drunk," that he now figures was a response to his immersion in a context of fear and violence. "You know . . . ," he paused for a moment and then continued with a subdued tone of voice, "brutality is something that you can get used to even though it's contrary to your deepest nature, you can get used to it. And I did. At least I was able to live through it without going out of my nut. Other people did go off their nuts. There was a lot of breakdowns amongst our troops. And I encountered that as an air policeman."

Powell found one way to mitigate the shame that was starting to eat at him. Kids—orphans of the war—seemed to be wandering everywhere. "I was having feelings for those kids when they were coming around our out-fit. And, I was really worried about them. Nobody was looking after them." Once, in the wintertime, Powell came across "two boys that were dead in a little shack they'd built, wrapped up in each other's arms, and that affected me pretty deeply." He met a local farming couple that was taking in orphaned kids. "They had nothing. They had absolutely nothing except their humanity, which really impressed me at that time because I was kind of losing it about humanity, you know." Powell decided to help. "They needed a dormitory. They needed a better place to sleep. They needed a lot of stuff and they needed food." He wrote a letter home that was published in the *Berkeley Gazette*. In response, "a mound of boxes" soon arrived from home, but the donations were mostly adult clothing, "unsuitable for the kids." Powell and his partner Scotty, also an air policeman, took the adult clothing to Taegu, where it was "worth a fortune on the black market. That bought us a whole bunch of bags of rice and building materials." With further support from a Methodist chaplain at the base who secured donations from a church in the States, Powell and his colleagues "arranged to have a dormitory built" for the kids. He "really needed that activity," he can see in retrospect, "as a counterpoint to the deadly, exhausting routine of nightly patrols."

The truce was signed on July 27, 1953. Powell was ordered on that very day to board a plane for a redeployment center in Fuji, Japan. He was surprised at how quickly this happened, and though he was "glad to get out of there. Glad it was over," he was also "deeply saddened" at having to leave Bodo behind. "That was terrible. I cried and Scotty cried even though his dog was a beast. I was really down about the dog. Leaving the dog."

Memories of his half year in Korea would stick with Woody Powell for the rest of his life, eventually fueling his peace activism. For most Americans, however, the three-year stalemate was mostly forgotten behind what historian John Tirman calls an "architecture of indifference," supported by "the McCarthy deluge" of the early 1950s, a combination of American beliefs in the frontier myth, racism, and ethnocentrism toward Asians, and a "just world theory" that posited the United States as always being on the side of right and good in the world.[15] "The tragedy," according to Cumings, was that after so many deaths "the war solved nothing." However, Cumings concluded, the Korean War did have one enduring impact. The United States was now "a very different country . . . one with hundreds of permanent military bases abroad, a large standing army and a permanent national security state at home. It was this war, and not World War II, that occasioned the enormous foreign military base structure and the domestic military-industrial complex to service it and has come to define the sinews of American global power since."[16] A "centrist consensus" on how to "contain" global communism had emerged in the United States, with a global chain of U.S. military bases that positioned the United States as "the policeman of the world." A few years later, this consensus "deeply shaped how the Vietnam War was fought."[17] But in the summer and fall of 1953, Airman First Class Wilson Powell had had it with "my war," and was keen to close out this Air Force chapter of his life.

Freshly home from Korea, Powell spent thirty days' leave in Berkeley, where he felt "out of sorts, that I didn't fit anywhere." The community where he'd come of age "felt strange to me, as though I didn't really belong. I was languishing, with another ten months to serve." Following his month of leave, Powell served out those final months of his enlistment stationed at a Strategic Air Command base in Limestone, Maine. Here, he guarded B-36 bombers grounded for maintenance. Powell chuckled in recalling that when he was ordered to do "chicken shit things like scrubbing the barracks floor," he refused. "[I] got into a fight with my sergeant. We took him into the luggage locker and he stood down and said, 'Well let's make it look like we had a fight.' He was saving face. I helped him save face but I wasn't about to do that chicken shit stuff that they had us do in basic training. After all, I'd been to Korea!" During his final months in Maine, Powell purchased a "secondhand '48 Indian motorcycle, and started rebuilding it." The day he finally got his discharge, "it was kind of anticlimactic." He "just wandered off the base, got on my motorcycle," and the U.S. Air Force receded in his rearview mirror. A month later, Woody Powell "got back to Berkeley with exactly ten cents in my pocket."

I Was an Imposter

One of the first things Woody Powell did when he got back to Berkeley was to get a dog—a German Shorthair he named Bodo II. He and his friend David Levins decided they would enroll at University of California, Berkeley, with support from the GI Bill. Powell also launched an ill-fated Jewish delicatessen with Levins. "When I started Cal," he recalls, "my intention was to get a degree in sociology and go back to Korea and take care of kids. But life intervened. And so I had to put that aside." The lion's share of the "life" that intervened in Powell's educational goals had to do with his "kind of rocky" new marriage with Annie in late 1955, and the birth of their daughter Heidi in 1956. After two years of university, he "left Cal" and "got a job at Fred Finch Children's Home in Oakland. Annie got on as a cook and I got on as a maintenance man and group worker. We lived over the kitchen. That's when we had a child. Had Heidi in 1956. But, Annie and I were not getting along."

At the time Powell had a "'52 Chevy pickup and I outfitted it with a canopy in the back and we decided we'd move. It was my dog, my daughter, and my wife. We headed for Connecticut." There, Powell enrolled at the University of Connecticut. He made a living first working nights at a local rubber plant, and then he became a copy editor for an education industry newsletter. Life, at the time, "was a god-awful mess." Annie was pregnant again, and she and he were separated. "It's a sure mess of time. I was out of work and separated, trying to get a divorce." During that messy stretch in 1958, Powell met and fell for Joan, a young woman who roomed with his sister. "We'd gotten together. The rubber broke, literally." Nine months later, Woody and Joan had a son, Christopher; at roughly the same time, Annie was giving birth to another son, Gordon. Powell's divorce with Annie finalized one week before he married Joan.

Woody, Joan, and Christopher moved back to California. Woody won custody of Heidi and Gordon, and their California family swelled to six with the birth of Benjamin in 1961. He found himself in a common position for a man in the postwar baby boom years: a family's breadwinner with lots of mouths to feed. He traversed a succession of jobs: selling household goods door-to-door, retail in a department store, selling frozen foods and home freezers, and a stint doing surveillance work for a private investigator. Then, he met a man who hired and trained him to work as a machinist. Powell moved his family to Southern California where he worked to establish a grab bar and hand rail manufacturing business called Safe Rail. The project failed, and Powell next worked for Master Builders between 1964 and 1968, with a specialty in laying concrete floors and factory construction. In 1968, a guy "who saw what I did with concrete" offered him a job processing fresh slag and selling it to Kaiser Steel. Powell worked the next seven years for International Mill Service before they lost their contract, after which he "tried to make a living wholesaling jewelry . . . setting up booths in Las Vegas and LA. It was a crazy thing but I was just trying to transition and keep money flowing."

Powell was mostly managing to meet his breadwinning obligations, but he wasn't feeling particularly good about life, or about himself. "I was an imposter. I mean, I've always been an imposter. I wasn't a machinist but I passed myself off as a machinist. I wasn't a literary person but I passed myself off as a copy editor. I always felt like a faker for what I was doing. That's where the drinking began, with Master Builders." When his old hip injury flared up, Powell acquired a prescription for Dexamyl,[18] and joined daily use of that drug with his growing habit of drinking $1.68-a-gallon jug wine he'd keep in the car. "I began carrying a bottle of red wine under the seat. I was on the road a lot going out to these remote areas in San Bernardino and Riverside counties, working on batch plants down to Yuma. All that time I rode I would be sucking off on a bottle of red wine and feeling pretty good. Then I hit the damn Dexamyl. I've often said I found God tooling down the San Bernardino freeway sucking on Silver Satin and popping Dexamyl."

For a time, Powell convinced himself that none of this was a problem. "I rarely had hangovers because I rarely sobered up." Red wine, he even joked to himself, "was pretty healthy: twenty-one vitamins and minerals!" But his lifestyle was far from healthy. He got a DUI (driving under the influence) conviction in 1967, and he can see in retrospect that "I was in poor physical condition and an emotional husk." At home, the implications were even more dire. "I was getting violent. I was having rages and really threatening my family." A doctor warned him, "You've got to get off that shit," so he quit the Dexamyl, but "I stayed with the wine."

As Powell was drinking and working his way through the late 1960s and early 1970s, the American War in Vietnam was raging, and a massive anti-war movement was rattling the foundations of American society and upending two successive presidents. Everyone seemed pressed to take a stand. Joan adopted an antiwar stance, and Powell's father was one of a group of Berkeley faculty to write to the president in opposition to the war.

In retrospect, Powell thinks the "risk" his father took in signing that anti-war letter "was a way for him to try to right some of the distress that he experienced from the dropping of the bomb." For his part, Powell preferred not to think about this war, nor did he engage with any of the antiwar efforts around him. "I kissed it off. I could understand what those guys were going through, but I kind of figured that's their war. I'd had mine. I still was politically ignorant. I was still, you know, I was boozing quite a bit by then and working for a boss I detested who was a bully I put up with because I couldn't think of anything else to do. I was making good money. So I just—I think I just narrowed my world down to making that living and getting through every fucking day, just feeling the most deep, deep depression. Just, the world was nothing. I really didn't give a shit."

By 1976, Powell's job had moved him to St. Louis, where he had "a large territory," stretching across parts of "Mexico, Canada, all over the place." Woody and Joan had now "been married twenty years and we were on the edge of divorce. I'm drinking all the time." Clearly, something had to give, and in 1978 Powell decided to get sober. "It changed my life and it changed my attitude towards my boss, towards the entire world. Joan went to Al-Anon at the same time, which is a good thing. We repaired our relationship, which was very badly broken at that time. I began opening up." The immediate focus of Powell's "opening up" concerned the repair of his family relationships. As he began to open to the world outside of work and family, he strove to understand, make sense of, and eventually make peace with his experience with war.

A LITTLE MORE HONORABLE

In 1983 Woody Powell embarked on a "fascinating expedition, three weeks railroading trough China" with the American Railway Engineering Association. "That trip wouldn't have happened if I weren't sober. Because how would I sustain all my drinking under those conditions? Sobriety just opened up the world." One night during that trip, while walking in the city of Chengndu with a fellow railroader who was also in Alcoholics Anonymous (AA), Powell had a serendipitous meeting with a Chinese man who would become a lifelong friend. "This guy rides up on his bicycle and asked if he could talk with us. He was practicing his English. That's when Ming-Fu and I discovered we'd been in the same war. I realized that we were about the same age and I had been wondering if I would run into anybody from China that had been in that war, and so I just asked him if he'd been in Korea and he said, 'Yeah, I was there 1,000 days.' Incredible. That broke the ice and we both agreed that it was the children that suffered the most. And we were just together that night, but we swore to write one another, which we did."

That chance meeting in Chengndu sparked a "huge correspondence" between Powell and Ming-Fu. By 1985, the two had "cooked up" a plan, working through the State Department, for Ming-Fu and his wife Xi-Shian to visit Powell and Joan in the United States. Ming-Fu delighted in viewing Chicago from the top of the Sears Tower; he visited with some Amish people; and Powell arranged for him to lecture in some high school international studies classes. During the visit, the two further solidified their friendship as Ming-Fu dictated his life story to Powell, who transcribed it on his Kaypro, one of the first personal computers. Powell would later collate Ming-Fu's story with his own for what would become a lovely coauthored memoir, *Two Walk the Golden Road: Two Soldiers, Two Cultures, Their Histories Intertwined*. Meanwhile, the two continued their long-distance friendship, with Powell helping in whatever ways he could when Ming-Fu's health declined and he was hospitalized.

As his friendship with Ming-Fu grew, Powell was also expanding his understanding of the war the two of them had fought in. "The book that really opened my eyes," Powell recalls, was Bruce Cumings's two-volume work, *Origins of the Korean War*.[19] By the time the Gulf War started in 1991, Powell's sobriety and his expanding education opened him to translating his "very visceral reaction" to what he was seeing on television into antiwar activism. "I saw people being blown up on cathode ray tubes and

I thought, how remote can you get from what the fuck you're really doing? I thought it was an abomination. It just was awful. I was seeing it on television. That had more of an effect on me than the Vietnam War did as far as awakening. I was in a position to be awakened. I was sober and opening up. My world was opening up."

Powell then spoke with a young man who was starting a chapter of VFP in St. Louis and decided he "wanted in." Through that same network, Powell met "an activist nun named Maggie Fischer," who was doing interfaith support work in Latin America. Fischer "really educated me and gave me books to read. It opened up my eyes to everything." Fischer put into Powell's hands Howard Zinn's powerful radical primer, *A People's History of the United States*,[20] and other works that illuminated the costs Americans pay for our government's open and secret acts of violence around the world, in support of empire. At first, Powell balked at some of the critical ideas he was reading, and he laughed as he recalled pushing back at his mentor. "I actually argued with her about America being an empire—ha! I couldn't accept it! But then, finally, I mean, the scales left my eyes and I realized it had always been a fucking empire." When it came to peace activism, Powell realized, "I was a late bloomer." Over the next two decades, he would more than make up for that.

In 1998, Powell represented VFP as part of a Global Exchange contingent that visited the Mexican state of Chiapas following the infamous December 1997 paramilitary massacre of forty-seven indigenous people—many of them women and children—who were attending a prayer meeting in the village of Acteal. Powell recalls it being scary, as "the Federales were in collusion with the state police" and against the indigenous people, and Powell's group "counted bullet holes and got chased around by men with guns just south of Oaxaca" in an area "riddled with marijuana fields." A second such trip that "was a real eye-opener" took Powell to Colombia, where he witnessed U.S. money—supposedly sent to stop coca farming—used by "the paramilitaries that were in collusion with the fucking army and they were running people off of their land where they were growing rice and other things and supporting 40,000 people and turning the land over to people who wanted to raise cows and it only supported 2,000 people. And they were just gunning these people down. It was a terrible, terrible thing." During these visits, Powell's group met with activist priests and displaced "rebels in the forests." Once back in the United States, Powell presented talks and slideshows "wherever I could find an audience," to "educate people as widely as possible, to make it clear that this money that's going in there from our government in support of Colombia was actually being used to displace civilian populations for the benefit of the elites."

In 2000, Powell and this friend Charlie Atkins, also a Korean War vet and a VFP member, took a trip to Asia. In China, they found Ming-Fu seriously ill and got him out of the hospital and situated at his daughter's home. "We stayed around for about a week and kind of brought him back to life." Ming-Fu was "fascinated" to see for the first time a copy of the book he and Powell had authored. From there, Powell went on to Korea, where in Kokan-Ri he had his moment of reconciliation with massacre survivor Hwang Jum Soon. In 2001, Powell visited Korea again, this time with a commission organized by human rights attorney and former U.S. attorney general Ramsey Clark. Visiting Taegu, a town he had patrolled during the war, Powell found another opportunity "to apologize in public."

We went and toured various sites where atrocities had occurred. In Taegu, there was a cobalt mine and at the top of the mine in the mountain there was an open shaft. This happened before the war where the National Police had taken prisoners. People that they considered insurgents, and tied them up in groups of seven. Lined them up next to that hole, shot one of them, dropped him down the hole and he pulled the rest of them down the hole after him. We went into that mine and you could see where they'd excavated and found the bones and looked at the bones, and we participated in a ceremony there for the dead. There were survivors of the war that were there, and I got a chance again to apologize. I had that opportunity in Taegu to talk to a bunch of students about war and the uselessness of it and my actions in it and my regrets.

On his return to the United States, Powell, Ramsey Clark, and others who had made the trip "gave testimony" at a tribunal at Riverside Church in New York. Powell cannot gauge how much impact this sort of witnessing and public education has had, concluding, "You know, it's a little pebble in a great big ocean." Wars and atrocities continue, despite these efforts. But he is confident what he did on his visits to Chiapas, Colombia, and South Korea was important and right.

I don't think anybody can go through life without doing some awful things at one time or another. I kind of believe in karma. What goes around comes around. I think later in life once you know a little bit more about your position in life, you get the opportunity to make amends. Of course, in the 12-step program, as you probably know, amends-making is a pretty big part of that and I think that's a very human thing. People are very uneasy until they've unburdened, and amends-making is part of the unburdening process. But you have to know what the hell you're unburdening first, and that means a lot of examination and a lot of growing up.

As Powell described his own "unburdening process" grounded in his belief in karma, I couldn't help but think that the wounds of moral injury may have run deeper for him than for many former soldiers. To be sure, his public apologies directly addressed his regret for his own acts of cruelty and for his complicity in atrocities committed against Korean civilians. But I wonder if on some more profound level, the powerful moral drive behind Powell's amends-making may also been fueled by a sort of intergenerational moral injury—inherited from the sins of the father, so to speak—still to be excavated from the rubble of Hiroshima and Nagasaki.

Wilson Powell speaks to veterans at the Korea Memorial in St. Louis, Missouri, 1991 (Wilson Powell)

Later, in 2000, Powell attended the annual VFP convention in Albuquerque. The organization's national membership had dwindled "down to 500 to 800 people." The national VFP office in Washington, DC, was disorganized, a "total disaster," and there was currently no executive director. Powell offered to assume that position and move the office to St. Louis. It was good timing for Powell. He had just retired from his consultancy work and was fired up "to do something meaningful in the interests of peace." He found a basement space available for $80 a month in the World Community Center. As one member packed a Ryder rental truck and drove the VFP files to St. Louis, Powell and local VFP member Bud Deraps cleaned, painted, and prepared the new space.

The day they were unloading the materials to set up the VFP office, another Korean War vet phoned and urged Powell, "Get a TV and turn it on." It was September 11, 2001. Things began to happen quickly for the new executive director of VFP. Soon following the attacks of 9/11, VFP placed a full-page ad in the New York Times featuring a letter written to President George W. Bush by retired marine Greg Nees. "The essence of it," according to Powell, "was don't go off half-cocked and attack anybody over this. Treat it like a criminal matter." The ad got the attention of the mass media, and before he knew it Woody Powell was on national television, being interviewed by the conservative Fox News commentator Bill O'Reilly, known for his glee in ripping liberals and progressives to shreds on air. It was different when he spoke with Powell. O'Reilly did attempt to label Powell a "compromiser" and implied that he may be a "socialist" with a "hidden agenda."[21] However, O'Reilly's tone when talking with Wilson Powell, the Korean War veteran, was more respectful than it likely would have been had he been speaking on air with other peace activists. For Powell, this was instructive. "I came away from that interview convinced that I was in the right place and doing the right thing because he deferred to me because I was a veteran. He tried to call me a socialist and this and that and I said, 'Come on,' you know. I blinked a lot because I was very tired, but I acquitted myself okay, you know. But, I came away convinced, more than ever, that I had a mission because of his deference to me as a veteran. And so that gives us a leg up. It gives us some power when we state our views on things."

Following this media attention, "The phones began ringing. Emails poured in. We invited lapsed members back into the fold and recruited new ones with our burgeoning campaigns against war cropping up all over the country." Woody Powell suddenly had a tiger by the tail. Still a relative newcomer to political activism, he was fortunate to learn from and team up with seasoned members of Vietnam Veterans Against the War (VVAW). Powell particularly credits veteran antiwar activist David Cline, who served as president of VFP at the time, for "energizing VFP" with his "organizing genius." Powell recalls feeling "pleased and humbled" when Cline called one day to say that "we made a good pair, a 'dynamic duo,' he said."

VFP grew like wildfire, from perhaps 800 when Powell took over as executive director in 2001 to about 10,000 members by 2005 when he left the position. New VFP "chapters were springing up everywhere." Members of the swelling organization were using their bully pulpit as U.S. military veterans to assert an agenda of peace that ran counter to the Bush-Cheney message of fear and the rapidly escalating U.S. war in the Middle East. The United States invasion of Afghanistan, Powell says, "was the war that Greg Nees was warning against in that letter in the *New York Times*. Don't go off half-cocked and attack somebody. But they did. Bless them. And, oh, God . . ." In response, VFP joined a massive antiwar demonstration in Washington, DC, of perhaps 500,000 people.

In a very short time, Woody Powell had gone from painting a basement office for what seemed to be a shrinking organization to becoming a very public leader in a vibrant and growing effort. "I did a lot of traveling around to help build chapters and talk at public events about ending the war in Afghanistan, and then also the coming war in Iraq. It's kind of a blur for me, because I was just on the road a lot. Sometimes I'd go to religious organizations. I did talk at schools, high schools, colleges I even talked at grammar schools. Sometimes I had media coverage, sometimes not. Sometimes local media wasn't interested." Meanwhile VFP's basement office was proving inadequate for the needs of a growing organization; besides, some heavy rains had flooded the space. Powell and some other VFP members moved the office to the "unfloodable" top floor of a converted apartment complex. The owner, "a very strong supporter," rented the space to VFP for a generously low fee.

Public education was an overarching goal of VFP during this time, and that meant creating a counterstory to the dominant U.S. government claim about the necessity of an all-out "War on Terror," a war largely supported on both sides of the aisle in Congress and echoed in the mass media. In 2004 Powell recalls that one of "the most amazing things we did during that period" was setting up "Arlington West lookalikes that cropped up around the country." In the St. Louis area, Powell's VFP chapter hammered into the grass 2,500 crosses, representing the current number of U.S. dead in the Afghanistan and Iraq Wars—"out in front of the slope in front of the art museum in Forest Park and held a rally there. And it was a big rally. We had a lot of people come." Soon after, they set up the crosses "in the quadrangle of a local community college and held a weeklong series of events, seminars, talks, and so forth trying to reach the students there." On college campuses and elsewhere, VFP members engaged in counterrecruiting, setting up VFP tables right next to military recruiters. "Usually it went very well. The recruiters, they weren't that upset by our presence. We were civil, cordial, and certainly willing to talk about anything that's on their minds." And when the military recruiters were talking with young people about joining up, Powell laughs in recalling, VFP members would say, "'Come over here, let me tell you what it's really like' [laughs]. All over the country we were doing that."

By 2005 Powell was wearing down. "I literally burned out. I had my knee replaced and I remember I was just on my ass for a while." Gulf War veteran Michael McPherson took over as VFP executive director, a position he continues to hold as I write.[22] Relieved of his leadership duties and recovering from surgery, the seventy-three-year-old Woody Powell was slowed, but not done with his work for peace and justice. He continued to attend VFP local and national meetings, and still delivered the occasional

public talk. He turned more to writing, embarking on a major project
chronicling the previous decade's public activism and internal struggles
of VFP, a document published in 2008 as *The Democratization of Veterans for Peace: 1995–2007.*[23]

    Powell also took to writing in a more personal vein. In 2005 he penned
"The Man in Uniform," a poem about the pain he still carries from his
time in war, that he read aloud at a Memorial Day event. A segment of the
poem laments, "I am a man / without a uniform / without significance /
without a shield / naked / and all too aware / of what I might have been."
The final stanza alludes to the decades of fog Powell drifted through before
finding sobriety and a community of veterans with whom to work for
peace. With a grieving tone, Powell describes himself as having been "a
spirit confused / looking for shelter / in a job, a family, a bottle / or just a
space where I need not think."[24]

    In recent years, Powell has retained his connection with VFP, occasion-
ally attending the national meetings. He became frustrated a couple of
years ago when the St. Louis chapter—headed today, he says, more by associate (nonveteran) members than by veterans—decided to spend the $800
Powell had raised to start a computer clinic for homeless vets to buy a
model drone for peace demonstrations. "By that time, I was not that hip
on demonstrations, you know. And I was more concerned about working
with people's lives in a very direct way. So, me and the chapter split and I
became a member-at-large and they bought that fucking drone."

    Today, Powell enjoys "walking the dog or reading, or working on the
house or going shopping with my wife." He and Joan "read Thich Nhat
Hanh [a Vietnamese Buddhist monk and peace activist] every morning.
It's a very simple spirituality, just becoming aware of everything around
you and seeing it for what it is." Powell also still works "four or five hours
a day" helping to run the Veterans Court Technology Clinic, the local nonprofit that assists recovering veterans to "achieve a certain level of com-
petency which qualifies them to get jobs they wouldn't otherwise qualify
to get." This work affords Powell the opportunity to put to good use his

lifetime of business skills, and it also allows him "to take advantage of the fact that I'm in recovery, I've fought depression and I'm a veteran. So I'm a mentor in the veterans drug court, and I can relate to these people on a couple of fronts. For me, it's something I can do, and my whole history has led up to it."

All of this—the spiritual self-awareness, the commitment to sobriety, the peace activism, the writing, the service to other veterans—has been central to Woody Powell's life project of becoming "a more honorable person." He can gaze back at his complicity in a war that he now sees as unjust, and he can lament his own brief descent into cruelty. He can regret his years of drinking and the ways that he neglected the people he was closest to. But reframing the meaning of his past does not mire Powell in a pool of lament and regret.

> Being honorable was always important for me even though I did dishonorable things. So I was an honorable person doing dishonorable things I guess you could say. When I had the chance to examine what I was doing and get out of that condition that caused me to do that, then I was able to make the change and become a little more honorable. I often ponder on that, and I realized that this is a matrix we're in, and all of us have our individual journeys though this matrix and we each reach a certain level of self-awareness and awareness of other things that's commensurate with who we are at that time. Some people become very advanced spiritually and some people don't. It argues in favor of reincarnation, where you can maybe go on from life to life, and in each life you improve your spirituality until eventually you become a bright light in the universe or just an energy spot. But who knows? Who the hell knows? But still the argument remains that we are all, it seems, destined to make a bunch of mistakes and to be very self-absorbed as we start off, and then become less so—or die being very self-absorbed.

Now in his mid-eighties, Woody Powell is satisfied with the contributions he can continue to make for as long as he can make them. He does not concern himself with the question of whether or when his efforts will succeed in helping VFP and allied organizations one day create a peaceful and just world. Instead, he anchors the meaning of his continuing work in his sense of honor and right. He works with others to promote peace and justice, he concludes, because "it's a necessary thing to do to retain my humanity. It's the right thing to do. It's the next right thing to do. And when I get tired, I don't do it [*laughs*]. I take a nap."

This business of burning human beings with napalm, of filling our nation's homes with orphans and widows, of injecting poisonous drugs of hate into the veins of peoples normally humane, of sending men home from dark and bloody battlefields physically handicapped and psychologically deranged, cannot be reconciled with wisdom, justice, and love. A nation that continues year after year to spend more money on military defense than on programs of social uplift is approaching spiritual death.

—Dr. Martin Luther King Jr., *"Beyond Vietnam"*

I can't stop being a veteran. All I can do is try and live with it. Sometimes I do better than others.

—*Gregory Ross*

CHAPTER 4

-《《◆》》-

Paying Off My Karmic Debt

GREGORY ROSS, THE AMERICAN WAR IN VIETNAM

The San-Francisco-Oakland Bay Bridge opened for traffic in 1936, its two spectacular spans, roughly equal in length, joining on Yerba Buena Island. In that same year, work commenced to build Treasure Island, connected with Yerba Buena Island by a narrow 900-foot causeway, and soon to be the site of the 1939 World's Fair. Treasure Island was a jewel, created to showcase modern technological progress, and framed by the local beauty of the San Francisco Bay Area. As the United States surged into World War II in 1941 and 1942, the island became home to Naval Station Treasure Island, a key departure-and-receiving port for ships and sub-marines, and a major naval air facility. Following the war, Treasure Island converted mostly to a naval training and administrative center.

Gregory Ross was not thinking much about the storied history of that lovely island as he sat with a handful of men in the Administration Build-ing of Treasure Island Naval Base, waiting to be discharged from his four-year stint in the Navy, six months of which was spent on the Navy's 7th Fleet gun line, "a floating artillery unit" that hammered the coast of Vietnam. "Sometimes," Ross recalled, "we were firing those guns 24/7 for a week or more." The clamor and thunder of those big guns would never fully leave Ross, but on this day, August 5, 1970, he sat quietly, relieved he had dodged the bullet of a dishonorable discharge due to a recent drug bust, which would have left him without any veterans' benefits. In recent months Ross had grown thin from amphetamine use; alienated and disillusioned, he embraced a singular sense of clarity that he was "anti-military and antiwar." This moment of transition to civilian life was anti-climactic: "When the admin personnel called our names, we went up and signed more paperwork and were handed our packet of discharge papers. That was it. No raising of right hands, no swearing in, or I guess in this case, swearing out; no orders to 'Take one step forward' to seal the deal. Just, 'Here are your papers.'"

Knowing he was heading to the brutal winter of his hometown Lancaster, New York, Ross traded on the spot his Navy-issue pea coat for a warmer all-weather jacket. And as he was leaving Treasure Island Naval Base, he pulled from his pocket his three medals of commendation: the National Defense Service Medal, the Vietnam Service Medal, and the Vietnam Commendation Medal. "I threw my medals away right after I was discharged, into the nearest garbage can, literally as I walked out the gates of Treasure Island, minutes after I was handed my discharge packet. My only regret about that was that when I was in the March on Washington, DC, in 1971, I had no medals to throw over the White House fence—but that's just a small regret."

On the day of Gregory Ross's discharge from the Navy, the American War in Vietnam was still raging. Over 6,000 American soldiers would return home in body bags that year, and U.S. bombs, napalm, and ground attacks were killing Vietnamese and Cambodians by the tens of thousands. The previous year, in January of 1969, Richard Nixon assumed the presidency, and by March of that year—right at the time Ross was assigned Temporary Auxiliary Duty on the floating gun line off the coast of Vietnam—Nixon announced the "Vietnamization" of the War, commencing with a withdrawal of 25,000 of the then 543,000 U.S. troops in the war zone. By then, resistance to the war among active military personnel—escalating desertions, refusals to fight, "fraggings" of superior officers, and the proliferation of antiwar GI newsletters and coffeehouses—was causing major problems for U.S. commanders in the field.[1]

Meanwhile, antiwar activism by organized veterans was increasingly visible and militant at home, and some individuals in the mass media were starting to ask critical questions about the war. In November 1969, Americans learned of the My Lai Massacre, where U.S. troops had systematically slaughtered 504 residents of a small Vietnamese hamlet, most of whom were women and children. Though officials first tried to cover up the massacre, and then attempted to frame the story as an aberration—for which Lieutenant William Calley was court-martialed—it became increasingly apparent that the civilian toll from U.S. bombing and ground forces was devastating the people of Vietnam. In his book *Kill Anything That Moves*, Nick Turse makes a convincing argument that My Lai was "no aberration" but part of a larger pattern of American atrocities, "the inevitable outcome of deliberate policies, dictated at the highest levels of the military." A foundation for this pattern was laid, Turse observed, in "Kill Kill Kill" GI training, and in the U.S. leadership's obsession with "body count" as an indicator of progress in the war.[2]

On November 15, 1969, roughly half a million people in New York City demonstrated against the war, with simultaneous massive demonstrations in San Francisco and elsewhere. On May 4, 1970, National Guard troops fired on antiwar demonstrators at Kent State University in Ohio, killing four. Eleven days later, police fired on student demonstrators at Jackson State College in Mississippi, killing two and injuring twelve. The growing understanding of atrocities like the My Lai Massacre, public weariness at the continuing death toll for U.S. troops, and mounting sympathy for antiwar protestors was eroding support for the war. Public opinion gradually tipped, from a high of 61 percent of Americans expressing support for the U.S. war in mid-1965, to 32 percent just before Nixon took office, and eventually plummeting to 28 percent in early 1971.[3]

After shedding his medals and his Navy pea coat at Treasure Island, Gregory Ross headed home to upstate New York. He grew his hair and beard, and began smoking much more pot than he had while in service. For a time, he joined VVAW and marched in peace demonstrations, but

he soon became disillusioned with the internal squabbling in the organization, and fell into a depressive and sometimes suicidal state. For much
of the next decade, Ross struggled to live in a world that made little sense
to him. Following a suicide attempt in 1980, a months-long VA hospital-
ization helped him commence to dig out from the rock bottom he'd hit,
and begin a steady climb to a meaningful life. Eventually Ross found
rewarding work as an acupuncturist, which gave him daily opportunities
to care for people who were poor, sick, addicted, down and out. During a
particularly low time in his life, in the late 1970s, Ross consulted a palm
reader. Her message resonated with his understanding of his working-class
background and became for him a foundation for building his life.

> She told me, "This lifetime, your issues are service versus servitude, and
> when you're stuck in a servitude kind of place, look out: It's not good
> for you, it's not good for them. So you really want to be of service this
> life." And [laughs], you know, the times that I've been happiest is being
> of service. I went from being in the Navy off the coast of Vietnam throw-
> ing 350-pound shells, to an acupuncturist, helping heal the poorest
> people around, working with HIV/AIDS clients. Most of my life till then
> I did grunt work. I was a mule, you know? I was paid to be a mule, and
> if I thought—if I showed any intelligence—they were pissed off, they
> didn't like that, like in the military.

Ross's mid-life shift "from servitude to service" coincided with his commitment to everyday peace activism—never leaving home without a VFP
button on his lapel, for one thing—and with finding self-expression
through writing and reciting antiwar and pro-peace poetry. All of this
coalesced into a life project Ross found both personally healing and meaningful as a "major payback on my karma in this life."

-«‹•›»-

I met Gregory Ross in 2011 when I interviewed him for *Some Men*, a book
I was writing about men's past and current efforts to stop sexual and

domestic violence against women.[4] For a time in 1978, Ross had been a member of the San Francisco Bay Area group Men Against Sexist Violence (MASV). Ross told me he was proud to have been a part of MASV but that he never felt he fit well. He was a working-class, non-college-educated man and a Vietnam veteran in a circle of progressive, educated men who had opposed the war and avoided the draft. In that 2011 interview, it became apparent to me that the most salient part of Ross's past story and current identity had not to do with his participation in that short-lived pro-feminist men's group. The VFP button on his lapel and the peace posters and art that decorated the walls of his Oakland home spoke to what was most important to Gregory Ross. Just a few years earlier, he told me, he'd made a commitment never to leave home without some VFP button, hat, shirt, or patch evident on his person, which he hoped would draw attention and open conversations.

When I decided to write this book on war veterans who became peace activists, I immediately thought of Gregory Ross. At first, he was reluctant to be interviewed; he was uncomfortable serving as the single representative of the tens of thousands who had served in the American War in Vietnam. "After all," he explained, "I was a REMF." My puzzled response drew a laugh and a quick explanation: "'Rear Echelon Mother Fucker'—you know, someone who was not on the front lines of combat." I understood his reluctance. Driven by popular culture and in literature—exemplified in the lovely semiautobiographical stories in novelist Tim O'Brien's *The Things They Carried*—we Americans tend to hold a certain image of "the Vietnam Veteran" in our minds—comrades fighting side by side in the steamy jungle, sometimes with tragic heroism, often in terror, as explosions and gunfire engulf them.[5] I told Ross I didn't believe that any one person's story could capture the range and depth of experiences in any one war, but assured him that from what I already knew, his story was well worth telling. I'm grateful he agreed to the interview.

On four subsequent occasions—once in the home in Oakland he shared with his wife Peggy, twice after they moved to nearby San Leandro, and once at a VFP national meeting in Berkeley—I spent time with Ross, listening to his stories of the past, and learning of his continuing struggles and joys. Now in his late sixties, retired and piecing together support from Social Security, Peggy's income as a social worker, and medical care from the VA, Ross deals with regular physical pain from past back surgery and other ailments. He walks with a careful and deliberate gait, with the aid of a cane, and suffers from partial hearing loss that he attributes to the continual booming of the big guns during his six months on ship off the coast of Vietnam. His PTSD symptoms—including startle responses to sudden clanking or crashing noises, and continued brushes with depression—are managed with talk therapy and medication from the VA, through his continued participation with the local chapter of VFP, through creative writing, and through his supportive partnership with Peggy. Ross frequently peppers conversation with sarcastic quips that reflect a critical sensibility coupled with a snarky sense of humor. At this stage of his life, this personality trait makes him a lively conversationalist; in the past, especially during his military career, it got him into more than his share of hot water.

Born in a Navy Hospital

Gregory Ross began his life already immersed in Navy life. "My dad was in the Navy. I was born in a Navy hospital," on July 19, 1947, at Chincoteague Naval Air Station in Virginia. There, Ross's father served as an aviation machinist mate, specializing in parts for planes, and his mother worked as a beautician. Ross was raised in Lancaster, New York, a suburb of Buffalo, in what he described as "a lower working-class" Catholic family. His father was of Scottish and Irish descent, and it was his mother's Sicilian family that Gregory credits (or blames) for his having absorbed a tendency to wear his emotions and his opinions on his sleeve: "They're loud and they are emotional and they scream and cry and yell and then they make up and cry some more."

In retrospect, Ross can also see how much of the emotional tenor of his young life was grounded in the fact that his father fought in two wars. A "retread," in the parlance of the time, Ross's father was a World War II combat veteran who was recalled for further combat duty in Korea. The trauma that his father internalized in his two wars reverberated through the family for the duration of Ross's childhood. "He saw a lot of shit. I don't know how else to put it. He joined the Navy when he was nineteen, in August of 1941. And he went through boot camp and his first duty station was Pearl Harbor. So he was there December 7 and it just stayed like that for him for the next four years. He was on two different planes that got shot down and a ship that got sunk. One of those times he spent seventeen hours in a life raft with another guy who died."

Ross's father was also on the USS *Shangri-La* in 1946, off of Bikini Atoll—"where they said 'cover your eyes' and then the atomic bomb test blast." Following what may have felt like a brief respite following the Japanese surrender, his father was recalled to active duty for the Korean War. "Basically they said, 'Hey this is a land war, we don't need squids, we don't need Navy personnel so we're going to make you a marine!' As if he had a choice. And so, he was a marine during that war." While his father was in Korea, his mom took him and his sister to live with her family, and four-year-old Gregory hung out with his mom and other women in the beauty parlor. His father loomed large in his imagination, but when he returned from the war, Gregory hardly recognized him.

In years following his return from Korea, Ross's father "really didn't want to talk about it that much, like many vets." He stuck with the Navy Reserve for a few years, partly because it added much needed income for the family, but the emotional costs were steep. "Every time he went up in an airplane he got deathly ill, throwing up and all kinds of stuff." Finally, Ross's mom told his father to quit the Navy. He did, but whenever money got scarce, he would blame his wife for having made him quit. Ross can see in retrospect that his father "had massive amounts of PTSD." Decades later, when Gregory returned from Vietnam, struggling with his own PTSD, his father counseled him.

> He said, "You know Greg, just remember the good times. That's the difference between me and the guys in the loony bin. I just remember the good times. That's all you gotta do. Just forget the bad times." But I had lived with him. He might have forgot them during the day but his nightmares and his PTSD at night were frightening to the family. And he wasn't always in a good mood. Those things came back to him. He drank at least a pint of whiskey a day. By that time, he was fucked up beyond recognition. But he somehow always managed to work as well. So he was an alcoholic and a rage-aholic, but functioned somehow through it all.

These experiences with his father did little to dissuade young Gregory from thinking fondly of the military. He loved to watch John Wayne war movies, and the popular TV show *Combat*: "Tuesday nights; we'd watch that religiously." He laughed, recalling his penchant for theatrics when he and his friends "played war games. Kids would come to the door and say, 'Mrs. Ross! Mrs. Ross! Can Gregory come out and play? He's the best die-er on the block!'"

But Gregory's small body size and lack of athletic ability made it tough for him with peers, especially in his teen years. "I didn't grow up easily as a boy," he recalls, "I just never fit in well as a boy." In high school, "I was a little guy"—5'5" and 110 pounds, as he recalls—and not very athletic. "I joined the drama club, not the football team." When he considered going out for the football team, his father reassured him that he did not have to do that to impress him, that he'd be just as proud of his son if he joined the drama club. Ross suspects that during that time his father "thought I was gay," but he never gave Gregory a hard time about it. "Between his PTSD and his alcoholism and his machoism, he was a pretty good dad, actually."

Gregory Ross graduated high school in the spring of 1965. That year, U.S. military involvement in Vietnam was escalating rapidly. In 1964 President Lyndon Johnson had used the August 4 North Vietnamese torpedo attack on a U.S. destroyer in the Gulf of Tonkin to demand support from Congress to rapidly escalate U.S. involvement in the war. Secretary of Defense Robert McNamara declared at the time that the incident in the Tonkin Gulf was a "deliberate and unprovoked" attack on a U.S. ship in international waters. Later secret government documents revealed that the U.S. Navy had engaged in a series of provocations in North Vietnamese waters.[6] In the words of historian John Marciano, "In a war filled with lies," the Gulf of Tonkin Incident "is one of the biggest."[7] Johnson and McNamara had, for the moment, secured what they wanted—what Senator J. William Fulbright later dubbed the "blank check of August 7, 1964" to wage war in Vietnam as the president saw fit.[8]

By early 1965 U.S. bombers were slamming North Vietnamese targets, including the Ho Chi Minh Trail, with Operation Rolling Thunder, and General William Westmoreland, commander of the U.S. war effort in Vietnam, had successfully lobbied the government for a dramatic escalation of the number of U.S. ground troops. That year, over 1,900 U.S. troops died in Vietnam, up from only 216 in 1964. The number of skeptics was growing, but widespread opposition to the war had not yet begun to coalesce. This was due in part to the fact that popular knowledge about the war was still thin, veiled in government secrecy and framed in patriotic terms by a still-slumbering mass media that mostly echoed the official government story that the war effort in Vietnam was a noble cause, needed to stop communist aggression and save democracy.[9]

Newly graduated from high school, Gregory Ross's knowledge of the war in Vietnam was similarly limited. "I knew it was a war. I knew people were getting killed on both sides. If you asked me to find Vietnam on a map I couldn't have." Ross did know that, as a college student, he would receive a draft deferment. He worked full-time at a produce market his dad managed, so he signed up for a full load of night classes at Canisius, a local Catholic college. He had "some vague notion I wanted to become a teacher." His parents—his father had a GED and his mother a Beautician School Certificate—liked his going to college, but they weren't equipped to provide financial support or academic advice. Ross had no car, and eventually "working full-time days, going to school full-time nights until 10 p.m. and taking the bus home," and then getting up the next morning "at 6 a.m. or so and go in with my dad and open up" was impossible to sustain. Like so many young, working-class guys before him, Ross soon found the road ahead aiming toward boot camp.

> About five days before I got my "Greetings," I got the notice from Canisius College that I was flunking out and they were getting rid of me. The day I got my notice, I ran down to the Navy recruiter and I said, "Look, I just got my Greetings. Can I join the Navy?" Now, you don't believe anything a recruiter says but I didn't know that then. So he said, "You know, you're one lucky son of a bitch. We get a mimeograph printout once a day that says whether or not we can accept draftees into the Navy. Boy, you're lucky! It's been 'no' for the last six weeks. Today it was 'yes.' So sign on the dotted line." Ha! It was either good timing or it was bullshit.

Ross's father, he recalls, "was quite proud of me; I was going to be a man now. My mother was terrified and she blamed him." Within ninety days of signing with the Navy recruiter, he was called up. "They said, 'Be here in thirty-six hours or we'll hunt you down and put you in jail.' They said it in a slightly more polite way." In a downtown building in Buffalo, Ross had his physical with fifty or sixty other guys, after which they were ordered to line up and count off by threes. "Luckily, I was a two. 'All the threes step forward. Go over there and talk to that Marine recruiter. You're now in the Marines.' That was the beginning of understanding that the bears at Yellowstone had more rights than you did at some level. They were more protected than you were by the U.S. government."

At that point in his young life, Gregory Ross barely knew the half of it, when it came to fully understanding his government's level of disregard for the thousands of young men it was sending into battle. By the end of 1966, as Ross headed for boot camp, student deferments and resistance to the draft was straining the military's ability to put enough young men in uniform for the escalating war effort. As chronicled by Vietnam veteran, writer and veterans' health advocate Hamilton Gregory, President Lyndon Johnson and Secretary of Defense Robert McNamara sought to alleviate this shortage with what McNamara dubbed "Project 100,000"—a plan to, in Johnson's words, draft "second-class fellows," men with lower IQs who would previously have been considered unfit for duty. Ultimately, 345,000 such men—called "McNamara's Boys" or, disparagingly, "McNamara's Morons"—were drafted into the Army; their fatality rate in the War was three times higher than that of other soldiers.[10]

AN ABSURDIST EXPERIENCE

Nineteen-year-old Gregory Ross was delivered by bus on October 11, 1966, to Great Lakes, Illinois, where he completed basic training at the U.S. Naval Training Center. The Navy internal recruiter noted that Ross did well with languages, and suggested sending him to the language school at Fort Ord, in California. That sounded good at first, until Ross was told, "'Well, you've got to sign up for another two years though, because it's a two-year school.' All the sudden it doesn't sound so good to me anymore." Next, the Navy said he should become a medic, but Ross knew that as a Navy medic "you're attached to the Marines. They had a life expectancy of about fourteen seconds. I think in '67 they still had those helmets with the white circle and the Red Cross, which is like a bull's-eye." Finally, they settled on training Ross as a communications technician, for radio intelligence. Following his training in Pensacola, Florida, he recalls, "They gave me a 'Top Secret, Eyes Only' clearance which means I was seeing shit from the captain of the base to the Department of Defense."

Ross's first overseas assignment was in Morocco, which, he joked, might have been a cool place to be in 1967 if you were a hippie buying hash. But for him, "it wasn't that cool. . . . We were there in secret, actually. Our base was not officially there. Our primary mission—and once I tell you this I have to kill you [laughs]—our primary mission was to spy on the Russian

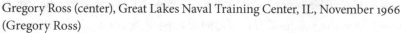
Gregory Ross (center), Great Lakes Naval Training Center, IL, November 1966 (Gregory Ross)

satellite stuff. Whenever the Russians set something up, lights would flash, bells would ring, everything would stop and we would—those of us who were communications technicians—would scramble to get all that information and then to send it immediately to the Department of Defense."

Ross did his job in Morocco, but could not help but feel a sense of absurdity that wearing a coat and tie instead of his uniform when he was in public was "supposed to camouflage us" and keep under wraps the "unofficial" and "secret" U.S. mission. Echoing the sensibility of Joseph Heller's fictional World War II-character Captain John Yossarian in the popular antiwar novel *Catch-22*, Ross was coming to feel that "the military is absurd.

It is an absurdist experience." During his time in Morocco, Ross was aware of the growing antiwar movement both inside the military and at home, but he didn't pay a lot of attention to it. On one of his first leaves home, he smoked marijuana for the first time with a former high school classmate who had been drafted into the Army had had returned with "a sea bag full of Vietnamese pot."

After seventeen months in Morocco, Ross was transferred to the Philippines. The moment he arrived, his smoldering "antimilitary" sentiments were stoked by the racial tensions in his unit. "When the bus pulled into the base, they take you immediately to the admin building to orient you. I swear this is not a joke. The very first thing they said after they told us to sit down and shut up is that all liberty had been canceled until morale improved. I'm serious! They said it! But the morale improvement involved racial tensions. There were blacks and whites—mostly Southern whites— beating on each other. That started me being pissed off that I was in the Navy, basically."

In the Philippines, it became more and more clear that "lifers"—those committed to careers in the military—were a major source of irritation and torment for recruits like Ross. Though he came to respect a handful of lifers along the way, his disdain for most of them was palpable. Many lifers, he said, were guys from the South with little formal education. For them, "the Navy was a good job. They could get fucked any time they want for money. They had people who did their laundry, people who cooked for them, a place to live. And as they got more rank, they got to boss people around." When Ross arrived in the Philippines wearing a pair of round-framed "John Lennon glasses" he'd purchased while on leave, this apparently rankled a chief petty officer. "The lifer that checked me in says, 'Why do you wear those subversive glasses?' I said, 'Well, Chief, because I need them to see' [laughs]. Subversive glasses? I didn't view them that way, but when I found out they did, that was cool. I harassed lifers basically."

Radio work in the Philippines "was part of a network that communicated between a Navy base in Vietnam, the 7th Fleet, and the Philippines."

Ross's unit's job was to monitor "every single MiG [Russian-built fighter plane] in the air," and give warnings to the American weather planes that were constantly in the air gathering information, so that if necessary "they could get out and get away. It was a very stressful job when you knew that."

Ross's antiwar position germinated within his more developed antimilitary sentiments. "I didn't have a political analysis. I hadn't figured it out yet. I just hated being in and I didn't like the military and I didn't really think it was such a great idea to be part of a war." He witnessed a radioman in another section get court-martialed—in Ross's view, unfairly—after a U.S. plane was shot down. "Somebody has to be blamed and certainly it is not going to be an officer." Ross did his job, "just typing messages," and got consistently good performance marks for his work running the Philippine Island link of the network. But his antimilitary and antiauthority gestures eventually got him in trouble.

> I was abrasive. I used to wear a teardrop silver peace medallion and a headband. I bought a toy gun just for the hell of it and I put it in a shoulder holster and I would go to work and I'd walk up to the lifer guys and go [*mimics shooting*] with a cap gun: "That's what I think of lifers." I was a pain in the ass; I had what was called a bad attitude. One day I pissed off my duty officer, and he called me into his office at zero four-thirty. I was like "Sir yes sir what do you want sir?" You gotta say "sir" a lot. "You're going out TAD [Temporary Auxiliary Duty], you're going out to the 7th Fleet." And I was like, "Yes sir. When will I be leaving?" He said, "Zero eight-thirty this morning." I had pissed him off, so this was his punishment.

THAT'S HOW NUMB YOU GET

Third Class Petty Officer Gregory Ross packed his sea bag and reported to Subic Bay to board ship and head to the coast of Vietnam. "You're there on the gangplank and you go, 'Sir request permission to come aboard sir!' I'm thinking, 'Request permission to turn around and run,' but you can't say that! You have to be complicit in your torture. Please torture me! Please send me to the war zone!" Within a few days, Ross joined 1,660 other crew members aboard the USS *Newport News*, a cruiser in the 7th Fleet's gun line of destroyers, cruisers, a battleship, and an aircraft carrier that were "strung out a mile off the coast of Vietnam." Following three months on ship, Ross had a thirty-six-hour layover, and was then reassigned to another cruiser on the gun line, the USS *Saint Paul*.

In total, Ross spent six months on the gun line, from the beginning of March to the end of August 1969. "Basically," he said, "we were a floating artillery unit. Sometimes we were firing those guns 24/7 for a week or more." That six-month stretch was a particularly hellish time in the war. U.S. troop numbers in-country had peaked in April, at 543,000, as President Richard Nixon's "Vietnamization" of the war commenced with a gradual drawdown of troops. Several thousand other Americans came home that year, in body bags. Nixon had vastly escalated the bombing of North Vietnam, and—unknown to the American people—had extended massive bombing into Cambodia. Tom Hayden recalled 1969 as the start of "the cynical Nixon-Kissinger doctrine of 'winding down' the conflict . . . as weary and demoralized American troops were dramatically withdrawn while U.S. bombing . . . actually escalated."[11]

In addition to dropping more tonnage of bombs on Vietnam, Cambodia, and Laos than the United States had dropped during all of World War II, U.S. planes and helicopters rained napalm fire on Vietnamese villages and saturated the Vietnamese countryside with Agent Orange, an herbicide that defoliated over 7.5 million acres of forest, making it easier for U.S. forces to track and target the movement of Vietnamese forces. Exposure to the powerful Dow Chemical-manufactured defoliant also created severe health problems in the Vietnamese population, including elevated levels of leukemia and Hodgkin's lymphoma, and abnormally high numbers of stillborn deaths and birth defects. An estimated 3 million

Vietnamese, Cambodians, and Laotians were directly killed in the war—roughly 2 million of them civilians. More than 5 million more Vietnamese were wounded; about a quarter of them children under the age of thirteen.[12] Untold more suffered the long-term debilitating effects of Agent Orange, and of death or injury years or even decades later, from still-unexploded bombs, mortar shells, and landmines that littered the countryside and villages.

U.S. bombs and defoliants managed to impede the movement of North Vietnamese troops and supplies on key inland routes like the Ho Chi Minh Trail. The 7th Fleet gun line was charged with hammering the roads and rivers of the North Vietnamese coastal plain, to further hamper the movement of personnel and supplies. Gregory Ross's job on ship as one of four communications technicians was to relay radioed information to the captain or the admiral, so that the ships could properly aim their big guns. The space Ross worked in was "like a giant bank vault, two decks below the guns. When the guns fired, everything rattled—the walls, the floor, everything. The ship, if it was straight, would go like this and bounce back [*waves arms vertical to diagonal*]. That would go on, with everything rattling like crazy." Though Ross found some camaraderie on ship, coping with the daily stresses was mostly a private affair. When he could get it, Ross would smoke some pot. "I was aware I was self-medicating. I was drinking, doing pot. It was such a macho environment. You know what I mean? Yeah, some of us talked about 'Wow, it's really hard to have this,' but mostly we didn't." Ross recalls coping during that time by "shutting it down, shutting it down, shutting it down until there were little things that happened that broke through." One of those things was hearing the "screaming, screaming, screaming" of an electrician who got electrocuted on the ship. "That sort of kicked a little bit of a hole in my denial. But still, there was this major denial. It's like, okay, that's happening over there. I've got nothing to do with it. I have no culpability somehow, is what I kept telling myself, and believing on some level that all I do is pass these messages. What I do is save lives, sort of like the sniper in that movie *American Sniper*. What I do saves American lives kind of thing."

On some level, Ross understood that the shells he and his shipmates were launching were causing death and destruction. But his physical distance from the shoreline, coupled with his denial at times, left Ross experiencing the war from offshore as a spectator. "We'd go hang out up on the captain's deck and watch the war. You could see tracers, and they're flipping over and over and over, and when they hit someone they tear the hell out of them. We could see mortars, yeah, it was a big explosion. And we had sort of gotten numb enough, that it was like, okay we're here. I can't watch *The Graduate* another time; I've seen it fifteen times. It was the only movie they played for like six weeks. We would go to the movie to buy popcorn and then go up there. That's how numb you get in a way."

After nearly six months on the gun line, Ross was returned on August 26, 1969, to work at the Naval Communications Center in the Philippines. It was a relief to be away from the constant roar of the guns, but for Ross life just "got more stressful." On leave with some money in his pocket, he went to a bazaar on the outskirts of Olongapo City, near Subic Bay. He recalls that it was "a beautiful tropical day; I'd just gotten off board ship, and I was feeling good. I was going to go get my money exchanged and meet some guys later in the day and go drinking and buy some pot and go smoke it and find bar girls and go fucking." Instead, he witnessed an act of brutal violence. In the bazaar, Ross saw a U.S. fleet sailor, perhaps nineteen years old, in uniform, purchasing a "knockoff watch," worth maybe $10, and holding the watch in his hand, smiling in satisfaction at the deal he believed he has just made. What happened next still feels to Ross as though it was in slow motion.

This roughly ten-year-old Filipina girl comes from behind him and grabs it and starts running. So he yells at her. She gets roughly 10 feet from me, and this Philippine Constabulary—they're part of the military but they're like cops and they don't fool around—pulled out his .45

and shot her in the back and she just exploded 10 feet from me. Her white shirt started turning red. She hit face-down into the dirt and slid a little bit. Didn't take that long, all of her body fluids—blood, piss, lymph—everything came out. So, she started to sink a little bit into this mud puddle that her body fluids were creating. I didn't even register the gunshot at first—and then I turned and I looked and the PC guy walked up to her, grabbed the watch, holstered his .45. The guy whose watch was stolen was just in shock and you could understand why. And the PC keeps trying to give him his watch—he's like grinning, like "Oh, I'm so proud."

Stunned, Ross caught the first bus back to base, went to the enlisted men's club and drank several rum and Cokes. "Then I went to the barracks, rolled myself a big fat joint, grabbed a handful of pot, stuck it in my mouth, started chewing, went down to the beach, smoked the whole joint, headed back towards my barracks, stopped off at the enlistment men's club and had some more rum and Coke. When I got to my barracks I just passed out."

For the next fourteen months, Ross continued to do his job efficiently, in part he thinks because he was speeding up with amphetamines. He lost twenty-five pounds, and recalls that he "stopped talking to people because people would say, 'Hey Ross, how's it going?' And I'd be like, 'What the fuck do you mean by that?!' I was paranoid as shit, but I also could crank out so many messages so fast and they were like 98 percent accurate, so at some level they weren't going to mess with me either." Busted with pot, he and two other enlisted men were arrested, taken to the Military Police (MP) station where they were "grilled" and then released. They immediately flushed and dumped all of their drugs down the toilet, so when the MPs came the next day to ransack their place, they found nothing. On August 5, 1970, Ross discarded his medals in that garbage can outside Treasure Island, hoping that he had left the military and the war in his rearview mirror.

CONTAIN IT, GREG

Back in Lancaster, New York, Gregory Ross, his girlfriend Marci, his two sisters, and their boyfriends rented a ramshackle two-story house that became the local "hippie crash pad." He "took great pride in the fact that I could drink almost anybody under the table" and if someone else ingested three magic mushrooms, Ross would eat five. "I communicated with God. Generally he was a somewhat stern God. My old Catholic God." It was months before he told Marci he was a Vietnam veteran. "Every once in a while, I would just, like melt down, and she was just like, 'What the fuck, what is this?'"

Ross hung out with his parents a bit after he returned, and once his father asked if he would like to join him for his regular Tuesday night visit to the VFW lodge to have a couple of beers and play some poker. Ross was reluctant, but his dad talked him into going. When he walked in the place, he could feel the cold stares of the older vets as they assessed his long hair and hippie attire. "I walked in and about four guys were like, 'Gene, who the hell is that and what is he doing in here?' [My father] just said, 'Shut up, asshole, he's my son and he's a veteran and he has every right to be here just like me' [*laughs*]. I was like, 'Okay! Yeah, I'll take a beer!'"

It was good to feel supported by his father and mother, but Ross would not be seeking connections with other veterans at the VFW lodge, a place for older, more conservative vets who for the most part supported the war and disparaged antiwar protestors. Soon after his discharge, he joined VVAW, a growing and vibrant voice in the national antiwar movement. According to historian Andrew Hunt, VVAW had about 2,000 members in 1970 and grew rapidly, peaking in 1972 at over 25,000 members, most of them veterans from working-class backgrounds.[13] VVAW orchestrated high-profile, antiwar demonstrations and provocations, issued position papers and newsletters, took out a full-page ad in the February 1971 issue of *Playboy* magazine (which yielded about 5,000 new members), and organized counseling and other health services for veterans.

VVAW's central and visible role in the larger antiwar movement also tossed a monkey wrench into government and pro-war groups' efforts to label the antiwar movement as a bunch of spoiled rich kids who were disrespecting the troops. Vietnam veteran turned antiwar activist John Kerry, later the senator from Massachusetts and a presidential candidate, chronicled a poignant moment in a 1971 antiwar march in Washington, DC. "A Daughter of the American Revolution approached one of the VVAWers and said, 'Son, I don't think what you are doing is good for the troops.' Replied the VVAWer: 'Lady, we *are* the troops.'"[14] In April 1971, as thousands watched and TV cameras rolled, hundreds of veterans, one by one, threw their medals over the chain-link fence that had been hastily constructed to keep them away from the Capitol building, gradually creating a "garbage heap of honor" with their discarded decorations.

Gregory Ross appreciated that there were veterans who were putting themselves on the line to end the war. On his return to his hometown, he attended five or six meetings of the Buffalo chapter of VVAW but decided "I can't deal with this because *every* meeting would degenerate" into squabbling about the "correct" theory and tactics of resistance. Ross was annoyed that the Revolutionary Communist Party (RCP), a fringe Marxist-Leninist group, was active in VVAW, constantly pressing the organization to accept what they saw as the "correct" revolutionary line and promoting tactics that provoked street conflicts with police. Ross was against the war, but his working-class sensibilities left him little patience with the revolutionary posturing of what he dubbed the "Royal Communist Party," whose members were, in his view, a bunch of spoiled "trust fund kids." What Ross didn't know was that VVAW had also been infiltrated by COINTELPRO (short for Counterintelligence Program), a Federal Bureau of Investigation (FBI) operation designed to surveil, disrupt, and discredit antiwar organizations. Andrew Hunt notes that orders to spy upon and disrupt VVAW came straight from the top; Attorney General John Mitchell had instructed the FBI to destabilize the antiwar movement, and had "scores of agents" investigating Vietnam veterans.[15]

Between the manipulative antics of the RCP and the underhanded disruptions of COINTELPRO, Ross recalls, "Every meeting was totally disruptive and full of shit, and then I quit. I just said I can't deal with this. This is not helping me; it's making it worse. Many people hung on though and cleaned house, hung on, and turned [VVAW] into something good, but I—that wasn't me. I fell further into drug and alcohol use."

What he needed most, Ross came to realize, was help digging out from a deep well of cynicism and depression. Within four months of his discharge, Ross realized he "was extremely depressed and suicidal." He did not trust the VA, so he called a suicide prevention hotline for help, and was set up with a young psychology student at the University of Buffalo, whom he saw five times. "The fifth time I saw her she said, 'This will be our last session, Mr. Ross. I'm leaving this profession. It's just not for me. I'm going back to Connecticut and marrying my high school boyfriend whose family has owned a farm for three generations and I'm going to raise soybeans.' No, seriously! So, what I came back with was: I broke my therapist! Part of me was like, I can't even tell professionals about my experience. It was another thing that said, 'Contain it, Greg. Contain it. Don't walk around with this. Don't put this out.'"

Ross did his best to "contain" his turbulent feelings with drugs and alcohol, but he also found his way to helpful rap groups, informal and often leaderless therapeutic discussion groups the VVAW had organized as an alternative to VA services. After his unemployment insurance benefits ran out, Ross found a job through his father, doing demolition "grunt work," and then landed in a hospital job he received because of his veteran status. There, he worked with other vets, including "an ex-Marine known as 'Semper Fi' who put his Harley Davidson 'Hog' and himself through a chain-link fence at a hundred miles an hour, one of the most creative suicides I'd heard of." Ross and some other vets drove together to the March on Washington. "I marched and chanted. It didn't mean that much to me at that time; not the least reason being I was stoned all the time."

A common story we tell ourselves about the contentious politics surrounding "the war at home" during the American War in Vietnam is that
a clear dividing line appeared between "hard hats"—patriotic, hardwork-
ing, blue-collar people who supported the president and the war effort—
and the "hippies"—young, college-educated liberals who opposed the
war and the "establishment." This dichotomy was exemplified weekly on
the popular TV show *All in the Family*, which, starting in 1971, regularly
featured verbal jousting about the war, race relations, and other current
issues between Archie Bunker, the conservative hard hat, and his long-
haired liberal son-in-law studying sociology. In her book *Hardhats, Hippies and Hawks*, historian Penny Lewis argues that this popular view of
the dichotomous class basis of support for and against the war "contains
only half-truths, and overall it is a falsehood."[16] Instead, Lewis argues that
"support for the war came from the privileged elite," while some working-
class labor unions, racial-justice groups, and working-class-based veterans
groups like VVAW were central to the antiwar movement.[17]

Still, a substantial part of the distance Gregory Ross felt as he joined in
the antiwar movement was grounded in his sense that many college students and hippie demonstrators didn't understand the experiences of
working-class veterans like him. Ross found it "confusing" when he witnessed a "long-haired hippie peace freak wearing a part of the uniform,"
like an Army jacket. When a peacenik told him that wearing military garb
was a form of "sarcasm," or "irony," it angered Ross. "I tried to contain
myself. You can probably guess that did not go over well."

I asked Ross what he thought about the argument that Vietnam veteran-
turned-sociologist Jerry Lembcke asserts in his 1998 book, *The Spitting
Image*. Lembcke argues that the popularly accepted story that Vietnam
vets returned from the war and were spat upon in airports and called baby
killers by peace activists is a myth, propagated to drive a wedge between
antiwar veterans and civilians, and to defuse popular opposition to future
wars.[18] More recently, VFP activist and Vietnam veteran W. D. Erhardt

made a similar argument, asserting that when he returned from the war, he was never "confronted by civilians out to denigrate and abuse me. No one called me 'baby killer' or spat on me. When I later became active in the antiwar movement, I never once saw or heard any antiwar demonstrator blame soldiers for the war, let alone act out verbally or physically toward soldiers or veterans."[19] Gregory Ross has a more nuanced view, saying that he had not been spat upon, to be sure, but that he had received plenty of scorn as a veteran of a lost war. In retrospect, he sees his differences with civilian antiwar activists as based in their lack of knowledge about the GI resistance,[20] and their naive belief that hippie love-ins and peace demonstrations had ended the war.

> You know, people would tell me that's how they ended the Vietnam War, and I'd say, "You know, I knew a guy who filed the firing pin off his weapon, so in a fire fight he couldn't kill anyone." You know, I think they're the ones that ended that war. I know guys that refused to go out, had .45s stuck in their heads and said, "Hey I'm dead either way, go ahead, Sarge, shoot me." You know, and they refused to fight the damn war. I think they had a little something to do with this, while you were marching here stoned on pot and fucking, you know [laughs]. That was, you know, that was unfair. But they had no idea that there were people in the military who resisted the war, you know? They had no idea.

COMPLETELY UNMOORED

By the time the war in Vietnam officially ended in 1975, Gregory Ross and his girlfriend Marci had relocated to the San Francisco Bay Area. Not long after that, they broke up, and while Ross was selling "feather and leather and natural beads and bone jewelry" in an outdoor crafts market in San Francisco, he met Peggy, another street artist who was selling "deer antler dope pipes." Peggy had moved from Detroit, and "she'd experienced some

Gregory Ross ca. 1977, Berkeley, CA (Gregory Ross)

shit in her life too." Peggy's steady presence was somewhat stabilizing for Ross, but he nevertheless remained in depression, containing his welter of negative feelings as best he could with pot and booze.

In 1978 Ross discovered MASV, the Eastbay men's anti-rape group, and he joined in part because violence prevention work felt so hopeful and positive. But he also found the same sorts of sectarian squabbling in MASV.

"It was all these polemics—people were doing position papers in the meetings. What's the primary contradiction? Is it sexism, racism, classism, or stupidity-ism, I don't [*laughs*]—I mean, who cares, you know?" Ross felt his working-class and veteran status gave him "a right to be angry" with these educated, middle-class men. But his interventions were mostly unproductive, and the group process wasn't making him feel any healthier, so he pulled back from MASV.

Ross connected briefly with the War Resisters League, a Quaker organization through which he did some public antiwar poetry readings—actions that his poet/veteran partner Steve Hassna called "choking America." Ross's work with the War Resisters League didn't last long either, but poetry writing planted a seed he would later cultivate as a source of personal healing and self-expression. By spring 1980, though, Gregory Ross had become, in his words, "completely unmoored." "It was a very bad time in my life. My PTSD was really bad, I was clinically depressed, I was suicidal, I was probably somewhat homicidal. I felt like I was unlovable because of it, that I had no right to be alive at some level. It was just too painful to be alive. Even Peggy's love didn't work anymore. I felt like there was no place to go; I just wanted out. One night at Point Reyes, I waded into the water with the idea that I would just keep swimming until I couldn't, but it was so damn cold I turned around and came out [*laughs ironically*]. That water was too damn cold!"

On April 2, 1980, Ross checked himself into the VA hospital in Menlo Park, where he would remain for the next nine months. On admission, VA doctors diagnosed him as having suffered from "a ten-year history of chronic depression and post traumatic symptoms," including a "syndrome of weakness, fatigue, anorexia, sweats," and "moderate suicidal ideation." Ross got with the program. "I went to groups. I interacted. That program saved my life." When his therapist told him he should join the Vietnam group, Ross balked, fearing that his REMF status would mark him as an outsider where "everybody else in that group is a combat vet." Ross agreed to try, knowing that the five others in the group would have to vote him in. Two or three were reluctant, but a Marine Corps vet for whom Ross had done a favor a few weeks earlier intervened. "'You know, here's the thing,' he said. 'You're right, Ross didn't see the same kind of shit I did or that you did, but I think we should let him in,' and the other guys said okay." In the group, Ross discovered, "I was a good listener and I could analyze things and I would put out my stuff. Eventually as I felt more accepted, I would talk about my feelings of guilt and my feelings of survival guilt."

There, Ross also began to grapple with the moral injury he had absorbed as part of the gun line in Vietnam. Unlike the other men in his VA group who had been in direct ground combat in Vietnam, the people Ross had helped to kill were distant, and thus more abstract. He recalls feeling, "You have no right to have this kind of guilt. You were never in direct combat. You did kill those people long-distance, but you're just being grandiose. You're making it more than it is for your own ego or whatever. I don't know exactly. So I denied the hell out of it." Ross came to realize, as Dave Grossman observed in his book *On Killing*, that one's internalized shame from being an "accessory to killing" can fester as a continuing source of moral injury.[21] This understanding, eventually, became a source of Ross's efforts to link his own self-healing with "absolution" for his role in killing Vietnamese people in what he came to realize was an unjust war.

Following four months of what Ross's VA report called "intensive personality reorganization," he was transferred to a VA work rehabilitation program. He received his release from the VA program on January 22, 1981. Soon, he and Peggy were married, and in December 1982 their son Nick was born. Ross reconnected a bit with peace activism—of which there was plenty in the Bay Area, including protests against nuclear weapons and "Reagan's dirty little wars" in Central America and the 1983 U.S. invasion of Grenada. Shortly after his discharge from the VA, Ross did a "reading/ performance" of "Shell Shocked"—a poem about his own war-caused PTSD and startle response ("How I dread the sound of the 4th of July")— at a 1981 "Welcome Back to the Vietnam Veteran Celebration" in Menlo

Gregory Ross reading his poem "Shell Shocked" at the Welcome Back to
Vietnam Vets Celebration, Menlo Park, CA, 1981 (Gregory Ross)

Park, California. The performance required him not just to read the piece
aloud, but to "scream, cry, whisper, and scream again," a form of public
self-expression that coupled Ross's growing passion for writing with the
raw emotionally expressive skills he'd begun to develop during his months
in therapy.

Ross was working part time doing shiatsu and Swedish massage when he heard about an opportunity for "middle- and working-class people to become acupuncturists." He "went to school on credit cards," supported in part by Peggy and by his own part-time employment. It took him seven years, but he was finally licensed as an acupuncturist, and by 1990 he was "doing detox work" in local hospitals.

KARMIC PAYBACK

For much of his young adulthood, Gregory Ross had trouble envisioning a future that stretched beyond his working-class roots: "I was supposed to work in a factory. That was my tape. The best I could do was get a union job in a factory and try not to drink myself to death before I retired." In 1990, he began a twenty-year stretch working as an acupuncturist. He started with pregnant women and their children at a detox clinic in Children's Hospital in Oakland, and from there he got a job setting up an acupuncture program at a methadone clinic. Oakland's Highland Hospital was starting a new detox program, and the director asked Ross—who lived only a half mile from the hospital—to join them. Soon he was working at Highland with what many would call "the quote-unquote 'dregs of society.' It's a county hospital. I worked with poor, very poor people, people of color. I started working with junkies, you know, heroin addicts, alcoholics, crack addicts, crank, and oxycodone."

For Ross, the work provided far more than a regular income; it became a deeply satisfying source of self-esteem, and his pivot point "from servitude to service" as he continued to deal with his own PTSD and moral injury. "I wasn't that conscious of it then, but it was like—a karmic payback, so to speak. It was a way of paying off my karmic debt around all that, for my part in the war; for the people I killed."

Ross continued to write—short pieces and poetry, mostly. Nearly twenty years after the end of the war in Vietnam, National Book-award-winning writer Maxine Hong Kingston started a veterans writing group in the San Francisco Bay Area. Ross joined and found a community of fellow veteran writers, and an encouraging mentor in Kingston. He wrote the short piece, "Atonement" at one of the group's writing workshops.

Atonement One:

Soldiers kill to live
But to survive will dredge their
Souls of grief and cry

Atonement Two:

Soldiers kill to live
But to survive will dredge their
Souls for peace and cry

Ross felt that the piece "formed a healing arc from grief to peace by way of tears," and he was amazed when "Maxine remarked that it was a perfect poem. Nothing needed to be added. Nothing needed to be taken away. The statement took my breath away." In 2006, Kingston published *Veterans of War, Veterans of Peace*, a thick anthology of works by the veterans in her writing workshop; the book includes two pieces by Gregory Ross.[22] Whenever he had the opportunity, Ross would read his poetry aloud at public events "because it felt like the right thing to do karmically."

Following the first Gulf War, and then ramping up following U.S. invasions of Afghanistan and Iraq, Ross rekindled his connection with the veterans' peace movement. For a few years, Ross attended meetings of the San Francisco chapter of VFP, but given his job at the hospital, the roundtrip BART (Bay Area Rapid Transit) commute from the East Bay, and his mounting health troubles, it was hard to stay attached. When he learned in 2010 that there was an East Bay chapter of VFP forming, he decided, "I want to be a part of this." He went to the initial organizing meeting of VFP, East Bay Chapter 162, and has been an integral part of the group since. He decided too that from then on he would literally wear VFP on his sleeve everywhere he went. "I thought, now I need to do something every day, and I decided that I would wear something that said Veterans for Peace out in the public every day, as a penance, a balance, you know, a karmic balance. I always wear something that says Veterans for Peace." His VFP garb or buttons occasionally draw him "the stare, the *how-dare-you* kind of thing" from some people. But for the most part, Ross finds that his VFP insignia spark supportive and productive conversation with strangers. Ross purchased fifty VFP buttons, so when someone commented that they like his button, he could reach into his pack and give them one of their own. It was gratifying when he noticed that the guy manning the desk at the VA clinic was wearing a button Ross had gifted him. "And I'm like, 'Yay!' That felt really good, as you can imagine. Next time I see him if he's wearing it, I'll ask him if he wants to join 162. What the hell!"

The Dead Have No Use for Our Silence

In 2011 Gregory Ross was laid off from his acupuncture job at the hospital. Besides the financial concerns this raised—at age sixty-four, he had no pension from his years of work—the loss of his job also wrenched Ross away from his long-standing means of providing service to others, and finding absolution for his past. "When I was laid off, my life was severely disrupted. Emotionally jarring. But an added twist that I did not recognize until I was confronted with it was that the job was a way of paying off my karmic debt. A way to atone. An absolution. A way to balance out my life in the world. Now, I had no place to put my guilt. I no longer had the service outlet." PTSD symptoms Ross had held at bay for years stormed back. Memories of witnessing that young girl shot in the back in

the Philippines haunted him. Ross's startle response to loud noises—
even the sound of two glass bottles clinking together—amplified. "On
the fourth of July, I got under the bed with our dog half of the night. I just
couldn't deal with it." Ross returned to the VA, and after all these years
he was pleasantly surprised to find that he was treated by VA staff with
great respect, "like a hero." He saw an individual therapist, joined a PTSD
group, and eventually settled on some medications he found helpful.

Still, Ross is frustrated with the fact that he has only a 10 percent disability rating for his partial hearing loss—which yields about $133 a month
in disability income. Even his VA therapist, Ross says, is "flabbergasted"
that despite his longtime PTSD diagnosis and struggles, Ross has no PTSD
disability rating. "I've asked for compensation three times and they've
turned me down." As I write this, Ross's appeal is still pending, and he
worries that if Republicans' efforts to privatize the VA are successful,
he will never win the benefits he deserves.

Once again—now in retirement from the job that had given his life
such meaning—Gregory Ross finds himself reconstructing a life project
of personal healing and promoting peace through his daily actions and
his poetry. He is gratified that his family life, including his relationship
with Peggy and their son Nick, now in his early thirties, is solid. He's happy
to have a young grandson, Levi. He is managing his health troubles,
including his PTSD and chronic back pain, with help from the VA. And
he remains engaged with VFP, in part because he loves the organization's
inclusivity and its positive pro-peace message. "I do little things here and
there. I feel less and less like I've got to change the whole world to make
up for what I did. Where my heart is, is with Veterans for Peace; it's *for*
something, not against something. It's *for* peace. We're here to try and
foster peace everywhere. Not just in our own selves, but in the world. I
just think war is ridiculous. I don't understand why we do it. I believe
that the top 1 percent pay the middle 98 percent to send off the bottom
1 percent, that way they didn't have to get their hands dirty."

Ross's aging body now limits what he can do as a peace activist. He continues to wear his VFP button every day, and he attends his monthly VFP chapter meetings. A couple of years ago, he told the members of his VFP chapter that he wanted to cut a deal with them.

> I said look, here's the deal: I'll facilitate every meeting from now on. I'll even have a title for myself called Facilitator for Life. But here's the thing: I'm semidisabled here. I will not chain myself to any fences in Livermore. I will not march or ride on the truck on Veteran's Day or Gay Pride Day. I can't. Even if I could, I can't run for shit. I can't fight back anymore and I'm not going to jail, partly because I'm in pain a lot and I don't want to do it. So my deal with you guys is I'll facilitate every goddamn meeting, but nobody better give me shit about not doing any of that stuff. It's good stuff, and those of you that want to do it—great. But I'm not doing it. Man, people were standing up on their chairs—"Yes! Yes!"

Ross also continues to write poetry—he and Peggy recently joined a new writing group—and on occasion, he'll recite his work publicly. I witnessed him reading a poem to kick off a plenary at the national VFP convention in 2016, to a packed auditorium in Berkeley.

Part of what was so satisfying about being on stage that day, he told me later, was that "I was requested to read that. I was asked to read that. Not just, 'We need a poet for the opening plenary,' but, 'Can we have Gregory read this one?' It's been an amazing experience. One, I get to talk to people in a way that I don't get to in the 'normal' world. Two, I attained a little bit of notoriety from the poetry readings. People come up. I've sold some books."[23] The poem he was asked to read was "A Moment of Silence in a Forest of White Crosses." The title references the VFP's Arlington West project, and the subject and tone express Gregory Ross's lifelong commitment to absolution for past wars, and peace for the future.

Gregory Ross reads one of his poems at the 2016 VFP convention, Berkeley, CA (author)

The Dead

do not require our silence to be honored

do not require our silence to be remembered.

do not accept our silence as remembrance, as honor.

do not expect our silence to end

the carnage of war

the child starved

the woman raped

the virulence of intolerance

the Earth desecrated

It is the living who require our silence

in a lifetime of fear and complicity

The Dead

do require our courage to defy the powerful and the greedy.

do require our lives to be loud, compassionate, courageous.

do require our anger at the continuance of war in their name.

do require our shock at the maiming of the Earth in their name.

do require our outrage to be honored, to be remembered.

The Dead

have no use for our silence

Peace in ourselves; peace in the world.
— Thich Nhat Hanh, *Peace Is Every Step*

I was brought up on this "duty, honor, country" stuff. But I didn't serve my country. My god, I killed people for these goddamned lies.

—Daniel Craig

CHAPTER 5

-◄◄◄◆►►►-

You Clock In, You Go
Kill People

DANIEL CRAIG, THE GULF WAR

By the time Lieutenant Daniel Craig finally returned stateside following his 1991 combat deployment in Operation Desert Storm, the echoes of the massive victory parades in Washington, DC, and New York City had long since receded. The tens of thousands of yellow ribbons that had bedecked trees and poles during the war—symbols of citizens' support for the troops—were now faded, tattered, and fallen. Even President George H. W. Bush's triumphant proclamation following the lightning-quick U.S. victory, "By God we've kicked the Vietnam Syndrome once and for all," was now being second-guessed by more hawkish politicians and pundits who wondered why U.S. forces hadn't marched into Baghdad while Saddam Hussein's forces were shattered and in disarray in the desert.

Daniel Craig didn't much care about any of that. Following his role as an artillery battery fire direction officer in the war that historian Andrew J. Bacevich described as having taken "a nice, tidy, one hundred hours," Craig remained in the desert another two months as burning Kuwaiti oil wells belched noxious smoke like massive funeral pyres.[1] The first month in theater, he said, it was freezing cold; the final month it seemed never to drop below a scorching 110 degrees. Whether hot or cold, Craig said, most every day was boring; the soldiers whiled the time away with lazy games of hacky sack between stints of cleaning the relentless desert sand from the gears and wheels of their armored vehicles.

As he and his wife, Lee, who was then five months pregnant, transitioned from Germany back to the States in the spring of 1992, Craig faced a challenge more personal than boredom or faded yellow ribbons. Lee fell ill and was diagnosed with preeclampsia, a condition that endangered her life if the pregnancy were to go to term. Amniocentesis revealed that their unborn son—whom they named Aaron—had not developed kidneys or a bladder. The doctor's grim news was that the baby would not live, and worse, taking the pregnancy to term would also threaten the mother's life. Their decision was wrenching but clear: "We decided to induce labor, and he died right away." Craig, already "emotionally numb" from his war experience and drinking heavily—"partying," he called it then—struggled to come to grips with his son's death. "I used to think it was God punishing me. I grew up Catholic so there's this whole guilt-shame thing going on. You know: You went to Iraq, you killed people, this is your punishment. Like karma."

Craig and Lee had another son, Jordan, in 1993, but the marriage did not survive. Mother and child moved out in 1995. Craig had quit drinking by then, but "getting clean" was not the same as having it together. He was still "a mess," and absent the daily numbing effect of alcohol, his anger amplified, especially as he educated himself about U.S. foreign policy, the military, and the experience of Gulf War vets like himself. His shame—that perhaps his son's death was his own bad karma—had now converted to rage over how his government had used him and what it had cost him. Aaron had died, Craig became convinced, "as a result of [my] being in a toxic environment" during the war—inhaling the smoky air from burning oil wells, ingesting the PB pills[2] the troops were given to protect against expected nerve gas attacks, being exposed to depleted uranium found to be in tank rounds, and being in proximity with stockpiled Iraqi chemical weapons that U.S. engineers had destroyed in place. All of this, Craig said, was "just toxic," for him and for thousands of his fellow soldiers.

I found out there were thousands, potentially tens of thousands of [Gulf War Veterans] in my position where they had children who were born without internal organs. They had children that were born physically deformed and mentally handicapped. I never really delved into detailed statistics about this because I get pissed off all over again, because I'm just a fucking number to someone in the government somewhere. We're all just a bunch of numbers, we're like line items in an inventory. You know they call us "GI?" It means "General Issue"—you're a piece of equipment on an inventory list. You get killed, all they do is replace the part like when you get a flat tire.

Anger tugs at Daniel Craig's narrative like a continually cramping muscle. Through the many hours we spent talking, he would return again and again to the account of his son's death. This story, I came to realize, serves as a locus of Craig's fury over being lied to by authority figures, being treated as a "peon" by the government and the military, and firing the big guns that killed an unknown number of Iraqis. Recounting Aaron's death is also the pivot point in Craig's narrative, the jolt after which he began to awaken from numbness, gradually devoting himself to a conscious project of recovery. Craig's individual recovery melded with collective activism in late 2002 after he crossed paths with some local World War II and Vietnam veterans who were active in VFP. The older veterans became mentors, and Craig's VFP activism accelerated following the 2003 U.S. invasion and escalation of war in Iraq. Craig's work with VFP provided a group context for what had until then felt like a purely individual struggle. Working for peace facilitated Craig's efforts, "to channel this—*uggh!*—*energy* into something more positive than just my little-by-little self-destruction."

-«‹‹◆››»-

I was put in touch with Daniel Craig by longtime VFP activist Ken Mayers, who told me that Craig, a veteran of the Gulf War, worked with the homeless population, and was currently serving as president of the Santa Fe, New Mexico, chapter of VFP. Our initial interview took place on a warm summer day at a local café and yoga studio where Craig practices yoga and sometimes subs as a yoga teacher. Craig greeted me with a firm handshake, his intense hazel eyes locking with mine. His initial manner was not unfriendly, though he seemed a bit tense or guarded. Perhaps his manner and attire put me a bit on guard as well: A striking fifty-two-year-old guy with a compact muscular body, Craig's shaved head was offset by the fluffy goat patch on his chin, now mostly gray. He had ripped the sleeves and collar from his T-shirt—"it's cooler in this hot weather," he explained—and across his broad chest a provocative message was emblazoned in bold caps:

MILITARY
RECRUITERS
LIE

Craig said he wears this shirt frequently, and it draws frowns from some and smiles and a thumbs-up from others. At times the T-shirt starts a conversation, and when it does he immediately personalizes it to tell his story of being lied to when he was recruited into the Army as a seventeen-year-old who had yet to finish high school.

As Daniel Craig opened his life story to me on this first day and on several subsequent sittings at the dining room table of his home, I also opened to him. It did not take long for me to learn that Craig is a man in recovery, devoted to sobriety, yoga, service to others, and channeling his once-debilitating anger into healthy and peaceful avenues. It also became apparent that he has a sophisticated understanding of the history and politics of America's wars, and of the importance and responsibility for veterans to stand up and tell their truths about war and peace. Like many of the vets I've met in VFP, Daniel Craig's commitment to peace, to social-justice activism, to his own physical, emotional, and spiritual health, and to serving others are interconnected parts of a coherent life project. But it was never a simple or straightforward road getting to this place, and it still isn't.

Turmoil in My House

Springer, New Mexico, where Daniel Craig was raised, was a "very small ranching, farming community, so small it's not even a one-horse town." Born in December 1963, just weeks after the assassination of President John F. Kennedy, the early years of Craig's youth seemed insulated and isolated from what many have called the "social turmoil" of the 1960s. Springer was "pretty small," with about 1,500 people in the 1970s, "mostly white and brown."[3] Craig's Mexican American mother worked as a nurse; his schoolteacher father was "a mix of Scottish and Mexican American." His parents identified as Hispanic, but his mixed background placed him between ethnicities, "always in the middle," unsure where he fit in among other kids. "Here in New Mexico the term is 'coyote.' Half and half. A mixed-breed type. Being mixed ethnicity always sucked. My last name is Craig, which is Scottish. So the Hispanic surname kids were like, 'You're white,' and then the white kids said, 'You are brown,' and it's like holy shit, it's a tug of war in myself about who and what the hell I am."

Clarity about his place in the world didn't come from home. Craig recalls witnessing continual "turmoil in my house; my father drank a lot." He remembers from a very young age "just picking up on the dissension, the tenseness" in the house, when his mother returned from work to find her husband once again had been drinking with his friends. Nor did a Catholic upbringing provide much of a "moral compass" for young Daniel. "We'd go to catechism classes in the evening . . . and the priest would come into the little classroom in the little school building near the church totally fucked up. I mean, drunk as hell, he's holding onto a chair." The lessons of the church weren't much different from those he was learning at home: "I'm being told one thing and shown another. Like in my house being told to act a certain way and then watching my mom and my dad argue and my dad drink. It was a lot of 'do as I say not as I do.'"

Young Daniel felt boxed in—"There's all this shit going in within myself as a child and then in my teens"—but there were few avenues of escape in tiny Springer. For a while, he found solace in the town library, pouring through Edgar Rice Burroughs's *Tarzan* series, and devouring numerous volumes of *The Hardy Boys*, Edward Stratemeyer's popular adventure novels written for boys. "Reading was total escape, to be somewhere other than where I was, and in some cases to be someone other than who I was." By his early teens, Daniel had found another source of escape that echoed the adult behavior around him: "partying . . . I was really invested in that."

Something else besides books connected young Daniel to a larger world outside of tiny Springer—the U.S. military. As a boy, Daniel orchestrated fantasy wars with "a gigantic array of little green army men," and then got into building models of "World War II tanks, airplanes, ships." With BB guns in hand, Daniel and his childhood friends utilized the "hundreds of square miles of open land" surrounding Springer, to "go out there and play war. That was what we called it—playing war." The boys found ready-made storylines of wartime bravery and heroism in popular entertainment of the time. Daniel enjoyed watching *Combat*—a World War II TV series that ran on ABC from 1962 to 1967—and movies like *Battle of the Bulge* and *A Bridge Too Far*, which "implanted, really young, this patriotism flag-waving stuff."

Daniel was, he can see in retrospect, "primed to go into the military." After all, his father had served three years in the Air Force, and Daniel had been told that he had a cousin who had served in World War II at Pearl Harbor. Others in his Springer community had fought in Korea and Vietnam, and though few of them wanted to talk about their experiences,

Daniel could see that these men were respected by others in the town. "I was raised with this whole duty, honor, country thing, just that mentality of serving your country." By the time he was sixteen, Daniel had already decided to enlist in the army, but he learned that he'd have to wait until he was seventeen to do so. "So, I turned seventeen and, within a week, I was down in Albuquerque at the MEPS [Military Entrance Processing Center], and I enlisted. In part I joined the military out of this sense of duty, because that's what I was conditioned for. But at the same time, I was seventeen years old, I partied a lot, I had no direction. I had no great plan like I'm going to do this, this, and this. What the hell, I'll join the military."

In July 1981 Daniel Craig left Springer for basic training at Fort Leonard Wood, Missouri. His description of his decision to enlist gives insight into a question that led to a good deal of late-1970s hand-wringing, following the end of the American War in Vietnam: With an Army draft no longer in place, how will the nation find enough willing soldiers to populate an all-volunteer Army? Part of the answer, of course, lay in stepping up the investment and effort of military recruitment via television commercials and in schools, especially in poor and working-class communities.[4] But in listening to Daniel Craig's story, one would be hard pressed to say that he was forced or even manipulated into joining up. Instead, we see in his story an example of how many young men find what the sociologist Max Weber called an "elective affinity" between the military and their own developing identities as young men. Take a generation of boys—especially those in rural small towns or poor inner cities that offer few avenues for gainful employment or economic mobility. Engage these boys in fantasy warrior play, and immerse them in TV and movie images that glorify war as sites for the enactment of manly patriotic heroism. Teach them to see the older men around them who served in the military as having done their duty to serve their country. By the time they are in their late teens, many such young men, like Daniel Craig, will see joining the military as the patriotic thing to do, a rational decision. Joining the Army, Craig recalls thinking, was "the next right step. This is natural, this is normal, this is what you do."

THIS IS WHERE YOU'RE GOING TO DIE

Daniel Craig's twelve-year military career would eventually span the end of the Cold War and the shift in national focus to a desert war waged mostly in the Middle East. From the age of seventeen, when he enlisted, until he was nearly thirty years old, Craig said, "I was never a civilian. My twenties was all military." At first, though, he was only vaguely aware of the sociopolitical forces that would move him from the United States to Germany and back, and eventually to the Middle East.

As noted above, Daniel Craig rolled in to basic training at Fort Leonard Wood, Missouri, in July 1981. Six months earlier, Ronald Reagan had assumed the United States presidency, trumpeting the moment as "Morning in America," promising a new dawn of prosperity at home and renewed American boldness on the world stage. Reagan, Secretary of Defense Caspar Weinberger, and their team forced a dramatic escalation in military spending, reviving the B-1 bomber program and giving the green light to the production of the so-called MX Peacekeeper Missile. Reagan proposed costly new weapons systems, including his pet (eventually abandoned) Strategic Defense Initiative, dubbed "Star Wars," a satellite laser-guided system designed to shoot down incoming enemy nuclear missiles. And it wasn't all buildup and bluster. In 1983, the United States invaded and quickly overwhelmed the light forces of the tiny Caribbean island of Grenada and installed a new government. During the next few years, the United States prosecuted semisecret proxy wars to fight back popular insurgencies in Central America. All of this—the arms buildup, the waging of what some called "Reagan's dirty little wars," and a good deal of rhetorical saber rattling was part of a larger strategy, a final Cold War push to defeat the Soviet Union. Included in this was Reagan's 1983 approval of NATO's deployment of Pershing II missiles in West Germany.

Basic training and advanced individual training in engineer school took five months at Fort Leonard Wood, and then at the start of 1982 "it was off to Germany" for Private Daniel Craig. The young "coyote" from a "tiny town from the middle of nowhere" hoped that being in the military would give him some identity, and perhaps some purpose. "I thought, 'I'm joining the military. Well shit, I will get some definition here.' And I did, to a degree. Everyone is a GI and everyone is a soldier. But have you ever seen *The Jerk* with Steve Martin? He's like, 'I'm in the phone book! I am somebody!' For me it was like, 'I'm in the military, I belong to something bigger than myself. I'm a soldier!' And then I found out that within that big happy family bullshit, the divisions, the hierarchical stuff, the color lines stuff, the religion line stuff, it's all there too."

It was "a big eye-opener" for Craig to live amid "this explosion of languages, ethnicities." The level of diversity he experienced in the Army amounted to "shell shock, culture shock, it was like wow!" He saw black people for the first time, and a couple of them were scary "badasses, street-tough gangbangers from Baltimore." Eventually he connected with some black guys from small rural towns, with whom he felt some kinship. Echoing Ernie Sanchez's World War II Army experience, Daniel Craig discovered his in-between racial status in the military to be a location of both confusion and creative learning. He found himself "fitting in with the black guys more than the white guys. Some of these white guys were incredibly racist. And the black guys were like well, you're not black, obviously, but they were more accepting. So I was the token not-black guy for a long time."

Craig's first eighteen-month stint in Germany was spent as a combat engineer with the 4th Infantry. He drove an armored vehicle-launched bridge in support of an antitank and mortar platoon that guarded the Czechoslovakian border, in preparation for the possibility of the Cold War suddenly becoming a hot tank war. "You look right across the Fulda Gap, that's where the bad guys are, the enemy." Once, his commander pointed across the Fulda Gap and told Craig and the others, "This is where you are going to die." As tensions escalated and Soviet troops massed near the border, Craig was jolted awake by sirens at 2 a.m. "You load up all your shit: all your personal gear, your weapon, your protective mask, your other weapon systems, and you get down to the mortar pool, you get your entire unit, your entire battalion brigade, division ready to go to the border to protect against a Soviet invasion. But it never happened." Such moments of crisis and tension stand out in any veteran's memory. But much of the day-to-day in the military is routine mundanity. Just as he had at home, Daniel filled the emptiness with partying.

> I was continually in trouble, and I had been that sort of person my entire life. The partying: alcohol and other illegal drug use when I was in Germany. I'm seventeen, and in Germany they serve beer to fourteen-year-olds. So just like, the partying, we're drinking and smoking hash-ish until four in the morning then waking up at five and running PT [physical training]. And I could do that. I could be totally wasted and get up. I'm seventeen, so I'm in reasonably decent health because of basic training and all. So I'd get up still drunk and go run 2 miles or I'd go to PT. We'd be running PT in the morning and invariably someone is popping out of formation to go throw up because the running is getting the best of you when you've been drinking heavily.

Craig wasn't the only one showing up to morning formation still drunk. It was obvious to the young recruits that some of their older superiors who were Vietnam vets were "just self-medicating and getting loaded." So it didn't seem so off for Craig and other recruits to do the same. "That was an eye-opener. It's like god, once final formation [ends], 17:00, 5 p.m., no adult supervision. So that do you do? You go chase women and get loaded."

SICK OF BEING A PEON

Craig's stint in Germany ended when he was shipped back to Fort Riley, Kansas, where in 1984 he faced a fork in the road: either to reenlist or to become a civilian. He decided to stay with the familiar, but with a twist that he hoped would improve his life. "For lack of common sense, I liked the military. The bizarre part was I liked the structure. I was a little kid playing war; I'm twenty-one, twenty-two now but without an adult brain." Craig may have "liked the structure" of Army life, but he did not like his lowly position within it. "I didn't want to do more time as an enlisted man; I'm sick of being a peon. I didn't reenlist, so I had the bright idea to go to university and get commissioned as an officer."

It was a rocky start at New Mexico State University, when Craig discovered that the promises of educational support that had been made to him three years earlier by his Army recruiter had been "lies." As part of an enlistment bonus, Craig had signed up for the GI Bill, but when he reported to the VA for his expected college support, he was met with a rude awakening. "I put in my paperwork and the woman there says you don't have the GI Bill. And what happened is the recruiter, his lie to me when I enlisted was I was going to get X amount of money for college, based on the fact that I met all of my requirements, and that I was good-conduct discharged. That was my end of the bargain. Their end of the bargain was I get this money to go to college. Well the bastard had lied to me." Craig's father helped him to appeal his case to New Mexico's U.S. senator Pete Domenici, who forwarded the case to the inspector general of the military. Craig's appeal was upheld: "They said it in so many words: Since he lied and you met your requirements, you fulfilled your contract obligations, you get the money." Craig was able to begin college, but the incident stuck in his craw, adding insult to earlier injuries and betrayals by authority figures. "He had lied to me. And it's like, 'What an asshole!' So add another one to I'm told one thing and then treated another way. Do as I say not as I do, type of thing. Another experience of another reason to hate authority, at the very least question authority."

During his first two years at New Mexico State, Craig served in the National Guard, doing a "weekend warrior thing" and being a Reserve Officer Training Corps (ROTC) cadet. During his final two years of college, Craig continued in ROTC. Throughout his years in college, there was one familiar theme: "Partying! Party until two in the morning, then go run PT with ROTC at 7 a.m. Party was the number-one thing: Go party, get loaded, get a college degree."

In one of his psychology classes, Craig met Lee, a fellow student who would become his wife. A "military brat" whose career Army father had taken his family to tours of duty in Korea, Germany, and various locations in the United States, Lee "knew what the military life was all about. The military life as a dependent." When he left university in 1988 with his bachelor's degree in psychology, Craig reentered active duty as commissioned second lieutenant in the U.S. Army. Craig's next stop would be Fort Sill, Oklahoma, for six months of officer training and artillery school, but not before the young couple married in January 1989. That summer, Craig was deployed again to Germany, now as a married man and as an artillery officer with the 2nd Armored Division.

SAME PLACE, NEW ENEMY

During Daniel Craig's four years in college, the United States' strategic and military maneuvering within a rapidly changing world had been shifting dramatically. When the 1990s began, Germany was still a major site of U.S. military strategic power. But the Cold War was rapidly coming to a close. Shortly after the Soviet Politburo elected him Communist Party general secretary in 1985, Mikhail Gorbachev joined with a younger generation of Communist Party leaders to institute glasnost—a liberalization of openness in Soviet political life—and perestroika—reforms aimed at decentralizing the Soviet political economy. These domestic changes were coupled with a thawing of relations with the United States and the West. Gorbachev's negotiations with Reagan resulted in the 1987 Intermediate-Range Nuclear Forces Treaty, a key moment in the slowing of the dangerous and costly 1980s escalation of nuclear arms. Fears of nuclear war, especially in Europe, were subsiding.

By 1989 and 1990, facilitated by the economic, human, and political costs of a disastrous decade-long war in Afghanistan, the Soviet Bloc that had arisen in the post–World War II years was crumbing from within and breaking away at its edges. Mass protests for labor rights, calls for democratic political reform, and revolts against Soviet rule spread with simultaneous urgency in Poland, Czechoslovakia, East Germany, Bulgaria, Hungary, Romania, and the Baltic states. German citizens began to tear down the Berlin Wall in November 1989. By December 1991, the Soviet Union had dissolved into fifteen separate independent nations.

Hopes in the United States for a post–Cold War "peace dividend" dampened almost immediately, however. "In a nearly seamless transition," historian Andrew Bacevich wrote, "Saddam Hussein's Iraq now replaced the once-mighty USSR as the chief threat."[5] This shift was fueled by several factors, including U.S. desires to control access to Middle Eastern oil and the U.S. military-industrial complex's need to find new global enemies to justify a continuing flow of taxpayer dollars into arms manufacturing. There was also the lingering fear that the post-Vietnam-War-era United States had become soft. When Iraq invaded Kuwait in February 1990, it provided the spark for U.S. action.

President George H. W. Bush, Secretary of Defense Dick Cheney, and Generals Colin Powell and Norman Schwarzkopf saw the need for a quick and decisive U.S. military: quick in order to minimize the risk of generating antiwar sentiment likely to result from large-scale U.S. casualties in a protracted conflict; decisive because an overwhelming victory could recharge a flagging national self-confidence and prop up a sagging American manhood. "Like some ghostly presence," Bacevich wrote, "Vietnam hovered over the entire proceedings. . . . A war against Iraq would be

Lt. Daniel Craig, Garlstedt, West Germany, 1993 (Daniel Craig)

Vietnam done right, with decisive victory the result. No shillyshallying around."[6]

Second Lieutenant Daniel Craig arrived in Garlstedt, West Germany in the fall of 1989 for a three-year tour during this moment of diminishing Cold War conflict and rapidly escalating discord in the Middle East. In November 1990, he recalls, "We got told that we were getting deployed to Iraq." As their vehicles made their way to the battlefields by sea, Craig and his 2nd Armored Forward Brigade flew from Germany, where "we became the 3rd Brigade of the 1st Infantry Division out of Fort Riley, Kansas. The Big Red One." In early January 1991, they downloaded and prepared their battle equipment, and "then we moved out into the western desert where we just waited."

A World of Hurt

In the weeks that Daniel Craig waited in the Saudi desert with the Big Red One, staged and ready to roll, they watched B-52s overhead, "flying north into Iraq to bombing missions, to pound on them from the air." What Craig and his cohorts were witnessing from the ground was indeed a pounding. The air offensive of Operation Desert Storm began at midnight on January 17, 1991, with helicopter, cruise missile, and F-117 stealth bomber attacks that took out Iraqi radar installations, hit government buildings in Baghdad, and quickly disabled the thin Iraqi air force. That first night, according to Bacevich, "nearly seven hundred combat aircraft, the vast majority of them American, penetrated Iraqi airspace . . . a coalition air offensive that would continue with minimal interruption for the next forty days."[7] With Iraqi air defenses demolished, U.S. planes turned to "tank plinking"—hitting and disabling from the air Iraqi ground forces. It was, according to the Army's 900-page *Final Report to Congress* on the conduct of Operation Desert Storm, a "huge air armada" that succeeded in launching "the biggest air strike since World War II."[8]

"We started shooting," Craig recalls, "on Valentine's Day, February 14 of '91." After Army engineers broke through a huge earthen berm the Iraqis had built to slow an invasion, the coalition tanks—Bradleys that "could go 40, 50 miles per hour"—powered from Saudi Arabia into Iraq. Craig was right on the Bradleys' heels with the somewhat slower built-up armored personnel carrier used to haul, set up, and "fire a mission," and then again haul forward the powerful "and pretty damned accurate" howitzer artillery that "could reach up to 34 kilometers with a rocket-assisted projectile."

As they pushed further into Iraq, Craig saw the wreckage of destroyed Iraqi tanks and trucks, but he assumed coalition tanks had dished out most of that destruction, not his artillery, which he knew was deployed "mostly against troops." He didn't see many bodies as they rolled forward. But he understood the hell he and his unit were raining on the enemy. "The artillery is nasty. The basic round is 95.5 pounds, and it's steel and high explosives, basically. When the fuse detonates it explodes and you've just got 95 pounds of steel just scattering in big chunks and tiny slivers, and I know the killing radius for a 155-milimeter round is like 50 meters so anything in a 50-meter radius is pretty much just vaporized. They'd call in a fire mission and we'd fire a mission, knowing the people on the other end are in a world of hurt."

Morale in Craig's unit, he recalls, was "very high" as they forged ahead. They were doing "everything we were trained to do," with great efficiency, and with no discernible opposition. "We just rolled over the Iraqi army. Just superior firepower." He could not see it directly, but Craig knew that their artillery fire missions were "just killing people." He recalls feeling no remorse at the time, but he expresses incredulity today in recalling how, as a young man in his mid-twenties, he experienced war as a routine job: "It was just matter of fact. Fuck it. This is the job. We get to go out here and shoot people and get paid for it. There's no 'you're going to jail and trial for murder.' It was just sanctioned. It was like matter of fact. You clock in, you go kill people." Craig experienced some of what John Gray, writing in the aftermath of fighting in World War II, called "the mad excitement

of destroying."⁹ "Shit, they're paying me to do this! It doesn't get any better than this. We're killing people. I get to participate in killing people
and not get in trouble. It was that ultimate getting away with something,
like when I'd steal things or when I would be dishonest and get away with
it. It's like using. The dopamine. The adrenaline, all that rush. Here's like,
what's the ultimate thing people can do is kill other people. There was that
sick part of me, that dark side of me that was like, 'Fuck! And they are paying us for this!'"

It would be some months before Craig and other victorious U.S. troops
were honored with "ribbons and awards and unit cred, battalion citations,"
but he did receive one form of recognition while in the battlefield, when
he "got promoted to first lieutenant somewhere in the middle of the
Euphrates River Valley in Iraq."

In the end, coalition and U.S. casualties were light, relative to the carnage dealt to the enemy. Estimates of Iraqi combat deaths range from
20,000 to 26,000. Coalition bombings killed roughly 3,500 Iraqi civilians,
and many thousands of Iraqis perished from other effects of the war.¹⁰ By
contrast, U.S. forces suffered 145 deaths due to noncombat accidents, and
148 battle-related deaths. Of this latter number, thirty-five deaths were due
to "friendly fire." Craig knew two of these friendly-fire casualties, men
from the tank battalion he had worked with. It still enrages him that his
brigade commander, a colonel, and a battalion commander, a lieutenant
colonel, addressed the entire battalion to "dispel the rumors that these
men were killed by friendly fire."

But everyone knew that they had been killed by U.S. forces, killed by
another tank company who engaged them thinking they were an Iraqi
tank company. It happens. It happens in every damn war. It happens.
It's how they came up with the term friendly fire! Holy shit. Call it
what it is. But you have this colonel and lieutenant colonel sitting here
saying that's not true when everyone knows it's true. So here's another
experience: you've got The Man, authority, just blatantly lying to you.

And what am I? At that point, I think I had become a first lieutenant.
But what are you going to do? Call a colonel a liar? The structure doesn't
work like that. There's a chain of command. You don't speak unless
spoken to.

Reenlisting as a commissioned officer, it turned out, hadn't changed the
experience of the military all that much for Daniel Craig. "It didn't
dawn on me that as a second lieutenant you're still a peon, bottom of
the barrel."

Once the Iraqis had surrendered, once the hundred hours of battle had
ended and his unit had set up a perimeter around their battalion and hun-
kered down in the desert, Craig encountered live Iraqi soldiers for the first
time. "We started seeing Iraqis walking towards our perimeter surrender-
ing in the hundreds. They'd been out there starved. No water. No support
to speak of. They're the ones who had people behind them that if they
tried to run away they would shoot them. So these guys were just surren-
dering in the hundreds, and what we ended up doing at the end was
transporting them to prisoner-of-war compounds to be processed."

After the hurry-up of preparation, fighting, and transporting prisoners, two months of waiting began. As celebrations of a victorious "hundred-
hour war" erupted at home, the fighting's aftermath dragged on for many
soldiers like Craig. From February through the end of May, Craig recalls,
"It became a matter of waiting to come home. It was just vehicle weapons
equipment maintenance, because all that sand, it just wears on everything." It's only in retrospect that he realizes that this "down time" in the
desert was "just toxic. . . .We were out in the middle of nowhere in
Kuwait, just waiting to get back to Saudi Arabia. We just lived in the
middle of oil fields for I don't know how many weeks just watching oil
wells burn and breathing oil-well smoke. I'm sitting on our truck and I
counted a hundred points of light all around us, the oil wells burning."
The constant smoke in the hot desert air was not the only toxin to which
Craig and his colleagues were exposed.

One morning, 2 a.m., 3 a.m., our chemical sensors went off and we'd pop into protective gear, and, "Oh, false alarm." But as years have passed we know that they had engineer units destroying Iraqi weapons dumps with chemical weapons in them, just blowing them up. There's all this shit in the air. We took PB pills—pyridostigmine bromide I think is the word—which was for chemical weapons so if we were to be hit by nerve gas you'd already have this stuff in your system. You introduce a little into the body so that way a bigger dose doesn't kill you. We are taking PD pills, we're putting on sunscreen crap, we are living in the oil fields. Depleted uranium is widely used [in] tank rounds, the A-10 Warthog, that's how they killed tanks because the damn thing is depleted uranium. So there's all these toxins out there and the Iraqis had all the chemical war ammunition which they got from the United States in the '80s so they could kill the Iranians. Just toxic.

After five months in the Middle East, Craig was sent back to Germany via Saudi Arabia. That his return was not met with public celebrations "like the people who came back to the States to the parades and the hero's welcome," didn't seem to bother him. The job that he and other coalition forces had accomplished was "very straightforward. We went in. We did what they said we were going to do." Craig was vaguely aware that back home, President Bush was being criticized for stopping at the Iraqi border, not "finishing the job" by rolling the tanks right into Baghdad and toppling Saddam Hussein. Those criticisms, Craig scoffed, came from "a bunch of people whose asses weren't out there."

The U.S. government decided not to invade and occupy Iraq in 1991—a wise decision, Craig still believes. However, this does not mean that U.S. presence in the region came to even a temporary end. "Whenever the American Army shows up, it tends to stay a while," Andrew Bacevich observed. "[Dick] Cheney's promises notwithstanding, U.S. troops were never going to 'go home.' From this point forward, U.S. military engagement in the Greater Middle East became permanent and sustained, rather than occasional and episodic."[11] Daniel Craig, however, would soon be going home.

DISILLUSIONED, DISENCHANTED, PISSED OFF

After more than four years duty as a commissioned officer, Daniel Craig "got out of the military in May 1993, completely." His separation from the Army was not voluntary. "After the Gulf War in '91, the Army contracted immensely. It halved its size. I was part of that. At that point, they're booting people out left and right so I ended up RIF, Reduction in Force." The goal of reducing U.S. military forces by 25 percent was first announced by President George H. W. Bush in August 1990. The troop drawdown and the reduction in the defense budget was widely viewed as a welcome outcome of the United States winning the Cold War, a shift in budgetary priorities that promised to cut the federal deficit and facilitate a shift toward domestic spending on human needs like education and health, and rebuilding a crumbling infrastructure. By the time Bill Clinton assumed the presidency in January 1993, the number of active-duty military personnel had dropped from 2.2 million in 1989 to close to 1.8 million. Clinton continued this shift in national priorities, and by the end of his term active-duty troops in the U.S. military numbered 1.4 million.[12]

Asked if he would have stayed in the Army had he been given the choice, Craig shrugged. "Part of me wanted to stay in, and part of me didn't care about anything. I didn't give a shit. So, yeah. It wasn't either/or; it was either this, or I didn't care. I just look back and I was so fucking numb."

The numbness, Craig can see in hindsight, had much to do with his inability to deal with his feelings surrounding the stillbirth of his son Aaron a year earlier and the impact of that tragedy on his marriage with Lee. "So, she came back a month before me, and then as soon as I got back we had to deal with the decision to induce labor or do we go to full-term and he's dying anyway, but she could die. It was like, that's the conundrum. Dilemma. That's what we were facing and our marriage just didn't survive that." Craig found a job in Santa Fe that he thought might make use of his psychology degree, working with young people in a drug and alcohol treatment center. He'd take the kids to their AA or Narcotics Anonymous (NA) meetings and watch the clock until it was time for him to leave work and go party.

> Get out of work at ten, and go partying. Partying. And then drive home, and then rolling into the house at one or two, or even eleven-thirty, earlier, but just loaded as hell because I went out drinking. I didn't know how to deal with shit other than to be shut down and get loaded. That was me dealing with things back then. And work. I showed up. I did all the required stuff but emotionally, mentally, spiritually all to hell. I was just going through the motions. My coping mechanism was to get loaded and stay numb and then [Lee] had to deal with her own grief, her own turmoil, and then deal with me always loaded and emotionally unavailable to her. I had no idea.

The fog Craig recalls being mired in was fueled by his continued partying—mostly with booze and marijuana—in the two or three years following the war. "When I came back to Germany and then a year later back to the States and then a year later out of the Army, I was using. That was my coping mechanism without saying I feel x, y, or z and this is my tool that I'm using to take care of myself. The partying, the using, was the coping mechanism to deal with Iraq. Just killing people." After Craig was let go by the Army, he continued to self-medicate, his way of coping with the baffling transition to civilian life.

> When I got out of the military in '93 and moved here, I had never been a civilian. I never lived out here and paid rent or had electric bills or dealt with the civilian world. That didn't happen until I was twenty-nine. Santa Fe was like a foreign world to me. I'd been in the military basically from seventeen to twenty-nine. These friends of mine I remember telling me, "Well you went in [the Army] at seventeen and you

learned all this discipline." I didn't learn discipline. I was disciplined. It was just conditioning: Do this, it's acceptable; get out of that range of behavior, you're punished. It wasn't that I gained this deep internal structure of discipline. I was just told what to do.

For several months, a major part of Craig's job at the residential rehab center was "taking kids to NA and AA meetings, drinking coffee, and not giving a shit because I'm on the clock and it's a job." But, gradually, all of those tales of ruin and hitting bottom he was hearing at the meetings began to jab Craig with a troubling ring of familiarity. One day, he recalls, "I woke up and just went, 'Holy shit, all those stories sound familiar.' I just realized that if you don't get your shit together you're going to have stories like you're hearing. Like my story is already bad enough. The years of partying and using and Aaron dying was like, I just saw the writing on the wall. Like, if you don't stop using drugs it's just going to get worse." He went cold turkey on January 6, 1994.

Meanwhile, Craig and Lee had a son, Jordan, born in September 1993. But neither the arrival of a healthy baby nor Craig's newfound recovery would usher in immediate emotional health or a stabilized marriage. Craig began to attend NA meetings two, sometimes three nights a week, and he realizes in retrospect that "I'm literally not here at home with her. Here I am not using, but it's becoming more and more apparent how much of a mess I am. I mean, internally, because I'm in fog all the time." Lee moved out with Jordan on Labor Day Weekend, September 1995.

During Craig's first years in Santa Fe, he recalls being "clueless" and going through the motions at work. "I was disillusioned, disenchanted, pissed off. I got clean not long after I got here. I wasn't using, but I was still pretty screwed up. It was more like I was abstinent. In AA they called it 'dry drunk.'" His growing anger and resentment about his part in the war kept him from seeking counseling and other health services. "I didn't think, oh you should go to the VA because you have benefits coming your way. I was like fuck it all. I just wanted to not have a damn thing to do with the government. So I hadn't even gone and checked in with the VA to get a physical. No services at all." Craig's anger amplified as he began to educate himself about some of the underlying realities of the Gulf War, and the costs that he and many other troops were continuing to pay, long after the hundred hours of combat passed. Craig began to reframe his understanding of why Aaron had died, and to redirect his feelings: from anger toward himself to anger toward the military and the politicians who had sent him into battle. "I spent years and years thinking it's my fault. This Jewish friend of mine told me Jews invented guilt and Catholics perfected it. I had all this guilt about my drug use. It never occurred to me in that time frame that my exposure to toxins on the battlefield [had] led to Aaron's death. So I'm walking around confused, angry, feeling shame and guilt and all that shit, and then I find out that it was more than likely— you know, they have to prove it to me that it didn't happen versus that I have to prove that it did—we were poisoned."

Indeed, from the mid-1990s on, patterns of health problems among U.S. and other coalition troops deployed during Desert Storm became increasingly apparent. In 2016 a twenty-five-year study of 15,000 U.S. Gulf War veterans concluded that 44 percent of deployed veterans experienced symptoms of "Gulf War Syndrome," described by researchers as a "cluster of medically unexplained symptoms including fatigue, pain, gastrointestinal disorders, and neurological symptoms." The fact that far fewer nondeployed Gulf War era vets reported such symptoms led the researchers to conclude that the experiences of deployed veterans in Desert Storm provide "a potent example of the hazards associated with military deployments [including] hazards that were unique to this conflict . . . the frequent threat of chemical weapons exposure, challenging operational conditions including temperature extremes, sand and dust storms, and smoke and fire from burning oil wells."[13] The U.S. Department of Veterans Affairs is, of course, more cautious in its conclusions, using terms like "chronic multisymptom illness" and "undiagnosed illnesses," and emphasizing that research has not connected these symptoms with specific causal

factors, and citing studies, for example, that show no link between inges-
tion of PB pills and veterans' subsequent health troubles.[14] Pertinent to
Craig's situation, several U.S. and British studies have concluded that
deployed Gulf War veterans and their spouses have suffered from significantly higher rates of miscarriage and birth defects, compared with
nondeployed Gulf War-era vets.[15]

It's neither possible nor necessary to prove that Daniel Craig's ingesting PB pills, inhaling oilfield smoke, and being exposed to chemical and
radioactive materials during the Gulf War caused Aaron Craig's death.
Statistically speaking, a certain proportion of all pregnancies result in mis-
carriages or stillbirths. However, the research showing that deployed
Gulf War vets and their spouses suffered elevated levels of such suffering
means that Craig's take on the cause of his son's death is more than plausible. And it's this plausible connection between his toxic exposures during the war, his son's death, and the dissolution of his marriage that fueled
much of his anger and despair in the decade following the war.

In the years following the breakup of his marriage, when February 14, the anniversary of the start of Desert Storm ground combat rolled
around, Craig would feel even more "down, depressed, sad. Everyone was
like, 'Oh, Valentine's Day!' Go to hell. Valentine's Day just sucked." From
1995 to 1998 Craig drove a delivery truck for FedEx. He was "clean," but still
living "in a fog," just "going through the motions." There were moments
when, he recalls, "I just wanted to kill myself. I'm not using, [but] I'm not
really in recovery. I'm just emotionally and spiritually all to hell. I remember there were times when I was driving FedEx and I would drive to
Pecos going up to Terrerro, there was this one curve and this rocky out-
crop around this almost 90-degree turn, and [one] day I just felt like
accelerating and not taking the turn, and just ride into that rock wall."
Craig's decision twenty years ago not to drive into that rock wall was not
based on anything he would now consider a rational calculation. He
now thinks his decision to carry on was propelled by an unconscious
"curiosity," a desire to witness "what's gonna happen next" in his life.

A HEALTHY OUTLET FOR MY OWN TRAUMA

A cartoon character can undergo a 180-degree transformation with the sudden click of a light bulb. On TV sitcoms, a deep misunderstanding, conflict, or even an evil person can suddenly flip into its opposite in a span of about eight minutes, when the protagonist suddenly learns an important piece of information or is exposed to the kindness of others. Personal-growth hucksters promise to invent a new you or bring out the "real you" for a few thousand dollars.

For most of us, most of the time, dramatic personal change doesn't happen with that kind of ease or rapidity. Deep personal change takes time; it doesn't occur with the flip of a switch nor can it be purchased in a weekend seminar. We can recognize personal transformation in retrospect, over considerable time, and dramatic personal change never results in becoming a totally new or entirely different person. Our past baggage—including mistakes, loss, heartache, injury, and betrayals suffered and perpetrated—never entirely disappears. Over time, the meaning of experiences and events can be rewoven into our life's fabric as we learn and experience new perspectives. And as the threads of our past are redefined, change becomes possible.

For Daniel Craig, the end of the 1990s and the early 2000s was such a time of gradual and wrenching recomposition. His life didn't change overnight; at times, he felt he was still just "going through the motions," his anger subdued but always threatening to burst to the surface. But he can see now, in retrospect, how some key commitments he made during those years created the basis for building a healthier life. A cornerstone in this foundation was Craig's decision to move beyond remaining a dry drunk: "I'd been clean for a few years but not ever really working a program, just basically abstinent." He committed himself to "working a program," and he began to develop supportive relationships with others in recovery. The meetings, he found, were places where he learned to "talk about sharing experience, strength, and hope. Not opinions. Not advice."

He was determined to no longer remain mired in "that mentality of negativity."

In the meetings, Craig met two older men, both veterans of the American War in Vietnam who were in recovery and dealing with their own trauma. He laughs with a sense of irony as he recalls these guys telling him, "'You need to get fucking help. You need to get involved with the health care system and get screened for PTSD.' I spent all these years not doing that. I guess I was starting to act dumb enough that they both said, 'You need to go to the VA now, because there's some parts of you that are just not okay.' Ha! Just the anger." Taking his friends' advice, Craig saw a VA psychiatrist in Albuquerque, was diagnosed with PTSD, and did a short course called PTSD 101. He then connected with a therapist at the Santa Fe VA clinic, and began regular sessions that continued for the next two or three years.

His therapy ended around the same time he was turning toward healing practices based in Eastern spiritual traditions. Similar to Vietnam vet Gregory Ross before him, Craig was drawn to acupuncture. For three years, he studied and worked in a student clinic, eventually earning the title of Doctor of Oriental Medicine. While working in the acupuncture clinic, Craig also started doing yoga, a practice that assumed a growing importance in his life in subsequent years.

Daniel Craig's growth at the turn of the millennium was not limited to inner work. During the years he was studying acupuncture, he also sought to learn about the world around him. As a boy in Springer, he had found refuge and escape reading in the local library. Now, he was reading to connect with and make sense of the world. In 2001 two books had a big impact on him. The first was Howard Zinn's *A People's History of the United States*. The second, which he read "almost concurrently," was a quirky and less-known novel, *Ishmael* by Daniel Quinn, a story of a silverback gorilla who communicates telepathically as an ethical philosopher and seeks, Craig recalls, to teach human beings "how we have such great potential, but how it just slowly shed in our species; about the haves and

the have-nots—he called them the takers and the leavers; how we are acting like idiots when we have so much potential."[16] For Craig, the lessons of
the two books helped him to make sense of "the government, the military, my experience with everything, my history."

At the turn of the millennium, Craig's personal history with the Gulf
War was still raw, the memories barely below the surface, always poised to
trigger a sense of hopelessness, despair, or anger. The revelations from
these two books jolted him to his core. Now seeing his experience of
military service within the big picture of American history and politics, it
was hard to contain his rage over the price he'd paid for "goddamned lies."
"I was brought up on duty, honor, country stuff. I never really questioned
anything. I was getting loaded and chasing women and no one said, there's
another story besides the one you're being told about military service,
about duty, honor, country. The way I look at it today, I served the economic
interests of a segment of this society, but I didn't serve my country. Conoco,
you know, Exxon, Chevron, Monsanto. That's who we were fighting for.
My God, I killed people for these goddamn lies. Had I known, not the
truth per se, but a bigger picture, I might not have made the choice to join
the military in the first place."

There was also an empowering element to the history Craig was learning. In addition to becoming more knowledgeable about the corporate
interests that drive U.S. foreign policy, Craig was also reading about the
rich history of grassroots resistance: "the peace movements in World
War I, hell, during the Civil War, World War II, Vietnam." This knowledge opened a fissure of curiosity in Craig when he first saw two older
men at a public event sitting at a table, distributing VFP literature. But he
didn't speak with them. "I turned and ran in the other direction, because
I don't want to hear this shit. I wasn't like, pro-war, but I was just angry
and jaded and confused and lost." A few months later, he saw the same
guys tabling at a talk by the Democratic representative Dennis Kucinich.
Craig thinks that having read the Zinn and Quinn books in the interim
served as a catalyst: "I said what the hell, and I went and stopped and talked

to them." Kip Corneli and Norm Budow, it turns out, were both World War II veterans and longtime peace activists in Santa Fe.[17] Craig recalls the two men greeting him enthusiastically; they seemed especially eager to kindle a "young" Gulf War veteran's interest in VFP, an organization made up mostly of older vets. That was September 2002. By October Craig had attended his first VFP chapter meeting and joined up. It seemed like he had discovered VFP just in time. "And then I run into VFP and it gives me a healthy outlet for my own trauma. My own anger. My own guilt, shame, confusion, all that stuff in a positive way instead of look, another GI went postal. I run into VFP in a pivotal part of my life: Here's a healthier outlet than what you are thinking about doing, which will get you dead or in prison because you're so angry and so feeling betrayed, which is the underlying theme of my life. The priest says this is God's work and the priest comes into our class drunk as hell! [laughs] This betrayal." In VFP Craig found a welcome counterpoint to the betrayal he had repeatedly experienced with older men in his life—his father, his priest, military recruiters, and superior officers. Here, perhaps for the first time, Craig found men who would become his mentors— men twenty, thirty years his senior like Kip Corneli, Norm Budow, and Ken Mayers—whom he learned to trust, respect, and emulate.

Craig's joining up with VFP in 2002 was timely in another sense. The United States was jumping into another war feet-first, and VFP was positioning itself to contribute significantly to the opposition. The September 11, 2001, terrorist attacks in New York and Washington had killed nearly 3,000 people and injured roughly 6,000. The day that came to be called 9/11 presented Bush and Cheney with fertile ground to ramp up military spending and rapidly prepare U.S. troops for war. Barely a month after 9/11, the United States invaded Afghanistan, and in March 2003 the United States expanded its war in the Middle East by again invading Iraq. For veterans of past wars, it was a galvanizing moment. Just as Ernie Sanchez was blindsided by his half century–delayed PTSD in Los Angeles

Public action against the U.S. War in Iraq, Santa Fe, NM, 2007 (Daniel Craig)

and Woody Powell was stepping up his antiwar work in St. Louis, Daniel
Craig was diving into a flurry of peace activism in Santa Fe.

YOUR RECRUITER TOLD YOU THIS, RIGHT?
HERE'S MORE OF THE STORY

As the United States escalated its military presence and actions in Afghanistan and Iraq, VFP ramped up its peace activism. The Santa Fe chapter
grew rapidly, and their actions multiplied, doing one event a month,

hosting speakers and movies, and creating a regular presence at public events.

In August 2002, during the run-up to the U.S. invasion of Iraq, the Santa Fe VFP chapter began a Friday noon peace vigil, waving VFP banners and antiwar signs to passing traffic on the busiest corner in town, Cerrillos Road and Saint Francis Drive. During the height of the war's escalation, the VFP vigil would draw fifty, even a hundred demonstrators. Mostly, Craig said, the demonstrators were well received by local people driving by, often honking or throwing the peace sign. On the few occasions a passerby gave them a hard time, Craig would have to work to contain his tendency to strike back. "I remember having a brief discussion with a twenty-something-year-old guy when I was out there on the corner, and they are at a stoplight and he is badmouthing us, and I said, 'Why aren't you in a uniform in Iraq?' He's like, 'Well I'm doing stuff here.' He's like Trump, rather than being one of the dumbasses who enlisted and got drafted. And I'm like, 'Well, you talk all this shit, you could be over there putting your money where your mouth is.' And then they drove off."

During those years, Craig and his VFP colleagues poured time into "Full Disclosure," a project close to Daniel's heart: talking to young people, mostly high school juniors and seniors in Santa Fe and small New Mexico towns about the military and war. "We decided not to call it counter-recruitment, so we called it Full Disclosure and we went and talked to the kids, not to dissuade anyone from joining, not to badmouth the military, just to say, 'Your recruiter told you this, right? Here's more of the story.'" They talked to young people about the sorts of moral dilemmas soldiers have to grapple with in times of war. They explained that even though the military might promise you a college education following your service, "when you come home you might be so screwed up you can't go sit in a college classroom because of your PTSD or because of your depression or because of your anxiety or because you're missing a couple of limbs." They also shared their personal experiences with military service, war, and its aftermath. "I would talk about having lost my son. Duffy talked about being raped by Air Force officers: not Vietcong, not Vietnamese civilians—her superiors. Tim was in Vietnam in '68 and lost his legs above the knees, blown up by an artillery shell. And other people, non-combat roles, talking about their experiences. And again, not to say don't join the military but to just say there is more to the story than what your recruiter is gonna tell you."

It's rarely possible to discern the impact of such educational work—such witnessing—on young people's life decisions, but we do know that by late 2005 the military was having a hard time keeping enough "boots on the ground" in the deepening and deadly morass the Iraq War had become. It's likely that VFP Full Disclosure efforts in New Mexico and elsewhere, in addition to the growing antiwar voices of Afghanistan and Iraq War vets, had something to do with the decrease of volunteers, as did the public knowledge of the rising toll of U.S. casualties in the Middle East.

When Arlington West, a high-profile initiative of the Santa Barbara and Santa Monica VFP chapters, came to Santa Fe, Craig and the local chapter enthusiastically took part. On what Craig recalls as a cold October day—the anniversary of the U.S. invasion of Afghanistan—VFP lined up row after row of white crosses, each to commemorate a U.S. soldier who had been killed in Afghanistan or Iraq, adding "a picture and a bio of the GIs who had been killed, where they were from, and circumstance of death." Arlington West, which is still assembled by the local VFP chapter every Sunday on the beach next to the Santa Monica Pier, is an emotionally arresting visual display that captures the growing numbers of casualties in an ongoing war, while zeroing in on the human face of each individual killed soldier.[18] New Mexico photographer Jennifer Esperanza captured these feelings in her portrait of Daniel Craig during the Santa Fe event.

During the Obama presidency, the wars in Iraq and Afghanistan continued, but they were waged in a way that resulted in far fewer U.S. casualties. Public antiwar activism declined, and this was echoed in lower rates

Daniel Craig at the Santa Fe, NM, Arlington West demonstration,
October 2007 (Jennifer Esperanza)

of VFP activism. Perhaps it just wasn't possible for a relatively small number of veterans to sustain the frenetic level of activism they had managed
during the Bush years. Craig speculated, as Donald J. Trump was assuming the presidency in January 2017, that peace activism might once again
swell in the coming months and years. Like Bush and Cheney, Craig
expected that Trump "will give us something to push up against; he will
definitely give us something to oppose."

Meanwhile, Craig and a dwindling number of core VFP members continue the work of the local chapter. The Friday street-corner peace vigil
continues, albeit with fewer participants. Monthly chapter meetings focus
on planning national or regional events, like the annual veterans' protest
at Creech Air Force Base in Nevada, the center for U.S. drone warfare, or
antinuclear arms demonstrations in nearby Los Alamos, where research
on building nuclear warheads continues to this day.

The Santa Fe VFP chapter delivers flowers to the graves of deceased
members every Memorial Day. And for the past seven or eight years, the
chapter has marched with their VFP banners in the city's Veterans Day

Parade, where, Craig says, "We're well received as a veteran's group. The other veterans' groups look at us and probably their underlying thought about us is that we're the bastard stepchild of the veterans world. But we're well received by the people who are there to watch the parade."

In 2016 Daniel Craig became president of the Santa Fe VFP chapter. He has contributed to a broadening of the chapter's efforts, beyond war and peace activism, thereby connecting to other progressive community and national organizations and grassroots movements. Given that the group is smaller and less active than it was ten years ago, it's crucial, Craig says, for VFP members to be "showing up for different events, cosponsoring events like with Amnesty International. VFP is known in town. We've been in the Gay Pride Parade for the past four or five years."

One afternoon when I was interviewing Craig in his home, I noticed he was wearing a T-shirt with "Black Lives Matter" written on the front, and "Veterans for Peace" in smaller letters below. I asked him if there was a Black Lives Matter/VFP coalition in Santa Fe, a small city with few blacks. "It's an alignment," he said. "We're all working towards basically common cause. We've aligned with different groups in support of the Black Lives Matter movement." Craig went on to remind me, "There's a VFP presence up in Standing Rock, North Dakota"—including his local colleague and mentor Ken Mayers—and he spoke enthusiastically about the national VFP effort to oppose Islamophobia. All these sorts of "alignments," he explained, were organically connected with VFP's emphasis on war and peace. "What we do and what we're about is finding that common cause. Basic human rights. Basic human dignity. For VFP, our forte is military issues. The veterans' experience. It's woven into Black Lives Matter, countering Islamophobia, countering this, that, the other. Racism, sexism, the LBGTQ community's persecution. They all weave into human rights issues." As broad and deep as VFP coalition politics has become, the issues of war and peace remain central and personal for Daniel Craig. He literally wears his politics on his clothing, an exercise in everyday activism that presents him with regular opportunities to talk with people about war and peace, and inform them about the existence and work of VFP. "I wear VFP T-shirts, and [from] people in general, I get a positive response. Like me, I had no idea there was a VFP. I was like, 'What the hell is the VFP?' And then I get a chance to explain it and they're like, 'Oh, right on!'"

Some of Craig's T-shirts, though, broadcast in-your-face messages that might be read as aggressive provocations. "Sometimes," Craig explained about his "Military Recruiters Lie" T-shirt, "I consciously specifically wear it to elicit a response from somebody. I've had a couple of good discussions with people when they say, 'That's a bullshit thing,' and I say, 'Actually it's not,' and that's my opening for us to talk if they are willing to talk instead of just having that knee-jerk reaction, 'You're full of shit, you're unpatriotic, how can you call yourself a veteran?'"

Today Craig seems able to manage the anger that risks bubbling up when he talks about such matters, even with "veterans who were like flag-waving, pro-war types. My job isn't to make you change your mind. My job is to just, like, do the footwork that's in front of me with Veterans for Peace. If you hear something we say and you relate to it, maybe you'll change your mind too."

HEART-OPENING WORK

As I sat in an auditorium with several hundred people, awaiting the start of the opening plenary for the 2016 VFP national meetings in Berkeley, I spotted the back of Daniel Craig's head fifteen rows in front of me. He stood for a moment, perhaps to let someone slide by him, and I read the message scrawled on the back of his shirt: "WHAT NOBLE CAUSE?" At that time I was halfway through my series of interviews with Craig, and I sensed what he sought to convey with this provocation: that the people he had killed and the price his family paid for his actions in the Gulf War were especially lamentable because the war turned out to be neither just nor noble.

The question on Craig's T-shirt led me to ponder more general questions. Perhaps the moral injury that is so common among soldiers who harbor deep shame at having killed others is sometimes mitigated (though not erased) when the man who pulled the trigger or fired the artillery round believes that the deaths he perpetrated served a just end: stopping tyranny, extending freedom, protecting the innocent. Perhaps the damage of this sort of moral injury can be managed with individual therapy. But what of cases like Daniel Craig's, where the deep cut of moral injury is compounded by a growing knowledge that "I killed people for these goddamned lies!"—that his actions were morally wrong, based on mendacities from leaders whose cause, it turns out, was far from noble?

When the pain of moral injury is amplified by such a maddening sense of betrayal, by the knowledge of having been used like a pawn in someone else's game, the combination can engender hopelessness and rage. Craig is aware that, despite all the growth he has experienced in the past fifteen years, he needs to consciously attend to the fact that his anger is still there, just below the surface of the calm demeanor he so carefully cultivates. "When we're at the corner and people flip us off or talk crap," he says, his tendency might be "to pick up a rock." So, he has to pause and think, "Okay, what would a healthy person do?"

> I go from zero to pissed and then from pissed to shut down and then I feel like beating—if I could find my chain of command from back then—beating them with a bat. Not very much Veterans for Peace language, but oh well! That's why I'm at VFP and not at the VFW drinking, and by now have acted out [laughs]. It's like, the VFP stuff, the yoga, being in recovery just keeps me grounded and from going off the deep end. I'm staying out of jail. I'm staying clean, because when this stuff comes up and it catches me by surprise, for instance, I just shut down, and fuck everything and everyone, and then I'm more likely to do dumb-ass moves from that place. From a place of anger, just like in the military.

Friday VFP peace vigil on the corner of Cerrillos Road and St. Francis Drive, Santa Fe, NM, 2016 (author)

Daniel Craig's current life project is a conscious "ongoing healing process" that combines recovery, yoga, service to others, and political activism with VFP. For the past five years, Craig's yoga practice has grown in importance. From the start, he found yoga to be just the sort of "heart-opening stuff" that nourished his "physical, mental, emotional, spiritual" healing. He recalls moments in some of his first yoga classes when "I'd just cry and cry and cry. I'm sitting there in child's pose, and I'm trying to cry as quietly as possible, trying to let it come out instead of stuffing it down."

This "heart-opening" spiritual and emotional yoga work meshes neatly with Craig's continuing commitment to recovery. He values his weekly coffee with "some guys in recovery that I'm close with." And for the past four years, his job as a case manager in a homeless clinic "gives me perspective." His modest salary puts him in a "working poor" category, he realizes, but "anytime I want to bitch and moan about my life, I look at some of the people we work with and it's like, you need to practice humility." In his job, he helps people apply for Medicaid. His clinic has a needle exchange program to help prevent HIV and hepatitis C transmission. They do street outreach, distributing "socks, peanut butter crackers, cheese crackers, toothbrushes, toothpaste, razors. In the winter, we get those chemical hand warmers, jackets when we get donations."

This service with the local homeless population not only helps Craig keep his own life problems in perspective, it's also part of turning outward that links his personal healing practice with socially engaged action. At the center of this social engagement is Craig's work with VFP, work that links him with supportive, like-minded people while also fueling his sense of connection and common cause with "the 99 percent," both in the United States and around the world. Craig hopes that, like many VFP members from the Vietnam War-era, he can one day engage in some form of healing reconciliation with the people he fought against in the Gulf War. But he recognizes that due to his country's continuing war-making in the region, "it will be a long time for it to be safe for anyone to go back to Iraq. But it would be interesting to have that experience, because the people I killed, we probably had more in common with each other than I had with my chain of command, way up there, up to and including the arms manufacturer, the arms salesman, and the congressmen they were in bed with. It's us peons. It's that 1 percent, 99 percent thing."

Late in 2016 Craig spent several weeks in India, deepening his yoga practice. He hopes to share his growing knowledge as a yoga teacher. There is research, he says, that meshes with his experience, showing how yoga can help with PTSD, "how it works physiologically to calm the nervous system." Perhaps, he thinks, one day he can conjure "a way in with the VA system to teach with veterans, or even with the National Guard unit. Working with military people, predominantly veterans I think, but to teach yoga because it's so beneficial." Meanwhile, Craig is determined to continue the "heart-opening work" of recovery, yoga, and VFP. Together, these practices are "melting away the bullshit. My beliefs, my biases, my worldview, you know. Like reading Zinn's book, reading *Ishmael*, peeling away the layers of the onion. It's ongoing, you know. I'm aware that I don't really know that much."

Like King before us, we are called today to break our silence on the madness and folly of a national policy that prioritizes weapons and war, while neglecting those in need here at home and abroad. As we speak out against war and militarism, it is important to remember another lesson from Dr. King, that our dissent is motivated by patriotism.

—David Cortright, *"Why Dr. King Was Right*
to Oppose the Vietnam War"

Muhammad Ali said, "I ain't got no quarrel with the Vietcong. The Vietcong never called me nigger." That was certainly an ethos that ran throughout my politicization. It was something my mother reinforced through both word and deed. I do not operate as a pacifist, but I am opposed to imperialist war.

—Jonathan W. Hutto Sr.

-◄◄◄•►►►-

CHAPTER 6

Laying the Tracks

JONATHAN W. HUTTO SR.,
OPERATION IRAQI FREEDOM

One by one, F-14 Tomcats roared from the deck of the USS *Theodore Roosevelt* (CVN-71) in support of U.S. and coalition forces on the ground in Iraq. Camera in hand, Seaman Jonathan Hutto performed his job dutifully. As a member of the media department's photo lab on ship, Hutto was tasked with writing stories for the ship newspaper and sometimes photographing the Tomcats as they took off and landed on the Navy's Nimitz-class aircraft carrier, dubbed "The Big Stick." It was January 2006, and fighting on the ground in Iraq was fierce. During the six-month stretch that Hutto was in theater, nearly 400 U.S. troops were killed in combat. As is usually the case in times of war, things were even worse for civilians on the ground: roughly 9,000 Iraqi civilians perished during the same six-month span.[1]

Jonathan Hutto understood that the jets he was photographing were raining hellfire on Iraqi targets on land, but the war still felt distant to him. It was below deck in the ship's cramped photo lab that the twenty-eight-year-old seaman was experiencing a conflict both visceral and immediate. At the outset of the ship's deployment in September, Hutto had been called into a "hostile meeting" with the senior chief petty officer in charge of his unit after Hutto had "laid out a litany" of examples itemizing how the photo lab was a hostile work environment, including "petty officers that feel very comfortable making derogatory remarks about

Dr. King, holding Adolf Hitler as a sign of someone who was a great person. Women and men were groped, what they call in the Navy 'grab ass.'" In response, the senior chief told Hutto, "'You're the problem. . . . You're the racist.'"

Things only got worse when Hutto entered the photo lab on January 10, 2006, to talk with his three colleagues—all of them higher rank than he and all of them white—to ask about a training program for military photographers. "All of the sudden, Boothby reaches on top of the vent and pulls down this noose that comes down. And everybody is just grinning, laughing and shit. I'm looking at him like, what, is that for me or something? I'm looking at them like, look that's some bullshit, and then Boothby says, he makes a comment that one of my colleagues, who was black, was deserving of a lynching. So I walked away in disgust. I was very hurt by it, both personally but also just from a broader social aspect. We're in a war zone, man! We're off the coast of Iraq bombing and shit, and they pull out a hanging noose!"

Hutto's first inclination was not to make the incident public, but to ask the three men for an apology. That evening, he typed a thoughtful email, telling his colleagues that "the hangman's noose has got to go," and explaining to them "the connotation the symbol has in this country." He appealed to them as fellow photographers, offering to share *Without Sanctuary*, a recently published book that graphically detailed the history of lynching photography in the United States.[2] Hutto concluded his letter with an olive branch: "We are all in the same boat and we have to find common ground." He received no response from any of the three men. When Hutto walked by one of the perpetrators a day later, the man greeted Hutto with "a half-assed smirk on his face." So Hutto concluded, "Fuck this, I'm going to the chain of command with this, including the command master chief, along with the equal opportunity adviser, departmental head, all the way down to the E6 lead petty officer in my shop."

In the early morning hours of January 12, Hutto emailed a four-page letter to "every level of my chain of command" in which he connected the hangman's noose incident "to the broader history of racism in this country and to the fact that we're at war and this is what the hell we've got going on on this ship towards an African American seaman." By midmorning, Hutto learned from the equal opportunity adviser chief that an investigation had been ordered. Hutto found that he had some allies, and eventually his complaints were validated when roughly one-third of his unit responded to a survey detailing various elements of a hostile work environment for women and for people of color. The main perpetrator of the noose incident was punished with a reduction in rank and other restrictions. Hutto felt that this was "some miniature accountability," but thought that the ruling fell far short of justice. He appealed the ruling, this time directly to Congressman John Lewis, whose office wrote a letter to the chief of legislative affairs of the Department of the Navy on Hutto's behalf.

For Jonathan Hutto, the hangman's noose incident on CVN-71 was a condensed moment in a history of racism in the United States and in the military. It was also a magnified moment of activism for Hutto, a moment in which his youthful immersion in Atlanta's rich history of civil rights activism and his experiences as a student activist leader at Howard University coalesced into a sense of clarity as to how to respond to a racist provocation. Having been inspired by central figures in the civil rights and black power movements, like Hosea Williams and Kwame Ture, Hutto was not about to allow racist intimidation to slide, nor would he overreact in a way that would make matters worse. As his shipmate and ally Chris Mason stated in his emails at the time, "The strong move quiet, the weak start riots." Hutto recalls, "I was no longer an undergraduate student at Howard with a bullhorn in my hand, but the spirit was not only still there, but more intensified."

Jonathan Hutto had entered the Navy two years earlier as a college graduate with a deep understanding of the history of racism. He was a seasoned community activist with a sense of efficacy based on concrete experiences that told him that when people organized, progressive change was possible. He had absorbed Ture's lesson that "the struggle is eternal," that there is never any final victory, no end to history; that each person has a responsibility, in his or her own historical moment, to stand up for justice. This knowledge served him well in the hangman's noose incident in early 2006. It also provided the foundation over the next year and beyond as Hutto cofounded "An Appeal for Redress," a high-profile public effort by active-duty military personnel to press the U.S. Congress to end the war in Iraq.

-⟪⟪•⟫⟫-

I caught my first glimpse of Jonathan Hutto on stage, moderating a session on Islamophobia in a packed auditorium at the VFP national convention in Berkeley in August 2016. Hutto's words about anti-Muslim racism in the United States and its links to the nearly two-decade "War on Terror" were as sharp as his appearance was imposing, dressed as he was all in black, topped with a black Kangol hat, his thick dark beard trimmed to a steep point well below his chin eliciting the first wisps of gray. Later that day, he and I sat down for a couple of hours at a local coffee shop for a preliminary interview. Hutto exuded warmth, shared an easy smile and laugh, and expressed support for my project.

Three months later, I spent the better part of two days interviewing Hutto in the home he shares with his wife, Yolanda, and their dog Noah. A short Metro ride from DC, their two-story house nestles in the tidy middle-class and mostly African American suburb of Suitland, Maryland, in Prince George's County. The first day I arrived at his home, Hutto again sported that black Kangol hat, with two buttons pinned on a black shirt: on his right breast the face of Martin Luther King Jr.; on his left, a VFP button. The next day Hutto wore a knit Howard University cap and denim coveralls on which he had pinned buttons depicting two of his heroes— Kwame Ture ("your generation knew him better as Stokely Carmichael") and the Reverend Hosea Williams hugging Jesse Jackson in 1984. Williams, Hutto explained, "was my first inspiration, my first example of a grassroots organizer, the first example I had of a true public servant. I'm wearing these coveralls because this is how Reverend Williams would dress when he was doing movement work. This was his movement uniform. I wear this in homage and respect for him."

Hutto's garb was the outward presentation of a deeply internalized sense of himself as part of a long history of struggle against racism, war, and injustice. The more I listened to him, the more impressed I became with how his commitment to contributing to a history of progressive struggle had been nurtured by deeply meaningful mentoring. I was also struck by the contrasts between Jonathan Hutto and the other veterans I had interviewed. Even as he was assuming a leadership position among the nation's active-duty ranks to oppose the war in Iraq, the war and its impact seemed distant, though connected, to be sure, with the proximate antiracism struggle on ship and in the nation. Hutto's antiwar stance and activism was sparked when a mentor sent him a new edition of David Cortright's *Soldiers in Revolt*, and it was then he began to connect the dots between racial oppression at home and what he came to see as a history of imperialist wars his nation was waging against people of color in other parts of the world.[3] Hutto's antiwar activism emerged as organically integrated with his long-standing antiracism proclivities.

Postwar, Jonathan Hutto did not exhibit hints of the internalized trauma, moral injury, or substance abuse suffered by the other veterans in this book. Though he was "in theater," his physical distance from ground combat is probably a factor here.[4] Hutto's differences from these other veterans for peace translates into a distinct postwar life trajectory. For one thing, Jonathan Hutto's life project is still a work in progress—thirty-nine-years old when I interviewed him, he is a young husband and father, committed to his family and still finding his way, still unclear as to how he will make a living in the world. Unlike veterans who experienced direct combat, Hutto seems to have little need for therapeutic self-healing, nor is he deeply engaged with reconciliation with former "enemies" in Iraq. Instead, more than anything, he is shaping his life project around community and national politics. His calling—learned from Ture, Williams, and others—is "serving the people" through a commitment to progressive activism. The edifice of Hutto's adult life is still being constructed, but this foundation of service to community through political activism, molded in his youth, seems rock solid.

WE WERE DR. KING'S KIDS

Atlanta is well known for its prominent black middle class, its role as an engine for the civil rights movement, and as a launching pad for national leadership for African Americans.[5] Jonathan Hutto was born in Atlanta on April 19, 1977, and as a young boy he was bathed in this legacy of black leadership, activism, and public service. His father never focused much on electoral politics; he immersed himself in church activities and worked steadily to build his heating ventilation and air conditioning business. His mother—a graduate of historically black Clark College—was "a stay-at-home mom," at least for the first eight years of Jonathan's life, until his parents divorced. She emphasized the importance of education for Jonathan and his brother Harold, and was "adamant" in exposing her children to "those daily grinding issues that we witnessed in our community: The pockets of poverty that existed near us, the homelessness."

Young Jonathan began his formal education in majority black public schools in Atlanta, but it was primarily from the church, the broader community, and especially from his mother that he learned about black history and politics. "My mother was my linchpin, the person who grounded me in our people's struggle through the oral history she passed down to me. I was fascinated." He also recalls that, at least until he was ten and his parents divorced, "church was compulsory in our house: Beulah Baptist Church on Griffin Street, a corner past Sunset Avenue where the King home was. The values, the connection of church to home to your school to your YMCA—it was all interconnected. Reverend W. L. Cottrell, the pastor of my church, was an alumnus of Morehouse College. These were very proud people in that they grew up in a segregated society." Part of it being "all interconnected" in Hutto's youth was the normalcy of crossing paths in daily life with black leaders who became household names both locally and nationally. "That was the social milieu I grew up in. We were Dr. King's kids. That's how we saw ourselves as children. I mean, Daddy King used to preach at our church. Andy Young was the mayor when I was a child, and he would come visit us at our church. Julian Bond was our state senator. He owned a Burger King not too far near the AU [Atlanta University] Center. Hosea Williams was on the city council at the time, and John Lewis was on the city council. Hank Aaron would visit my barbershop. So the people that were in history books were people that I saw quite a bit."

In this "predominantly black environment," Hutto recalls, "there was nothing that was enforcing racism" in the experience or eyes of a ten-year-old kid. That view was jolted in 1987, when nearby Forsyth County—a "sundown county" that earlier in the century had violently driven many blacks out—decided not to celebrate the still-new national holiday celebrating the late Dr. Martin Luther King.[6] The Reverend Hosea Williams would have none of that. His subsequent actions ascended him to the status of hero for young Jonathan Hutto.

Forsyth County was a place where blacks just understood you don't go. Hosea went in there on a bus with fifty demonstrators, and when they got to Forsyth, the size of the white-power rally overwhelmed the local police force out there trying to protect them. Hosea decided to turn the march around and get the folks back safely on the bus in the midst of bottles, glass, and a mass of angry whites shouting "Niggers go home." Hosea came back a week later with over 20,000 people with him from Atlanta—the largest civil rights march in Georgia history—that's when the governor sent in the National Guard. I'm in fourth grade. It's all over the local news. They are preaching about it in church. They talked about it on the street corners, and I'm just like, wow, you could see the pictures live on local news: "Niggers go home. Niggers go home." I look at my mom, and my mom is like, "Racism is still here honey."

The lesson for young Jonathan was clear: not only is racism "still here"; there is also a continuing legacy of courageous leadership and collective antiracist activism. For the first time, he could feel himself a part of it. "Everyone has this moment. For the Black Lives Matter generation, it might be Trayvon Martin. For my grandmother, it might have been the Scottsboro boys. For my mother, Emmett Till. For me, it was Forsyth County."

As his awareness of racism and activism grew, Hutto was less focused on war-and-peace issues, though he recalls that "the horrible legacy of Vietnam loomed large in the '80s and my mother spoke of it in a very disparaging way." The 1980s were a time of small and clandestine wars waged by the United States within the context of the final years of the Cold War, and Hutto recalls that several older men in his extended family had served in the military. But he does not recall growing up thinking he would join up. There was "nothing in my social milieu that even reinforced" the idea of military service, and he recalls how his mother "chased the army recruiter away from our house when I was a teenager when he was attempting to recruit my brother." Hutto recalls feeling a sense of "race pride" when he learned the story of the Tuskegee airmen during a second-grade field trip to the Tuskegee Institute in Alabama, but for the most part he did not grow up idolizing heroes of past wars celebrated in popular culture. "The heroes in my community, you know, were people like Dr. King, like Muhammad Ali, Julian Bond. Jesse Jackson running for president." In 1983, he visited the then new Vietnam War Memorial Wall in Washington, DC, and his predominant memory is his mother's weeping when she saw the name of an old friend on the wall.

After his parents divorced, Jonathan moved with his mom to South DeKalb County outside Atlanta. His mother married Joseph Winfield Cooper, a Vietnam veteran who "had visible wounds from Nam, a line that cut across his belly where he had been shot in the back and the bullet came out through his stomach. He would have horrible nightmares at least two to three times a year, along with terrible ulcers, pounding headaches." For young Jonathan, the move to DeKalb County also meant starting over at a different school, which "was very disruptive for me." He "didn't take the divorce that easily." In fifth grade, he "first started getting into trouble in school and becoming a little more insubordinate." By high school, he had grown a bit and played a little football. But in tenth grade, he made an important transition away from sports toward academics, and made a decision that he "wasn't going to be wayward anymore," that he would separate himself from "the disobedients and the derelicts." In the school library, he came upon *The Judas Factor*, a book about the murder of Malcolm X.[7] The book "just blew me wide open, man. From then on, I just kept on moving with it. I started to become more politicized. I really decided I was going to do something with my life. I didn't know exactly what, but I was going to do something."

Hutto tuned in to "progressive hip-hop" like Public Enemy, and was galvanized by the 1992 "Rodney King situation" in Los Angeles. "I remember vividly when the verdict came out. Everyone in our class was pretty stunned. The Atlanta University students were in the streets." He engaged at school, joining the Kappa League and Upward Bound. He was featured on local TV news after his school principal named him the most improved student in the school. He relocated with his mother to Chattanooga, Tennessee, and during his junior year at Brainerd High School he "tapped into a wealth of resources," and his essay on Jesse Jackson won the "Champions of Courage" essay contest.

As a high school senior, Hutto zeroed in on the goal of attending Howard University. He knew that Howard had "cranked out black folks that were going to be movers and shakers in society," including leaders like Vernon Jordan, Stokely Carmichael, and Ed Brown, the brother of the more famous H. Rap Brown. He worked hard to win several small scholarships that, cobbled together, would pay for a significant portion of his freshman year. As the selected faculty representative at his high school graduation, Hutto gave "a rousing speech that centered on Martin Luther King's ideas "about redefining greatness. That we all can be great because we all can serve." Three months later, in the fall of 1995, he arrived at Howard University and hit the ground running.

TAKING A WALK IN HISTORY

When Jonathan Hutto arrived at Howard, he was immediately galvanized by Minister Louis Farrakhan's call for a "Million Man March" of African American men in Washington, DC.[8] Hutto dove in to working with the student government and organizing the men in his dorm to bring a large contingent of Howard students to the march. "I was really ready to go, because the drumbeat for the Million Man March was pretty high. I remember when Mr. Farrakhan announced the march, he framed it as a march for atonement and reconciliation. I felt like I was taking a walk in history, you know? I was really, really fired up about it." The day of the March, October 16, 1995, Hutto showed up at the DC Mall at 5:30 a.m., and was thrilled already to see "at least 100,000 men there." He was proud when his mother called him later that night to say she'd seen him on television, "right there in the front by the stage. I was one in a million! That was the grand moment of my freshman year."

During his sophomore year, Hutto became a volunteer coordinator for Operation Vote Bison, a campus-based voter registration drive supported by the National Coalition on Black Civic Participation. His visibility in this campaign made Hutto "the face of the student government" for many Howard students. He subsequently ran and won a seat on a local DC Advisory Neighborhood Commission. Though he was mostly immersed in local politics, Hutto was certainly aware of the stakes of war and peace for young black men. There was a ROTC program on campus, and he was not a part of it, but when a fellow student, Kafele Sims, joined up, explaining that it could help him to get his education without "a plethora of student loans," Hutto recalls grilling him about this decision. "I asked him point blank, 'Are you willing to die for this country?'" Sims, Hutto added in a soft voice, "ended up getting killed in Iraq."

Jonathan Hutto with Kwame Ture, Howard University, February 17, 1998
(Jonathan Hutto)

When I asked Hutto what he majored in college, he laughed. "My major was the struggle, man. I signed up for political science courses with a minor in history." His education expanded in the summer of 1997 through a trip to the World Festival of Youth and Students in Havana. His time in Cuba was "a life-altering experience in the sense that for the first time I'm being challenged on what it means to be an American. How does America's power and its projection of it relate to other peoples? It's kind of hard to see people as enemies when you're right there, you're integrated with them you know, and they're opening their homes and their lives to you in that way."

Following his trip to Cuba, Hutto returned to Howard to complete his year as student body president. His effort to bring Howard alumnus Kwame Ture to campus for a featured lecture "was a watershed moment for me that I will talk about to the end of time." Hutto recalled his mother speaking of the central role that Ture—then known as Stokely Carmichael—had played in shaping the 1960s Civil Rights and Black Power movements, including leadership in the Student Nonviolent Coordinating

Committee (SNCC) and the Black Panther Party. But Hutto still had much to learn about Ture. Seeing Ture speak, and talking with him informally, Hutto can see in retrospect, "really changed the trajectory of why I even do what I do." A major lesson Hutto learned, condensed in Ture's slogan "The struggle is eternal," sparked a commitment to "collective responsibility for your people and humanity." Hutto was also moved by Ture's emphasis on service to the people. Compared with, for instance, high-profile public figures like Jesse Jackson or Louis Farrakhan, Ture was "an unleader leader: He came off as a servant. There was strong humility about him."

It was Ture's final speech at his alma mater; he would die nine months later. But his impact, along with mentors Bob Brown—a political comrade of Ture—and Lawrence Guyot, had a lasting effect on Jonathan Hutto.[9] Brown had challenged the twenty-year-old Hutto, asking him, "What do you want to do with the rest of your life? Are you trying to be of service to the movement? Are you trying to be a politician? Are you trying to be of service to the ruling class? Are you trying to be of service to the struggling African masses?" These questions would animate Hutto's life in his postcollege years and beyond.

A Rude Awakening

When Jonathan Hutto graduated from Howard University, he was already expressing a trait that would characterize his adult life: He had a clear and visceral commitment to the movement, but it was not coupled with an occupational direction. Had things been different, he might have spent the next couple of years in the Peace Corps, but in January 1999, during his final semester at Howard, he and his partner birthed a son, Jonathan II. Hutto recalls feeling "really afraid to be a dad." He and the baby's mother didn't make it as a couple, but Jonathan II's arrival forced the twenty-two-year-old Hutto to focus: "He helped me become a man. He helped me to become an adult. He helped me to fully embrace responsibility."

A key part of that adult responsibility was finding a way to generate a regular income, but it was also important for Hutto "to find some work that's got some purpose to it." He worked for a year with the American Civil Liberties Union organizing for and educating citizens on "civilian oversight of law enforcement," during a time of heightened awareness of police violence in the community. In 2000 and for the following three years Hutto worked with Amnesty International, doing "work of passion," including raising awareness about stopping torture and pressing the organization to take on the issue of police accountability, particularly in Prince George's County. This work made him proud, but when his son's mother decided to go back to school, Hutto assumed primary responsibility for the care of three-year-old Jonathan II, and he could no longer muster the time commitment the Amnesty job required.

So he decided to become a public school teacher and, following a "three-week crash course," he found himself in September 2003 in front of a fifth-grade classroom. It didn't take long before he realized he hadn't been properly prepared for the challenge of teaching kids. It was "a rude awakening," he recalls. "It felt like I'd gotten thrown in the oven. I couldn't handle it." By November, Hutto was "exhausted, beyond wasted," and he quit teaching. "For the first time in my life, I felt like a failure. I was twenty-six-years old. For the first time in my life, I had failed at something. I failed it bad. I still had a son to raise. I'm totally defeated."

Shortly after, Hutto was sitting "at the Atlanta Bread Company and just kind of chillin'" when he was approached by a Navy recruiter. He told the recruiter he had just quit teaching, had a son, and student loans to pay off, and was trying to figure out what to do next. Hutto's initial response to the idea of joining the Navy was "No, I'm not interested." But when the recruiter told Hutto that the Navy would pay off up to $65,000 in student loans, "that's when I started listening."

When Hutto enlisted in the Navy in January 2004, he was fully aware that the U.S. military was fighting in Afghanistan, and was "going into Iraq." Bush and Cheney, with the support of U.S. ambassador to the United

Nations, General Colin Powell, claimed there was ironclad evidence that Iraq had "weapons of mass destruction" (WMD) that threatened the stability of the region and U.S. interests. Congress rubber-stamped the war plan, even while U.S. and world public opinion differed. On February 15, 2003, roughly 12 million people took to the streets of major cities throughout the world to protest the imminent invasion. In the words of historian Andrew Bacevich, U.S. leaders acknowledged that "people are entitled to express their opinions, but these opinions didn't matter: The United States government was going to do what it wished to do."[10]

The WMD claim turned out to be false, a pretext for a war U.S. leaders were determined to fight—perhaps to retain access to Middle East oil; perhaps to sustain geopolitical dominance in the region; perhaps to provide the military-industrial complex a fresh enemy through which to bolster its profiteering; perhaps so Bush could "finish the job," after critics pointed to his dad's failure to close the door on Saddam Hussein following the Gulf War. On March 20, 2003, U.S. cruise missiles hammered Baghdad, and ground troops advanced into Iraq. By April 10 Baghdad had fallen and Saddam Hussein had fled into hiding. With typical hubris, Secretary of Defense Donald Rumsfeld brushed off public fears that the United States might find itself in another Vietnam-like quagmire, claiming that defeating Iraq should take "five days or five months, but it certainly isn't going to last any longer than that."[11] Indeed, by May 1, in a now infamous moment of premature self-congratulation, a flight-suit-clad President Bush declared "Mission accomplished" aboard the USS *Abraham Lincoln*. As it happened, bloody fighting would escalate in the coming months, and would continue for many years, as the United States waded deeper and deeper into the "Big Muddy" of a renewed war in the greater Middle East.

THE STRUGGLE INTENSIFIED

Jonathan Hutto's enlistment in the Navy just shy of his twenty-seventh birthday may seem, in retrospect, to have been impulsive and counter to his progressive values. "While I certainly was opposed to America's occupation in Iraq, my opposition to the war, in my mind, didn't preclude me from actually joining." For one thing, Hutto knew several veterans who were active in the movement. Joining the Navy, he was clear, was not about "leaving the movement behind." He was confident, too, that in joining the Navy, "I had no intentions of being in direct combat. I was totally looking at this from a resource standpoint of helping my own individual life." Rebounding from his "immense embarrassment and failure" as a teacher, and understanding his obligations as a father and breadwinner, Hutto recalls, "I thought going into the military would give me this opportunity to pay off my student loans and get myself together, potentially get me a new lease on life in a certain way. That's what I was thinking. That ain't what happened [*laughs*]. The struggle intensified is what happened, you know? Holy shit! The struggle intensified. It surely did."

When Jonathan Hutto rolled into Recruit Training Command in Great Lakes, Michigan, on January 16, 2004, he recalls "experiencing culture shock" in the "dehumanization and breaking down process" in which recruits were yelled at and called "maggots." It was "the most reactionary situation I had been in." The Navy Hutto joined was formally integrated. At that time, African Americans made up about 18 percent of the force, and in recent decades black women and men had moved up through officer ranks.[12] But it would soon become evident to Hutto that formal integration of the military—just as with other social institutions—had not eliminated covert discrimination; nor had ugly forms of overt racism evaporated. Hutto was also wading into a thorny historical debate within black communities about patriotism and black GIs' and sailors' participation in American wars. In essence, the debate runs along these lines: First, there is the argument put forth by W.E.B. Dubois during World War I, that black men should join and fight to prove their patriotism, and that doing so would contribute to whites' acceptance of blacks and thus to racial uplift. "*First* your country, then your rights," Dubois, an African American sociologist, civil rights activist, Pan-Africanist, writer, editor, and cofounder of the National Association for the Advancement of Colored People (NAACP), wrote in the publication *Crisis*. On the other hand—and Dubois leaned toward this position following World War I after witnessing with disappointment how black veterans were still treated as second-class citizens—some argued that black men should not travel to foreign shores to fight and die for "freedom" when the rights and respect of full citizenship were not extended to them at home.

During World War II, this debate continued. Sociologist Amy Lutz observed that the 900,000 blacks in the U.S. military during the war (167,000 of them in the Navy) served in segregated units. Many black GIs adopted the "Double V" symbol: All GIs knew that holding up the two-finger "V" signaled "Victory" over fascism. Using both hands to flash the "Double V" signaled the hope that one's service would contribute to victory over fascism abroad *and* victory over racism at home.[13] Toward the end of World War II, the military started to experiment with racial desegregation, including the Navy's decision to desegregate the general service, sleeping quarters, and mess halls.[14] The immediate results were mixed. Historian Douglas Walter Bristol Jr. documents how black GIs were too often met with discrimination and even violent backlash from white colleagues and officers.[15] Following the war, black veterans—and Latinos too, as we saw with Ernie Sanchez—too often returned home to jobs and communities still segregated in ways that protected the legacy of white privilege. In 1948 President Harry Truman issued Executive Order 9981, outlawing racial segregation in the military. The Korean War would be the first U.S. war fought with a formally desegregated military.

This debate within the African American community—to fight or not to fight—was revived and sharpened during the war in Vietnam. This war, Lutz observed, "was marked by racial strife."[16] African Americans made up a disproportionate number of draftees, as many of their white, middle-class counterparts escaped service with college deferments. Moreover, in the words of Lutz, "Discrimination against Black soldiers was rampant," and it was not uncommon to hear arguments that black soldiers were being placed in more dangerous positions in battle and used as "cannon fodder," resulting in higher casualty rates.[17] Meanwhile, at home, African Americans were an important driving force in the antiwar movement. Muhammad Ali's courageous stance against the war and Martin Luther King's famous antiwar speeches helped galvanize the peace movement, even as more cautious NAACP leaders distanced themselves from Ali's and King's positions.

Jonathan Hutto's future hero Kwame Ture—then Stokely Carmichael, whose SNCC had come out against the war two years earlier—lauded Martin Luther King for condemning the war.[18] Hutto recalls hearing Ture recount during that 1998 fireside chat at Howard how, during the Gulf War, a news reporter had asked Ture his opinion about General Colin Powell, then a trustee of Howard University:

> Kwame says he was a traitor. He and Colin both went to the same school in the Bronx when they were kids. He said that when it came time for the Vietnam War, Colin said yes and he said, "Hell no, I ain't going." He said, "I ain't got no problem with the Vietcong, I've got a problem with you. The Vietcong never lynched my mother." But then, he said the reporter said to him, "Maybe you're jealous of Colin Powell. He has power." And Kwame answered, "He's got power? When they ordered him to Grenada, he went. Ordered to Libya, he went. Ordered to Iraq, he went." Kwame said, "I want to know who's sending him. That's where the power is!"

Ture's radical perspective on African Americans' roles in American wars reflects a deep historical understanding of the ways that institutionalized racism at home and imperialist wars abroad are intertwined strands of our national DNA. Especially since World War II, U.S. bombs and napalm, ground assaults, invasions, occupations, and drone strikes have targeted almost exclusively people of color—in Asia, Central America, the Caribbean, Africa, and the Middle East.

Basic training, Great Lakes, MI, January 2004: "I was not a happy sailor" (Jonathan Hutto)

Many African Americans like Jonathan Hutto, past and present, have enlisted in hopes that the military would offer "a new lease on life." But his nine weeks of basic training had not ended before Hutto found himself thinking, "Oh man, I would have been better off going to a diner and waiting tables. What the hell am I doing here?"

Things did not get easier when Hutto was sent to Apprentice School (A-School) at Fort Meade, Maryland, for thirteen weeks to train as a photographer's mate. On the first day of class, he naively responded to the question of why he had enlisted in the Navy with a statement that "infuriated" the instructor and others. "I said due to some of the challenges in my personal life that I felt the United States Navy or the military in general was the best affirmative action employer in the country, and that I felt that I could use it as a second chance, as a launch or catapult to something a little better in my life. I didn't realize that using the words 'affirmative action' kind of got me targeted—that infuriated them. I was written up at least twenty times when I was at apprentice school. You know, minor stuff—anything. Hell if I'd breathe wrong, they came up with stuff."

After completing A-School, Hutto was to report by July 26, 2004, to CVN-71, then in a ten-month dry dock in Portsmouth, Virginia, for routine maintenance. During that time, Hutto remained "very much connected to the activist community in DC and Prince George's County, Maryland." In September Hutto met his first class petty officer for the first time. "I will never forget that dude. That was the most belligerent, racist, sexist, homophobic—this guy, he *embodied* oppressive culture. He *embodied it*. And he ruled the shop with an iron fist." The petty officer also tolerated his subordinates' making "jokes about Dr. King's holiday, talking about the merits of Adolf Hitler openly, around African American sailors." When Hutto complained to his equal opportunity adviser, the result was "that made me a super target. That put a bull's eye right over my head."

As the ship was transitioning from dry dock to operation mode in December 2004 at Norfolk Naval Station, Hutto was required to contribute to "workups"—preparation for the ship's next deployment. While in New York for a weekend to visit his son and see a woman he was dating, a heavy snowstorm kept him from returning to ship on time. He was written up for "missing movement, insubordination" and brought before a disciplinary review board that he described as a "shock-fright kind of thing, a draconian scream-your-head-off-type situation." The dressing down left Hutto thinking, "Why the hell did I join this Navy?" He recalled:

"I got shouted down, screamed out, called names. I was then sent back to the photo lab. I'm pretty heated now. I'm pretty heated. I was told to stay in the back of the photo lab and wait for more instruction. So, when the senior chief left I said, 'I've had it. I'm done. I'm getting out of this Navy. I can't stay in this.' This is pretty much it. When no one was looking I just left the ship."

Hutto rented a car, drove straight to DC and told his girlfriend, "I'm out of the Navy." He phoned an old Howard University mentor, Professor Rodney Green. A veteran himself, Green commiserated with Hutto's experiences with military hierarchy and discipline, but he also challenged Hutto to look at the big picture.

He said, "If you stay AWOL [absent without official leave], you're going to hurt yourself for the rest of your life in terms of your employment chances or whatever else you want to do with your life." He said, "What I would challenge you to do is to go back and take the punishment that is coming to you, and try to integrate yourself a little more deeply amongst your colleagues in the shop who are going through the same hell you're going through. They just choose to deal with it in a different way." He said, "If you do that over time, you'll begin to build some solidarity with folks, and the time will come where this situation will raise its ugly head again and there will be a different sort of situation that will take place, because you would have embedded yourself more deeply into the military culture; you'll have a deeper understanding and you'll have more solidarity."

At first, Green's advice "sounded kind of crazy," but soon Hutto saw the wisdom in it. He returned to ship, was brought before the Executive Officer Inquiry, where he was "screamed at so much so that I was in tears," and was punished with twenty-four hours of "extra military instruction: shining brass, waxing floors, very humbling, humiliating work." Subsequently, Hutto "kept my head low, didn't say a whole lot, just did my job."

Dropping Warheads on Foreheads

On September 1, 2005, CVN-71 was under way with roughly 5,000 Navy personnel and headed to the coast of Iraq in support of Operation Iraqi Freedom. Hutto got down to work with the photo shop, at times photographing the planes taking off from the deck, and mostly writing stories for the *Rough Rider*, the ship's in-house newsletter. Hutto would privately bristle when the ship's captain bragged, "We're going to kick Al Qaeda butt! Dirtbag, dirtball, Al Qaeda terrorist butt!" Heeding the lessons from Professor Green, Hutto remained "in quiet resistance mode, still building solid relationships."

Following brief port visits in Naples, Italy, and Paloma, Spain, the Big Stick made its way through the Suez Canal on September 27, and then up into the Persian Gulf. There it would remain for several months, serving as a launch site for two squadrons of F-14 Tomcat warplanes in support of Operation Iraqi Freedom. Hutto photographed bombs being loaded aboard Tomcats and saw the fighters returning emptied of their ordnance. He heard the captain's bluster about "kicking Al Qaeda terrorists' butt, snuffing out bad guys, and dropping warheads on foreheads," and he witnessed people "cheer when a plane went off." Hutto laments, "I didn't feel good about it. I would even raise certain contradictions in one-on-one conversations with friends about how cavalier it is" for people to cheer after "the captain would report that we had killed so many terrorists on the ground." But for the most part, Hutto recalls experiencing "somewhat of a separation between what the aircraft carrier is doing to folks on the ground and how it's affecting you. The trauma people are going through is more of a trauma of separation from their family."

Hutto felt that pain of family separation; he especially missed being with his son for such a long time. But he was also absorbing the trauma inflicted by racist and sexist actions of his colleagues, the exclamation point of which was that hangman's noose that his colleagues dangled in front of him that January day in the photo lab. Professor Green's sage advice served Hutto well; he'd learned how to respond to such incidents not with explosive rage that would get him further targeted, but by properly going through channels, and drawing on the goodwill he had developed with colleagues, some of whom turned out to be allies, and several of whom testified to various ways that the workplace was hostile to women and people of color. Before long, Hutto's antiracism work on ship would blossom into a national antiwar project.

Appeal for Redress

In response to my off-the-cuff lament about the declining relevance of books in public discourse, Korean War vet and author Woody Powell said, "Well, you never know when a book is going to turn up in somebody's hands at the time they need to read just that sort of thing." While on board CVN-71, Jonathan Hutto kept Professor Rodney Green abreast of his struggles, especially around the hangman's noose incident. Green, a veteran of the GI antiwar movement during the American War in Vietnam, knew that David Cortright had recently updated his classic on the GI movement, *Soldiers in Revolt*, with a new introduction by Howard Zinn, and he mailed a copy to Hutto. "I read it from cover to cover," Hutto recalled. "I mean, I just jumped into that book and I was like, gee, what a history. I'm connecting what's taken place to me right here in this micro-setting to what I figure has got to be happening across the military right now. And I'm looking at this movement, this historical movement of GIs that I didn't know anything about. The idea that there could be a collective mass movement amongst the active ranks just blew me wide open."

Hutto emailed David Cortright, and was amazed to receive an immediate and supportive reply. CVN-71 would return to Norfolk in March 2006, and Hutto invited Cortright to Norfolk, to "speak to both the broader peace and justice community but with a specific focus to active duty [personnel]." Cortright agreed, and a date was set for him to talk in May at the local YMCA. Once back in Norfolk, Hutto promoted the talk with fliers in coffee shops and elsewhere. Roughly seventy people showed up, fifteen of them active-duty military. "David gave an awesome talk about the history of the GI movement," Hutto recalls, and the talk got some coverage in the *GI Special* newspaper.

With Cortright serving as a "resource," Hutto assembled a group of interested active-duty military personnel at the home of Hampton University sociologist Steve Rosenthal to discuss "what we could possibly do in the midst of this current war." The core of the group included Hutto and Liam Madden, a marine who would later become active in IVAW. Hutto then recruited to the group Linsay Burnett who was with the 101st Army Airborne out of Fort Campbell, Kentucky. She and Hutto had worked together at Amnesty International. The group educated themselves about their legal rights, learning that "as long as you were off-duty, off-base, out of uniform, and not speaking seditiously of the president, you could activate, organize, go to demonstrations within the United States." The group's discussions continued into the summer of 2006. Cortright brought representatives from key organizations into the group: David Cline from VFP, Kelley Dougherty from IVAW, J. E. McNeil from the Center on Conscience & War, and Nancy Lessin from Military Families Speak Out.

The group decided to craft an antiwar statement that they hoped many active-duty military personnel would sign. Hutto's first inclination was to fashion a strongly worded statement that boldly underlined the fact that the basis of the U.S. invasion—Iraq's supposed cache of WMD—had been a lie, and that emphasized the horrors of the war: "IEDs [improvised explosive devices] blowing up our folks, that almost half a million Iraqis were being killed. Fallujah had happened; nearly decimated an entire city. Wouldn't even let noncombatants out. The purpose was to decimate everything in there." But Cortright believed that if the group hoped to garner wide appeal, their statement should be simply worded and "patriotic in tone." The result was an "Appeal for Redress." Hutto read it aloud to me: "'As a patriotic American proud to serve the nation in uniform, I respectfully urge my leaders in Congress to support the prompt withdrawal of all American military forces and bases from Iraq. Staying in Iraq will not work, and it's not worth the price. It is time for U.S. troops to come home.' That's the statement. That's it. We had no other demands or nothing. It was just a statement, and if you agree sign on. And we got the website set up in such a way where your signature went directly to your congressperson based on your zip code and address."

Hutto test-drove the Appeal over a weekend near his base in Norfolk, Virginia, and Linsay Burnett and Liam Madden did the same at their bases. Each of them got "a couple of dozen to sign on." The October 23, 2006, launch of the Appeal for Redress was covered in the *Navy Times*, which is distributed on every Navy base, and on Al Jazeera, as well as in the *New York Times*, the *Los Angeles Times*, and other newspapers. By November the Appeal had over 600 signatures. When *The Nation* magazine ran a December feature story on it, more signatures flowed in.[19] Roughly a third of the new signees, Hutto was happy to see, were from troops "on the ground in Afghanistan and Iraq."

Strategically well-conceived, the Appeal for Redress landed on fertile ground. For one thing, the war was not going well for the United States. The previous winter, Bush had admitted that the WMD claim had been based on what was now being called incorrect intelligence; but he and Dick Cheney simply shifted their justifications for the war and insisted on forging ahead as deaths of Americans and Iraqis piled up and revelations of U.S. torture became public. By 2006, political scientist Adam J. Berinsky observes, public support for the war had dipped well below 50 percent and was continuing to plummet.[20] Troop fatigue had long since set in. The demand for boots on the ground, coupled with the military's failure to meet its recruiting numbers, translated into an escalation of "Stop-Loss," a policy that forced thousands of existing military personnel to stay beyond the terms of their originally contracted agreements in exhausting, morale-crushing, multiple deployments.[21]

Meanwhile, antiwar veterans were organizing in multiple venues at home. IVAW formed in July 2004, and was growing in size and visibility.[22] VFP launched its emotionally wrenching Arlington West installations in Santa Barbara and Santa Monica, and VFP activists like Woody Powell, Daniel Craig, and Gregory Ross were working tirelessly in their local communities, doing counterrecruitment, attending public antiwar demonstrations, and pressing the mass media and the government to end the war.

In this growing antiwar context and with his ship now in eleven-month dry dock, Jonathan Hutto threw himself into antiwar activism. When the Appeal for Redress reached over 1,000 signatures, Hutto reflected on Cortright's wisdom in having argued to keep the wording brief and non-ideological.

> Keeping the statement simple so that you get different folks and different walks of life, he was right on with that. There were some people that were very ideological and some people said that "I really did embrace this war and I still do believe Saddam is a bad person. I just don't think we're doing a good job over here." One person signed the appeal because he just couldn't take seeing death anymore. One of his friends had just gotten killed, and he described it as a bullet to the head that he witnessed. He just couldn't take it no more. There were different reasons that people were coming in, particularly people on the ground in Iraq in terms of why they couldn't take it anymore.

Hutto and others then held a press conference at a Unitarian church in Norfolk, and not long after, leaders formally presented the Appeal for Redress to Congress, with visible support from Congressmen Dennis Kucinich and John Lewis. The number of signees rose to 1,270, and then a high-profile story on the TV newsmagazine *60 Minutes* "pushed it to about 1700 signees." As the Appeal became more visible, Hutto and a number of active duty signees placed themselves "out in front" for large

Jonathan Hutto "out in front," antiwar march, Washington, DC, January 2007
(Jonathan Hutto)

antiwar demonstrations in Washington, DC. While "mainstream" liberal
leaders and peace coalitions were at the heart of some of these demonstrations, other rallies pressed a more radical critique of the connections
between U.S. militarism, racism, and colonialism. Hutto joined any
and all such demonstrations, regardless of the ideological bent of their
leadership. His position was more than simply pragmatic; it reflected a
sophisticated understanding of how sectarianism has historically split
and undermined antiwar and other progressive efforts in the United
States. "I took the position that we should work with any and everyone.
I didn't take a sectarian approach to it. My thinking was we go to any
mass demonstration that is calling to end the war. I saw both as beneficial. I think you have to have an outside and inside game. I thought they
were complementary of each other, even if they didn't realize that."

In 2008, Hutto penned a book—part memoir, part history of the GI
movement, part practical manual for current and future dissenters within
the military—titled *Antiwar Soldier: How to Dissent Within the Ranks of
the Military*.[23] In it, Hutto proudly reported that over 2,000 active-duty
military personnel eventually signed the Appeal for Redress, roughly
85 percent of them from the enlisted ranks and the rest officers; 60 percent

of signees served at least one tour of duty in Iraq. The Appeal did not succeed in ending the war, to be sure. The Pentagon and President Bush's press
secretary Tony Snow had responded early on to questions about the Appeal
by pooh-poohing the "tiny" numbers of signees. But Hutto takes the long
view of a seasoned movement activist who sees his efforts as part of a continuing legacy:

> I saw the Appeal for Redress as having a distinct character in the
> sense that we were bringing forth the voices of actual active-duty
> service members. That's what I consider frontline activism. It chal-
> lenges the notion that you somehow complete your active-duty service
> and *then* you become a peacemaker when you're a veteran, when the
> risk is not as high, you know? You're risking something as active duty.
> You're putting your ass on the line. For me, looking forward—because
> there are going to be more wars of aggression, more imperialist wars—
> we're going to have to figure out how to do that type of work in a sus-
> taining way. It's the only way you're going to stop the war machine.

READY TO GET OFF THE SHIP

During the eleven-month dry dock of CVN-71, from January to November 2007, Jonathan Hutto reconnected with his son and immersed himself in political organizing while attending Old Dominion University for
a secondary education teaching credential with a concentration in social
studies. By the time the ship's workups toward the September deployment
resumed at the start of 2008, Hutto was clear that he wanted to request "a
new billet, a new job" before the ship sailed again. "By this time-period,
I'm ready to get off the ship. I've had enough. I've been there almost four
years now. And my son was getting bigger, and I'm at a point where I had
a want and a need to spend more time with him. I want to get some restruc-
turing going on in my life, so I'm looking forward to getting off this ship."
Just twenty-four days before the ship was once again to deploy for nine

months, Hutto received his new orders to report to the Naval Media Center in Washington, DC. "Whew! I still remember the feeling." But to get that assignment, Hutto had to extend his enlistment contract a year and a half, to August 2011.

In DC, Hutto got an apartment and began working at his new job with the Navy magazine *All Hands*, taking photos and writing feature stories. His co-workers, he recalls, liked to hang out together, "drinking, throwing back to about nine, ten at night on a weekday." Hutto rarely joined in. His ten-year-old son Jonathan had moved in with him in the summer of 2009, so when Hutto was not at work he was busy with "activities I'm doing with him around his school life." And Hutto's work with the Appeal for Redress was continuing.

> The Appeal is still going on, but it's not as revved up as it was. We are keeping the website functioning, we're still getting signatures coming in. Some people sign the Appeal, and they are really interested in being conscientious objectors, getting out of the military. So we get them counselors at the Center on Conscience & War. Some people want to join veterans' peace organizations, so we put them in contact there. Some people have basic grievances that they're facing within their chain of command—they've just got a belligerent situation like what I had. If I can't get to them, then I put them on to a GI Rights Hotline counselor who can work with them.

At the Naval Media Center, Hutto says, "I was doing my work and my assignments well. I didn't shirk anything. In fact, I wrote more articles, I believe, than anybody in there." He was especially proud of the *Navy Times* pieces he wrote that highlighted historical accomplishments of African Americans. One was "about Jesse Jackson freeing that the Navy bombardier Lieutenant Robert Goodman out of Syria in 1983. I did another article on the Golden Thirteen, the first African American naval officers. I did another piece on a naval officer, Jesse Brown, who crashed in the early '50s during the Korean War." Nevertheless—and perhaps it was due to his very public antiwar activities, or perhaps because he didn't hang out late with his colleagues—"I was not viewed as a team player." As the end of his enlistment period approached, Hutto made it clear that he did not want to reenlist. From the summer of 2010 through spring 2011, "I wasn't even really being assigned work anymore; the work assignments had totally diminished." During that stretch, Hutto recalls, "My sole focus was to get as smooth a transition out of the military as possible." After nearly eight years in the Navy, E5-Second Class Petty Officer Jonathan Hutto received an honorable discharge on August 16, 2011.

Activism for Me Is a Calling

In the months following his discharge from the Navy, Hutto again rehearsed familiar life themes. He remained crystal clear in his commitment to antiracism and antiwar movement organizing, and he cemented his commitment to his son, Jonathan, and his new wife, Yolanda. The question of how he would make a living remained a puzzle. The Navy had paid off "a significant amount" but not all of Hutto's accumulated student loans. He needed regular income. Hutto rekindled his plan to become a teacher, completed a student-teaching program, but then found that he couldn't land a local social studies teaching job. He took the "very intensive" three-month training to become an Amtrak conductor but decided he "didn't fit the billing" of the sort of employee Amtrak was looking for. At that point, he felt "kind of stuck. I'm pretty much living off of my savings and just being a full-time parent for a year." Eventually, he decided to "tap into my GI bill, take my activist experience and somehow parlay it into a doctoral program." He started the PhD program in political science at Howard University in fall 2012, but it was clear from the start that academia was tugging him away from his primary commitment to activism.

I would never abandon activism. The challenge though of pursuing the PhD is I found myself getting further and further and further away from activism to the point where I wasn't doing any activism at all. I was reading and writing quite a bit. And that felt strange. I felt somewhat divorced. And I think it really hit home to me when the tragedy of Trayvon Martin took place in Florida. Because although I was in a doctoral program, I felt driven to reorganize the People's Coalition here in Prince George's County. I used my energy to bring those activists back together, had a mass meeting at St. Paul Baptist Church, and it really reignited the Prince George's Coalition which hadn't met in some time.

Back in his element, Hutto thrived in helping to organize the local 10-mile march in the aftermath of the Trayvon Martin verdict that fed into a mass protest in front of the Department of Justice in July 2013. "That was quite a lot of work to pull that march off. I had to get permits from five police jurisdictions to make it happen. I had a bullhorn speaker on top of my head for a period of time when we got in front of the courthouse." Helping organize that Trayvon Martin protest invigorated Hutto, and helped him clarify his commitments. "That's when I realized—it reaffirmed—that activism for me is a calling. I'm one of those people where my résumé, if that's the word we want to use, is something that reflects not a careerist approach to life but a calling. I live my life based on what I feel called to do."

Hutto's antiracism work continued, and in 2015 he was called to reconnect with his peace work. "I was brought into a circle among the veterans of the Vietnam antiwar peace movement. Folks like Heather Booth. Folks like Bobby Seale. Folks like the late Tom Hayden, the late Julian Bond. David Cortright is a part of the circle. They were coming together to honor that movement in Washington, DC. I was brought into it because they wanted to connect with those generations of activists who had stepped forward during this last conflict. I honored Julian Bond at that opening Friday night piece, which was really, really profound for me. I was beyond moved by that. Beyond moved."

Jonathan Hutto (second from left) "honoring the elders" of the movement against the American War in Vietnam, 2015 (Jonathan Hutto)

At that Vietnam peace movement event, Hutto met Jim Driscoll of VFP. The organization had been a strong supporter and sponsor of the Appeal for Redress, and it was starting an initiative to confront the Islamophobia that was bubbling up in the nation, and which was erupting in and around the presidential candidacy of Donald Trump. Activists like Iranian American U.S. Navy veteran Nate Terani had already been protesting Trump's anti-Islamic rhetoric and his proposed "Muslim ban" at Trump rallies and in print.[24] VFP sought to develop an organized project to confront what they saw as a wave of hatred that might fuel violence against American Muslims at home and an escalation of war against predominantly Muslim nations in the Middle East and elsewhere. Driscoll invited Hutto to become a VFP field director for the anti-Islamophobia work. Hutto understood the importance of this work, and immediately agreed to help launch and promote the "Veterans Challenge Islamophobia" initiative.[25]

My job was to service and support the organizers on the ground. Working in conjunction with VFP and IVAW, we were able to choose organizing regions. Nate Terani [was] over in Phoenix. Deidra Cobb in Atlanta had been working a lot with the intersection between Islam and the broader African American community. I've been doing that myself here in the Northeast region. Just recently we did a program in a mosque here that looked at the adverse impact of law enforcement in both the Muslim and black communities and bringing a panel together to examine that and to look at some joint work we can do together.

In the effort to stem the tide of Islamophobia, Hutto and others sought to visibly utilize their status as military veterans to "bring a certain legitimatized voice to the struggle" and to highlight for the public that "Muslims are veterans and veterans are Muslims." The activists in Veterans Challenge Islamophobia are especially adamant in confronting the ways images of military veterans are used to bludgeon dissent into silence.

We speak forthrightly, to say to the forces out there—some aligned with Donald Trump but some are not but are still right-wing in their trajectory—that they are not speaking in our names when they say veterans support building walls. Veterans support ousting immigrants. Veterans support not building mosques in certain areas. Veterans support certain unjust zoning laws to keep out mosques. We provide a counterbalance to that, a countervoice, and that's essential. Without Veterans for Peace and Iraq Veterans Against the War, there probably wouldn't be an established countervoice right here in this moment. We have to do everything we can on a grassroots level to reeducate and to stop it.

Drawing from the lessons he learned in his youth, Jonathan Hutto points to clear connections between domestic police violence against African Americans and the nation's "long history of imperialism against darker peoples," most recently in predominantly Muslim nations. The role of VFP, Hutto says, is to "stand in the gap, if you will, calling for peace at home and abroad. Not just calling for it, but working for it. Working for it and putting our bodies on the line for it, both in terms of lobbying, agitation, and what Dr. King would call us to do, direct action. Not violent, but direct."

MAKING OUR CONTRIBUTION TO THE STRUGGLE

In the months after I interviewed Jonathan Hutto, while I was writing this book, he turned forty. He happily told me in an email that he and Yolanda are expecting a baby girl. He had decided to leave his PhD program, and instead had made a four-year commitment to teach secondary literacy with Urban Teachers, through the Johns Hopkins University School of Education. Time will tell if this latest shift in Hutto's occupational path will stick. Most likely it will if he experiences the work as being organically in sync with his "calling" of progressive movement organizing for peace and racial justice, and service to working-class and African American youth.

Hutto seems more optimistic about the prospect for progressive social change than the other veterans I interviewed for this book. In part, this optimism is grounded in his youthful experiences of success when he and others organized for justice.

> I was fortunate to have gotten some victories early on, to have been engaged in as an actor and agent and witnessed what mobilization coupled with pressure upon authorities can bring about in a micro way. Whether that was halting a street closing at a university, whether engaging in a process in the State of Maryland when I first started working for Amnesty International in 2000 when we were calling for a moratorium on the death penalty—Martin O'Malley fifteen years later as the governor signed the bill to abolish the death penalty in the State of Maryland. In the military as an active-duty member actually staying the course and being engaged in my shop and initiating an equal opportunity investigation, what it could do in a certain shop on a boat. One might say a small victory, but a victory nonetheless, one that reinforced the notion that—quoting the late abolitionist Frederick Douglass, "Where there is no struggle, there is no progress." And then with the Appeal for Redress, certainly we weren't able to stop the

war machine per se, but we certainly were able to affirm the right that we active duty could be engaged in the process and have our voices and our perspectives counted into the overall dialog and discussion.

Jonathan Hutto's optimism also rests on the solid foundation of the long view of history that he absorbed starting in his youth in Atlanta, and then from a continuing string of wise mentors stretching from his college years through his stint in the Navy. In this view of history, one does not expect to change the world overnight, or necessarily even in one's lifetime. At the center of this view of history rests an ethic of individual humility and a sense of service to a broader cause that Hutto learned from Kwame Ture and others.

We do what we do ultimately because we do want to change the world. We do want to have a peaceful society. A society that is nonviolent, that is free of nuclear weapons, a society that is free of war. We do work for that, but in working for it I believe people have to come to the understanding that they are laying tracks, if you will, for the next generation. Some people might think of themselves as indispensable to the struggle—no. We're making our contribution to the struggle. The struggle is eternal, as Kwame Ture taught us. And that means that it's going to take place from the day we are born to the day that we exit the earth. So, I'm hopeful. I'm optimistic, man. Dr. King, we certainly didn't get to the mountaintop. But then, we are a lot better than we were, I know we are. And we've got a far, far way to go.

You fight the war with guns, you fight the peace with stories.
—Omar El Akkad, *American War*

-«‹◆›»-

CHAPTER 7

This Is Our Service

The midday sun lit up the blue sky of Santa Fe, New Mexico, and three VFP banners whipped in a cool mid-October breeze. Cars and pickup trucks filed by, stopping and going with the traffic lights, some drivers honking and flashing the peace sign. It was a Friday, so members of the local VFP chapter stood on the state capital's busiest corner for their weekly peace vigil from noon to 1 p.m., a commitment they've kept—rain, shine, or snow—since 2002, following the U.S. invasion of Afghanistan. Back then—and especially following the invasion of Iraq—the local chapter's membership swelled, and they would often get forty, fifty, or more protestors on the corner. On numerous occasions between 2016 and 2018 when I joined the vigil, there were sometimes as many as ten or twelve, although normally five or six would show up. On this October day, I joined a thin group of three stalwarts: eighty-year-old former marine Ken Mayers; Ray Masterson, a Marine Corps Force Reconnaissance veteran of the American War in Vietnam, accompanied by his service dog, as always; and Army veteran of the Gulf War Daniel Craig, currently president of the chapter.

A pedestrian—a young guy with wiry red hair and a ruddy complexion, wearing an Oregon Ducks sweatshirt a size too large, paused to talk. He said that he'd seen the group there on previous Fridays, and appreciated their message of peace. And he added, "My grandfather served in Vietnam—at least that's where I think he was." And then, in a most earnest

(Left to right) Ray Masterson, Ken Mayers, and Daniel Craig at the weekly
VFP peace vigil, Santa Fe, NM, October 2016 (author)

tone he said, "I want to thank you for your service," adding, "I know you
don't hear that enough." Ray Masterson stood rail-still, with no visible
expression on his weathered face, the only movement his VFP flag flapping
in the wind. Daniel Craig turned aside and spit out a load of sunflower
seeds he'd been working on. Ken Mayers spoke without responding, at
least not immediately, to the young man's "thank you." Instead, Mayers
engaged in a brief discussion of the work of VFP, and answered the young
man's query about drone warfare.

I wondered if the three VFP demonstrators were simply going to ignore
the young man's "thank you" statement. I'd been following a lively discussion among VFP members, online and in their national newsletter, on
the conundrum veterans face when someone says, "Thank you for your
service."[1] For one who regrets his military actions and is critical of past
and current U.S. wars, the mantra "thank you for your service" is loaded

with ideological and emotional baggage. I had asked each of my interviewees how they respond when someone thanks them for their service. Ernie Sanchez shrugged: "I tell them I am not proud of killing people, that war is wrong," he said. It seemed to make Daniel Craig tired just to reply to my question about this: "It's become obligatory to thank a veteran. The thing is, people have no idea what they're talking about. They've been told a story about military service: duty, honor, serving your country, blah-blah-blah. When they say, 'Thanks for your service,' lots of times I don't have the energy to have a dialogue." Gregory Ross said he started noticing people thanking him for his service in the 1980s, and at first he'd "get really pissy about it." Then he shared a snarky fantasy response: "The people who would say 'Thank you for your service,' I would think, 'Oh you're welcome! Actually, I killed that one VC just for you!' But I never did it. I reminded myself that they mean well. It's a way for them to assuage their guilt, their survivor guilt. Usually they're middle-aged women and they mean well."

On that autumn day on the Santa Fe street corner, as the young redhead started to walk away, Ken Mayers added, casually, "Oh, you know, earlier you thanked us for our service. That was very nice of you. But you should know that the things we did when we were in the military, we did because we were told to. This work that we are doing right now—working for peace—*this* is our service." The young guy nodded, perhaps taken aback by Mayers's response, but he seemed to understand. He thanked them again, said "God bless you," and commenced to move on. Mayers tossed a friendly rejoinder as the guy walked away, "Oh, and Go Ducks!"

Some months later, I interviewed Ken Mayers and put the big question to him—a version of the same question I asked every veteran who works for peace. You dedicate a big part of your life to public activism for peace and justice, I observed, but year after year, decade after decade, our nation continues to wage wars as it prepares for new ones. What keeps you going? What keeps you coming to this vigil, week after week, year after year? Mayers smiled, nodded, and referenced a lesson he learned years ago from lifelong pacifist and peace activist A. J. Muste, who famously said, "There is no way to peace. Peace is the way." Every night the last couple years of his life, Muste legendarily stood vigil outside the White House holding a lit candle, protesting the escalation of the American War in Vietnam. Mayers continued: "He was asked, did he really think this was going to change the world? He says, 'You don't understand. I'm not doing this so that the world will be changed. I'm doing this so that the world won't change me.' That's what keeps me on the corner every Friday. If I stop doing it I have lost. As long as I'm in the fight, the fight goes on."

That in-it-for-the-long-haul perspective was a common thread that ran through the stories of each of the veterans I interviewed. I wondered whether this level of commitment goes beyond stubbornness in the face of unyielding power. Is there a sense of optimism that one's work is having an impact—that, in the long run, it might help shift the trajectory of history? The answer among the veterans I interviewed was not uniform. Ernie Sanchez suffered no illusions that wars would ever end, but his late-life project to talk peace, one to one, with each individual he met, surely gave *him* some peace and a sense of redemption for the many men he had killed. Woody Powell thinks of his peace and justice work as a way to battle depression and inject some positive spiritual energy back into the world. Every morning, he and his wife read a passage from the work of Thich Nhat Hanh to build mindfulness about "day-to-day stuff" that matters. Powell views this daily mindfulness, connected with his service to veterans and his peace activism, as necessary work, but he also understands its limits. "I realize that we're not going to stop wars. We're not going to stop people from being selfish, making stupid decisions that bring down whole populations with them, but we as individuals can become decent people and go on from there. I don't know what implications it's going to have, but I know what implications it has for me personally. It's not just enough to say it's a very satisfying thing to do. It's a necessary thing to do in order to retain my humanity."

Gregory Ross has a similar view, that his work for peace is therapeutically and spiritually meaningful for himself and those around him, and that in doing this work he hopes he is countering some bad karma from his past. When I asked if he thinks his work with VFP will ever end wars, Ross paused, fought back tears of despair, and spoke about how he is tired, and can't make it to marches any more due to his health.

> I saw firsthand how powerful the big picture is. You can't even call it the government, I mean it's like we're a feudal world [*laughs*] run by corporations. I did everything I could to try and change it, but I don't think it's going to change, not in my lifetime. It might change some-day. I'm glad everybody else, that they're out there chanting and march-ing, and more power to them. I work as hard as I can. I cry whenever I need to. I laugh as much as I can. And I do this kind of work, but I don't believe. I really don't. I just do it with some hope, but I don't believe. So, every time they go to war I feel bad for the ones that go. I try not to let it bother me. Things will bother me so much . . . that I just can't do it anymore. I'm one person.

All the VFP members I interviewed and met along the way shared Ross's understanding of the awesome inertia and power of the military-industrial complex, but some did not share his despair, grounded in that feeling that "I'm just one person." Those who expressed some optimism had a deep sense of how their individual life projects of peace and justice activism are linked to larger collective projects, to social movements with long historical roots and growing connections among progressive organizations. Though he had recently pulled back from working with VFP as I was com-pleting this book, Jonathan Hutto retained his sense of optimism that the progressive movement organizing he is committed to doing—working against racism, against police violence, against wars—is his contribution to "laying tracks" for future generations. Hutto understands that change will not happen overnight, but he holds to the dictum that he learned from Kwame Ture and other mentors: "We're making our contribution to the struggle. The struggle is eternal." Daniel Craig shares this long view of his work, focusing also on the inspiration he continues to receive from older vets who have been working for peace and justice for decades.

I think someone said it at the [VFP] convention: You're doing this knowing that there's no end in sight. Just keep doing the footwork, and there
will always be footwork to do. So, these guys have been doing it since
way back then. Me getting involved sort of like a late bloomer. Them
giving me the incentive and the—what's the word?—role models. As
examples. These guys, men and women, had been doing this since the
'50s, before Vietnam. These people who through Korea into Vietnam
were already veterans for peace, like Ken Mayers; and Norm and Kip,
World War II vets that are gone now; Anna Mae Daly, a World War II
and a Korean War veteran who died a few years ago. I'm like, man, this
is a damn marathon not a 100-meter sprint.

Craig's words about learning from older veteran activists to "just keep
doing the footwork" speaks to peace work not just as a personal life project, but as a collective, intergenerational project that—stretching his track
metaphor a bit further—is a marathon that requires passing the baton
across generations of activists. We've seen this intergenerational passing
of the baton throughout this book—from World War II and Korean War-
era activists to Gulf War veteran Daniel Craig; from David Cortright, a
leader of the GI resistance in the Vietnam War, to Jonathan Hutto, a leader
of the GI resistance in the Iraq War. At the national VFP meeting, executive director and Gulf War veteran Michael McPherson spoke of the
importance of this intergenerational connection between veterans of wars
long past, with those of recent and current wars. VFP members interrupted
McPherson's speech with thunderous applause and cheers when he
asserted, "We believe peace is possible. I don't spend time on something
unless I think it's possible. I like feeling good, I like feeling like I'm doing
the right thing, but I also like feeling effective." A clear part of McPherson's
optimism was his view that VFP does not stand alone fighting for justice
in the world, but is linked with other progressive groups, including Black
Lives Matter, anti-Islamophobia organizations, groups fighting for women's
and LGBTQ rights, and Native Americans' struggles for control of their

lands. VFP, McPherson emphasized, brings "the war part" to coalitions who might otherwise fail to see or understand the connections between their issues with war-and-peace issues. The VFP theme, "Peace at home; peace abroad," highlights this link.

The collective and coalitional nature of the quest for peace and justice can also generate personal joy that, for the activist, can transcend—at least in the moment—the despair he or she might feel about the ubiquity of wars and injustice. I watched in admiration in February 2017 as Ken Mayers joined about 2,000 other veterans who descended on wintry Standing Rock in support of Native American "water protectors" to resist the combined power of the oil industry and the government who were attempting to build the Dakota Access Pipeline. During the same year, Mayers traveled to Palestine with a VFP contingent and was roughed up by Israelis in the occupied territories. With another VFP group, he journeyed to Okinawa to join locals who had organized against the expansion of U.S. military bases. In the news clips and videos I watched of Japanese police physically cuffing and arresting Mayers and other protestors, I was struck with the way this eighty-year-old former marine always seemed to be smiling, projecting what looked like bliss. I asked him about it, and he told me that he was expressing the "joy of resistance," adding that when he's "getting busted," he is actually happy, because "I am in the best of company. You gotta love the work and you gotta love the people you're doing it with. If those things are there, it's not hard. For me, it would be hard not to do it. Have you read Ta-Nehisi Coates's letter to his son? He tells his son, 'You've got to learn to love the struggle.'"

Daniel Craig, nearly three decades younger than Mayers and still struggling with his own "darkness and negativity," hopes he is absorbing some of this "joy of resistance" from his mentor Mayers and others he's met in VFP who are "Quakers or Unitarians or Buddhists. That is their foundation, that bliss, that joy. I get the impression Ken brings that bliss and that joy to this. And for me it's . . . I'm feeling that shift of the fulfillment of it. The joy of resistance."

The ways in which Daniel Craig looks up to Ken Mayers is indicative of a key part of these individual veterans' life projects: the rejection of the self-destructive cultural images of male heroes as violent warriors and their replacement with mortal heroes who inspire with their humility, their fierce commitment to peace and justice, and their selfless, democratic styles of leadership. The men in this book mention some well-known heroes like Daniel Ellsberg or Kwame Ture, but they mostly talk of having been inspired by lesser-known women and men in their everyday lives who work tirelessly for peace and justice. I have come to see the men I profile in this book, and the many other women and men veterans for peace I met while conducting my research, as the sorts of heroes we so sorely need today.

In my email correspondences with Gregory Ross, I noticed that at the end of each message, he always signs his name followed by "Peace?" I asked him to explain the question mark. "'Peace question mark' is a progression. At first, I signed 'Peace and Light' from a Buddhist position that I was believing at that time. Then I began signing 'Peace Please' I guess to appease my mother who taught me to be polite. Then to 'Peace!' which you could say was my attempt to shout to the Universe that request. Finally, 'Peace?' because for the most part I've given up and I'm just asking the Universe to someday give me an answer, or give my son or his children or their children an answer." Ross wondered, too, if his "peace question mark" might also confront the reader with a question: *So what are you doing for peace?*

Acknowledgments

I grew up idealizing my grandfather's service in World War I and my father's in World War II. But as I came of age during the tail end of the American war in Vietnam, I considered myself lucky to have drawn a high draft lottery number—284—in a year when the numbers of draftees was dropping, but young men were still returning home in coffins. I never fought in a war, nor did I serve in the military. So I am especially grateful to the seven veterans whose voices and stories appear in this book: Wendy Barranco, Daniel Craig, Jonathan Hutto, Ken Mayers, Woody Powell, Gregory Ross, and Ernie Sanchez welcomed me into their homes and trusted me with their stories. Thanks also to the members of the Joan Duffy Chapter of Veterans for Peace in Santa Fe, New Mexico, for welcoming me in their chapter meetings and their weekly peace vigil.

Chelsea Johnson conducted valuable background research for me as I began this study. Chelsea Johnson and Michela Musto transcribed many hours of interviews. I thank Kristen Barber, Raewyn Connell, Nancy Dallett, Bob Dunn, Hugh Gusterson, Kathleen Hernandez, and Jim Messerschmidt for various forms of generous assistance, and for sharing ideas that deepened my thinking as I conducted the research for this project.

Support for this project was provided from an Ethel-Jane Westfeldt Bunting Summer Writing Fellowship at the School for Advanced Research in Santa Fe, New Mexico, and from a grant from the Advancing Scholarship in the Humanities and Social Sciences at the University of Southern California. My colleagues at USC, especially those in the Dornsife Office of the Dean, the department of Sociology, and the department of Gender and Sexuality Studies, were generous in helping me to arrange my teaching schedule to complete this project.

I appreciated sharing ideas as this study developed with students and colleagues at USC, Arizona State University's Pat Tillman Veterans Center, Saddleback College, the School for Advanced Research, and Ohio State University. Special thanks to friends and colleagues who read and commented on drafts of chapters, including Katie Hasson, Michela Musto, Laurie Narro, and Christine Williams. A full draft of each of the central chapters was read and commented on by the veteran who was the focus of the chapter. However, any errors in these chapters are my responsibility. The full manuscript was sharpened and improved with the professional editing of Arnie Kotler, and Blue Trimarchi expertly prepared the photos and contributed ideas for the cover design. I am grateful to the generosity and artistry of Jennifer Esperanza, who provided the cover photo. I so appreciate the expertise of Christina Frenzel, the creator of a companion web site at www.guyslikemebook.com that includes, among other things, short videos of each of the veterans I interviewed for the book. I extend many thanks to the production staff at Rutgers University Press, and deep gratitude to Peter Mickulas, my favorite editor, for his enthusiastic support for this book.

Finally, and as always, my deepest thanks to Pierrette Hondagneu-Sotelo. On many Santa Fe Fridays, Pierrette left her favorite yoga class early so I could make it to the noon VFP peace vigil. More, she listened to me worry and strategize about this project, from its inception through its conclusion, always supportive, always helpful. My work in this study broadened and deepened my understanding of how to live a life devoted to peace, justice, and love. I have never had to look far from home to find a living example of these principles in Pierrette.

Notes

PROLOGUE

1. The story about my grandfather that appears in this prologue is adapted from Michael A. Messner, *King of the Wild Suburb: A Memoir of Fathers, Sons and Guns* (Austin, TX: Plain View Press, 2011).

2. For Memorial Day in 1922, the VFW adopted the Buddy Poppy as its official memorial flower. To this day, disabled and needy veterans assemble Buddy Poppies in Veterans Affairs hospitals, and are paid by the VFW for their work.

3. The Kellogg-Briand Pact, outlawing war as a means of solving international disputes, was signed in 1928 by the United States, Germany and France, and most other nations. Oona A. Hathaway and Scott J. Shapiro, *The Internationalists: How a Radical Plan to Outlaw War Remade the World* (New York: Simon and Schuster, 2017); David Swanson, *When the World Outlawed War* (self-pub., eBookIt.com, 2011).

4. Veterans have continued to question the shift from Armistice Day to Veterans Day. See, for instance, Rory Fanning, "Why Doesn't the US Celebrate Armistice Day? We're More Comfortable with War Than Peace," *Guardian*, November 14, 2014, https://www.theguardian.com/commentisfree/2014/nov/11/us-observe-armistice-day-more-comfortable-war-than-peace.

5. Today, members of VFP insist on adopting the name used by the people of Vietnam for this war, "the American War in Vietnam." I adopt that practice throughout this book.

6. John Bodnar, *The "Good War" in American Memory* (Baltimore, MD: Johns Hopkins University Press, 2010), 11.

7. Smedley D. Butler, *War Is a Racket* (Port Townsend, WA: Feral House, 2003 [1935]).

8. Mike Hastie, "My Gift at My Lai," in VFP, *Full Disclosure: Truth about America's War in Viet Nam* (St. Louis, MO: VFP, 2017), 28.

9. On the cover page of *Full Disclosure*, the editorial staff writes, "The Full Disclosure campaign is a Veterans for Peace effort to speak truth to power and keep alive the antiwar perspective on the American War in Viet Nam. It is a clear alternative to the Department of Defense's efforts to sanitize and mythologize the U.S. role in the war, which legitimizes further unnecessary and destructive wars."

10. C. Wright Mills, *The Sociological Imagination* (New York: Oxford University Press, 1959).

CHAPTER 1 — PROJECTS OF PEACE

1. On the big screen, *American Sniper* (2014) and *Eye in the Sky* (2015) probed the moral, legal and emotional quandaries of contemporary U.S. wars in the Middle East, while *Whisky Tango Foxtrot* (2016) deployed actress Tina Fey for a "comedic drama" of the U.S. war in Afghanistan and Pakistan, and *Thank You for Your Service* (2017) probed postwar life of a seriously wounded soldier. Hollywood also continued to laud heroism in past wars, for instance *Unbroken* (2014) celebrated the "survival, resilience, redemption" of U.S. World War II soldier Louis Zamperini's ordeal as a prisoner of war. Meanwhile, current and past wars became small-screen entertainment. The popular HBO series *Homeland* (2011–) created an adventurous story line in portraying the complications of the United States' current borderless wars in the Middle East, while *The Man in the High Castle* (2015–) presented an alternative history of World War II and *The Americans* (2013–) entertains with a drama about Cold War–era Russian spies in the United States.

2. Irene Garza, "Advertising Patriotism: The 'Yo Soy El Army' Campaign and the Politics of Visibility for Latino/a Youth," *Latino Studies* 13 (2015): 245–268. In his book on the rise of televised college football, sociologist Jeffrey Montez de Oca shows how post–World War II fears of communist penetration and the softness of American boys manifested an escalating emphasis on physical education and sport, to create a "fortified masculinity" linked ideologically and bodily through sport, nationalism, and militarism. Jeffrey Montez de Oca, *Discipline and Indulgence: College Football, Media, and the American Way of Life during the Cold War* (New Brunswick, NJ: Rutgers University Press, 2013).

3. Adam Rugg, "America's Game: The NFL's 'Salute to Service' Campaign, the Diffused Military Presence, and Corporate Responsibility," *Popular Communication* 14 (2016): 21–29.

4. Brown University, "The Costs of War Project," Watson Institute, International and Public Affairs, http://watson.brown.edu/costsofwar/figures/2016/direct-war-death-toll-iraq-afghanistan-and-pakistan-2001-370000. Hereafter cited as "Costs

of War Project." Amy Belasco, "The Cost of Iraq, Afghanistan and Other Global War on Terror Operations since 9/11," Congressional Research Service, 7-5700, RL33110, December 8, 2014. These numbers continue to rise. A running ticker on the VFP home page states that "every hour taxpayers in the United States are paying $8,362,785 for Total Cost of Wars Since 2001." https://www.veteransfor peace.org.

5. "Costs of War Project." See also Nese F. DeBruyne and Anne Leland, "American War and Military Operations Casualties: Lists and Statistics," Congressional Research Service, 7-5700, RL32492, January 2, 2015.

6. Office of Public Health, Veterans Health Administration, *Report on VA Facilities Specific Operation Enduring Freedom (OEF), Operation Iraqi Freedom (OIF), and Operation New Dawn (OND) Veterans Diagnosed with Potential or Provisional PTSD (Cumulative from October 1, 2001, to September 30, 2014)* (Washington, DC: Department of Veterans Affairs, 2015).

7. "Costs of War Project." For a deep discussion of the various ways in which Americans remain indifferent to the high and continuing toll of civilian casualties for the wars that our nation wages, see John Tirman, *The Deaths of Others: The Fate of Civilians in America's Wars* (New York: Oxford University Press, 2011).

8. The impact of multiple redeployments on individuals and families became a frequent area of critical discussion during the Iraq War. Veteran Phil Klay's book of short stories *Redeployment* (New York: Penguin, 2014) won the 2014 National Book Award. And a 2008 feature-length film, *Stop-Loss*, probed the human cost of multiple redeployments.

9. William Ayers, "Hearts and Minds: Military Recruitment and the High School Battlefield," *Phi Delta Kappan* (April 2006): 597.

10. Damien Cave, "Growing Problem for Military Recruiters: Parents," *New York Times*, June 3, 2005, p. B-6.

11. Ayers, "Hearts and Minds," 597.

12. See Todd Gitlin, *The Whole World Is Watching: Mass Media in the Making and Unmaking of the New Left* (Berkeley: University of California Press, 1980); Jerry Lembcke, *The Spitting Image: Myth, Memory, and the Legacy of Vietnam* (New York: New York University Press, 1998).

13. Hugh Gusterson, *Drone: Remote Control Warfare* (Cambridge, MA: MIT Press, 2016), 145, 147–148.

14. David Zucchino and David S. Cloud, "U. S. Military and Civilians Are Increasingly Divided," *Los Angeles Times*, May 24, 2015.

15. Joseph R. Schwab, Michael A. Addis, Christopher S. Reigeluth, and Joshua L. Bergeret, "Silence and (In)visibility in Men's Accounts of Coping with Stressful Life Events," *Gender & Society* 30 (2016): 289–311.

16. The observation that adherence to narrow definitions of masculinity can both enhance a man's status and privilege, while also carrying emotional, interpersonal and health "costs" is a long-standing finding in social science studies of men and masculinities. For a summary, see Michael A. Messner, *Politics of Masculinities: Men in Movements* (Lanham, MD: Alta Mira Press, 1997).

17. Terrence Real, *I Don't Want to Talk about It: Overcoming the Secret Legacy of Male Depression* (New York: Scribner, 1998).

18. Will H. Courtenay, *Dying to Be Men: Psychosocial, Environmental, and Biobehavioral Directions in Promoting the Health of Men and Boys* (New York: Routledge, 2011); Donald Sabo and David Frederick Gordon, eds., *Men's Health and Illness: Gender, Power, and the Body* (Thousand Oaks, CA: Sage, 1995).

19. Lillian B. Rubin, *Intimate Strangers: Men and Women Together* (New York: Harper & Row, 1984).

20. Kang K. Han, Timothy A. Bullman, Derek J. Smolenski, Nancy A. Skopp, Gregory A. Gahm, and Mark A. Reger, "Suicide Risk among 1.3 Million Veterans Who Were on Active Duty during the Iraq and Afghanistan Wars," *Annals of Epidemiology* 25 (2015): 96–100.

21. Lizette Alvarez and Dan Frosch, "A Focus on Violence by Returning G.I.'s," *New York Times*, January 1, 2009. In a 2016 blog post, anthropologist Hugh Gusterson argues that analyses of the recent rash of mass shootings in the United States has failed to point out a common feature of many of the shooters: disproportionately, they are military veterans. Hugh Gusterson, "Understanding Mass Killings," *Sapiens: Anthropology/Everything Human* (blog), July 18, 2016, http://www.sapiens .org/blog/conflicted/mass-killers-military-service.

22. Leo Braudy, *From Chivalry to Terrorism: War and the Changing Nature of Masculinity* (New York: Vintage, 2003), 373.

23. George L. Mosse, "Shell Shock as a Social Disease," *Journal of Contemporary History* 35 (2000): 103–104. See also Roger J. Spillar, "Shellshock," *American Heritage* 41 (May–June 1990).

24. Mosse, "Shell Shock as a Social Disease," 107.

25. Jennifer L. Price, "Findings from the National Vietnam Veterans Readjustment Study," National Center for PTSD, U.S. Department of Veterans Affairs, 2003, http://www.ptsd.va.gov/professional/research-bio/research/vietnam-vets -study.asp.

26. Dave Grossman, *On Killing: The Psychological Cost of Learning to Kill in War and Society* (New York: Back Bay Books, 2009), 4.

27. Brett T. Litz, Nathan Stein, Eileen Delaney, Leslie Lebowitz, William P. Nash, Caroline Silva, and Shira Maguen, "Moral Injury and Moral Repair in Veterans:

A Preliminary Intervention Strategy," *Clinical Psychology Review* 29 (2009): 695–706.

28. Gusterson, *Drone*, 8, 79–80.

29. Cynthia Enloe, *Does Khaki Become You? The Militarization of Women's Lives* (London: Harper Collins, 1988); *Bananas, Beaches and Bases: Making Feminist Sense of International Politics* (Berkeley: University of California Press, 1989); *Maneuvers: The International Politics of Militarizing Women's Lives* (Berkeley: University of California Press, 2000).

30. Iraq Veterans Against the War and Aaron Glantz, *Winter Soldier: Iraq and Afghanistan: Eyewitness Accounts of the Occupations* (Chicago: Haymarket Books, 2008).

31. My coauthors and I summarize the increasingly visible problems of sexual assault, sexual harassment, and domestic violence in the military, and assess current efforts to end or mitigate these problems in the final chapter of a recent book. Michael A. Messner, Max A. Greenberg, and Tal Peretz, *Some Men: Feminist Allies and the Movement to End Violence against Women* (New York: Oxford University Press, 2015).

32. In their study of Iraq veterans sociologists Anjel Stough-Hunter and Julie Hart found that each man's shift to peace activism involved a "renegotiation of hegemonic masculinity." Though the study is limited in its focus on white veterans, the findings still offer valuable insights into veterans' different patterned "renegotiations" with hegemonic masculinity—some of them "feminist," some of them not. Anjel Stough-Hunter and Julie Hart, "Understanding Masculine Identity among Antiwar Veterans," *NORMA: International Journal for Masculinity Studies* 10 (2015): 219–235.

33. Howard Zinn, *A People's History of the United States* (New York: Harper Perennial, 2003).

34. Viet Thanh Nguyen, *Nothing Ever Dies: Vietnam and the Memory of War* (Cambridge, MA: Harvard University Press, 2016), 108.

35. Smedley D. Butler, *War Is a Racket* (Port Townsend, WA: Feral House, 2003 [1935]).

36. Many of these efforts are summarized on the VFP website and in VFP, *Full Disclosure: Truth about America's War in Viet Nam* (St. Louis, MO: VFP, 2017). See also https://www.veteransforpeace.org/our-work/vfp-national-projects/viet nam-full-disclosure-campaign.

37. Mike Hastie, "My Gift at My Lai," in VFP, *Full Disclosure: Truth about America's War in Viet Nam* (St. Louis, MO: VFP, 2017), 28; "My Lai Massacre, 49 Years Later," *Counterpunch*, March 21, 2017, https://www.counterpunch.org/2017/03/21 /my-lai-massacre-49-years-later.

38. For an example of the many articles circulated by the VFP listserv about what they saw as Ken Burns's "false moral equivalency" between the invaders and the invaded, see Patrick Martin, "The Contradictions of Ken Burns and Lynn Novick's *The Vietnam War*," *WSWS.org*, October 22, 2017, http://www.wsws.org/en/articles /2017/10/02/viet-002.html?view.

39. Tom Hayden, *Hell No: The Forgotten Power of the Vietnam Peace Movement* (New Haven, CT: Yale University Press, 2017), 5, 11, 17.

40. There had been many charges and revelations for years that the U.S. government had lied about the reasons for entering and escalating the war in Vietnam, but it was following Daniel Ellsberg's 1971 release of the Pentagon Papers—a secret Department of Defense study of the Vietnam War commissioned by Secretary of Defense Robert McNamara—that the public opinion scales began to tip toward a broad understanding that the American public had been lied to for years about the war in Vietnam. Neil Sheehan and Herick Smith, *The Pentagon Papers: The Secret History of the Vietnam War* (New York: Bantam Books, 1971).

41. Jerry Lembcke, *The Spitting Image: Myth, Memory, and the Legacy of Vietnam* (New York: New York University Press, 1998), 118.

42. R. Strayer and L. Ellenhorn, "Vietnam Veterans: A Study Exploring Adjustment Patterns and Attitudes," *Journal of Social Issues* 3 (1975): 81–94.

43. Andrew E. Hunt, *The Turning: A History of Vietnam Veterans Against the War* (New York: New York University Press, 1999); Penny Lewis, *Hardhats, Hippies and Hawks: The Vietnam Antiwar Movement as Myth and Memory* (Ithaca, NY: ILR Press, 2013); Richard Stacewicz, *Winter Soldiers: An Oral History of the Vietnam Veterans Against the War* (Chicago: Haymarket Books, 1997).

44. Hunt, *Turning*, 113.

45. Lembcke draws the concept of a "perfecting myth" from Virginia Carmichael, who argues that myths like the spat-upon veteran tend to reinforce "individuals' voluntary acquiescence to, support for, and daily investment in a specific history not of their choosing." Virginia Carmichael, *Framing History: The Rosenberg Story and the Cold War* (Minneapolis: University of Minnesota Press, 1990).

46. Lembcke, *Spitting Image*, 9.

47. Susan Jeffords, *The Remasculinization of America: Gender and the Vietnam War* (Indianapolis: Indiana University Press, 1989).

48. Klaus Theweleit, *Male Fantasies, Volume 1: Women, Floods, Bodies, History*, trans. Stephen Conway (Minneapolis: University of Minnesota Press, 1987).

49. Jeffords, *Remasculinization of America*, 130.

50. Lembcke, *Spitting Image*, 22.

51. George H. W. Bush: "Remarks to the American Legislative Exchange Council," March 1, 1991, *The American Presidency Project*, http://www.presidency.ucsb.edu/ws/?pid=19351.

52. Nguyen, *Nothing Ever Dies*, 4.

53. J. Glenn Gray, *The Warriors: Reflections on Men in Battle* (New York: Harper & Row, 1959), 23–24.

54. Simone De Beauvoir, *The Ethics of Ambiguity*, trans. Bernard Frechtman (New York: Open Road, 1948); Jean-Paul Sartre, *Search for a Method*, trans. Hazel Barnes (New York: Vintage, 1963); Sarah Bakewell, *At the Existentialist Café: Freedom, Being and Apricot Cocktails* (New York: Other Press, 2016).

55. Sartre, *Search for a Method*, 91.

56. Sartre, *Search for a Method*, 93.

57. Daniel J. Levinson, *The Seasons of a Man's Life* (New York: Random House, 1978).

58. Connell argues that "time seen in the life history is not only generational time, the cycle of reproduction, growth and ageing. It is also, crucially, *historical time* . . . the interviews reveal trajectories through an assemblage of institutions—families, schools, companies, clubs and so on . . . [but] this is not a matter of a traveller moving across an indifferent landscape. Our interview partners are telling us about the *making* of institutions." Raewyn Connell, "Lives of Businessmen: Reflections on Life-History Method and Contemporary Hegemonic Masculinity," *Osterreichische Zeitschrift für Soziologie* 35 (2010): 69. Connell's use of life history interviews is demonstrated in-depth in Raewyn Connell, *Masculinities* (Berkeley: University of California Press, 1995).

59. Historian John W. Dower presents a convincing argument that in the seventy-five years since the end of World War II, the many wars—large and small, overt and covert—fought by the United States are far from discrete events; rather, they are interconnected manifestations of ongoing U.S. efforts to maintain global hegemony, buttressed by an inflated defense budget and the widespread presence of U.S. military bases and overt or covert operations in roughly 150 nations. John W. Dower, *The Violent American Century: War and Terror* (Chicago: Haymarket Books, 2017).

CHAPTER 2 — THERE IS NO "GOOD WAR"

1. Pierre Bourdieu and Loïc J. D. Wacquant, *An Invitation to Reflexive Sociology* (Chicago: University of Chicago Press, 1992).

2. Geoffrey Canada, *Fist, Stick, Knife, Gun: A Personal History of Violence in America* (Boston: Beacon Press, 1995); Ann Arnett Ferguson, *Bad Boys: Public*

Schools and the Making of Black Masculinity (Ann Arbor: University of Michigan Press, 2000).

3. Hispanics were not then counted as a separate ethnic or racial group in the U.S. Census, so the numbers are uncertain, but estimates of the number of Hispanics (including Mexican Americans, Cubans, Puerto Ricans, and others of Latin American descent) serving in the military during World War II range from 250,000 to 500,000. See Raul Morin, *Among the Valiant: Mexican Americans in WWII and Korea* (Alhambra, CA: Borden Publishing, 1966); Maggie Rivas Rodriguez, Juliana Torres, Melissa Dipiero-D'Sa, and Lindsay Fitzpatrick, eds., *A Legacy Greater Than Words: Stories of U.S. Latinos and Latinas* (Austin, TX: U.S. Latino & Latina WWII Oral History Project, 2006).

4. See the many stories of Latino World War II veterans collected in Rivas Rodriguez et al., *Legacy Greater Than Words*.

5. John Bodnar, *The "Good War" in American Memory* (Baltimore, MD: Johns Hopkins University Press), 33.

6. Both of these books were eventually also made into feature films. The message of these books and films found their greatest cultural resonance during and following the American War in Vietnam. James Jones, *The Thin Red Line* (New York: Charles Scribner's Sons, 1962); Joseph Heller, *Catch-22* (New York: Simon & Schuster, 1961).

7. Paul Fussell was a prolific author of books about war and other topics. His highly acclaimed book on World War II is *Wartime: Understanding and Behavior in the Second World War* (New York: Oxford University Press, 1989).

8. Referring to Korea, the Legion's national commander and World War II veteran Erie Cocke declared in 1950 that America was "no place for weaklings" because the nation now faced an "unrelenting battle" against its enemies. Quoted in Bodnar, *"Good War" in American Memory*, 62–63.

9. Edward Orozco Flores, *God's Gangs: Barrio Ministry, Masculinity, and Gang Recovery* (New York: New York University Press, 2013).

10. Adia Harvey Wingfield, *No More Invisible Man: Race and Gender in Men's Work* (Philadelphia: Temple University Press, 2012).

11. Patricia Hill Collins, "Learning from the Outsider Within: The Sociological Significance of Black Feminist Thought," *Social Problems* 133 (1986): 4–32. See also Tristan Bridges and C. J. Pascoe, "Hybrid Masculinities: New Directions in the Sociology of Men and Masculinities," *Sociology Compass* 8 (2014): 246–258.

12. Richard Sennett and Jonathan Cobb, *The Hidden Injuries of Class* (New York: Random House, 1972), 171.

13. Lizabeth Cohen, *A Consumer's Republic: The Politics of Mass Consumption in Postwar America* (New York: Vintage, 2003).

14. Mario T. Garcia, *The Chicano Generation: Testimonios of the Movement* (Berkeley: University of California Press, 2015); George J. Sanchez, *Becoming Mexican American: Ethnicity, Culture and Identity in Chicano Los Angeles, 1900–1945* (New York: Oxford University Press, 1993).

15. Grossman, *On Killing*, 15, 86.

16. See, for instance, Thomas Childers, *Soldier from the War Returning: The Greatest Generation's Troubled Homecoming from World War II* (Boston: Houghton Mifflin Harcourt, 2009); Lori Rotskoff, *Love on the Rocks: Men, Women, and Alcohol in Post-World War II America* (Chapel Hill: University of North Carolina Press, 2002).

17. John F. Kihlstrom, "Trauma and Memory Revisited," in *Memory and Emotions: Interdisciplinary Perspectives*, ed. B. Uttl, N. Ohta, and A. L. Siegenthaler (New York: Blackwell, 2006), 259–291.

18. In chapter 1 I discuss the historical trajectory of the medicalization of wartime trauma, from "shell shock" to "combat fatigue" to "PTSD" and "moral injury." See Braudy, *From Chivalry to Terrorism*; Mosse, "Shell Shock as a Social Disease"; Allan Young, *The Harmony of Illusions: Inventing Post-Traumatic Stress Disorder* (Princeton, NJ: Princeton University Press, 1995).

19. Litz et al., "Moral Injury and Moral Repair in War Veterans," 696–697.

20. Nguyen, *Nothing Ever Dies*, 8–9.

CHAPTER 3 — BEING HONORABLE

1. Bruce Cumings, *The Korean War: A History* (New York: Modern Library, 2010), 63.

2. Here and throughout this chapter, I reproduce quotes from Wilson M. Powell primarily from the life history interview I conducted with him. But Powell is also a writer, so with his permission, I also interweave occasional quotes from his various writings, including his book coauthored with Zhou Ming-Fu, and here from a short piece he wrote for a newsletter in 2000 following his visit to Kokan-Ri. Wilson M. Powell and Zhou Ming-Fu, *Two Walk the Golden Road: Two Soldiers, Two Cultures, Their Histories Intertwined* (Mahoment, IL: Mayhaven Publishing, 2000); Wilson M. Powell, "Kokan-Ri," *The Veteran: Vietnam Veterans Against the War* 30, no. 2 (Winter–Spring 2000): 15.

3. Tirman, *Deaths of Others*, 92. In discussing the difficulty in estimating civilian war deaths, Tirman notes the common practice of writers to engage in a "circuitous replication of figures and citations" that they have read elsewhere; see 319–320.

4. Nguyen, *Nothing Ever Dies*, 51, 83.

5. Powell was in fact head of the Manhattan Project's magnet group, which developed magnets for the calutron, a device the lab developed in order to separate isotopes for uranium.

6. In the years following his government's dropping of two atomic bombs on major population centers, J. Robert Oppenheimer was outspoken about the importance of open scientific inquiry, but also frequently expressed grim ambivalence at his role in developing the deadly weapon. For instance, in a 1947 speech at MIT, later quoted in *Time* magazine, he stated, "In some sort of crude sense which no vulgarity, no humor, no overstatement can quite extinguish, the physicists have known sin; and this is a knowledge which they cannot lose." Oppenheimer's outspokenness about the need for nuclear nonproliferation drew critical scrutiny during the McCarthy era, as he was branded as a communist, brought in 1954 before red-hunting congressional committees, and wiretapped by the FBI. The definitive work on Oppenheimer is Kai Bird and Martin J. Sherwin, *American Prometheus: The Triumph and Tragedy of J. Robert Oppenheimer* (New York: Vintage, 2006); quote on loc. 7842 of the e-book.

7. Cumings, *Korean War*, 109.

8. Cumings, *Korean War*, 14.

9. Echoing the scholar Edward Said's critical examination of Western societies' embrace of racist "Orientalism," Tirman observes that in the United States at the start of the 1950s, "References to Koreans as 'gooks' or 'coolies' were commonplace. . . . The belief in the racial and moral inferiority of Koreans was rooted in a broader attitude about the 'Orient' . . . that Asians were morally vacuous, supine if not effeminate, prone to adopt despotism, and utterly devoid of democratic virtues. . . . The notion that Koreans did not value life as much as Americans do was at work as well." Tirman, *Deaths of Others*, 121.

10. Powell and Zhou, *Two Walk the Golden Road*, 101, 125–126.

11. The vast majority of scholarly works on war focuses on the experience of men. But a growing body of research—most notably that of feminist scholar Cynthia Enloe—examines the impact of war and militarism on women's lives. See Enloe, *Bananas, Beaches and Bases*; *Maneuvers*.

12. Cumings, *Korean War*, 152, 160.

13. In April 1951 the Truman administration had decided to retreat from confrontation, beginning peace talks and shifting to a strategy of containment that would leave North Korea in communist hands. When General Douglas MacArthur, who had earlier argued for the strategic use of atomic weapons in North Korea, openly contested the president's decision, Truman made the controversial decision to relieve MacArthur of his command. Dwight D. Eisenhower

then ran for president in 1952 on a platform that affirmed Truman's policy of coexistence rather than confrontation with China and the Soviet Union. Historian John Bodnar concludes that Eisenhower "was adamant about seeking a peace settlement in Korea instead of a complete conquest of the enemy—a position that helped him get elected." Eisenhower's nuclear saber rattling during the latter stages of the Korean War truce talks may seem ironic against that backdrop, but was probably viewed as an effective strategy to shake loose long-stalemated talks. See Bodnar, *"Good War" in American Memory*, 81.

14. Cumings, *Korean War*, 34.

15. Tirman, *Deaths of Others*, 119–120, 361.

16. Cumings, *Korean War*, 207.

17. Cumings, *Korean War*, 210–211, 243.

18. Dexamyl is a combination barbiturate and amphetamine drug frequently prescribed starting in the early 1950s, and discontinued in the 1970s.

19. This work appeared in two volumes, separated by nine years. Bruce Cumings, *Origins of the Korean War, I: Liberation and the Emergence of Separate Regimes, 1945–1947* (Princeton, NJ: Princeton University Press, 1981); *Origins of the Korean War, II: The Roaring of the Cataract, 1947–1950* (Princeton, NJ: Princeton University Press, 1990).

20. First published in 1980, with several subsequent editions, Zinn's *People's History* has sold more than 2 million copies. It is difficult to overstate the importance of the impact the book has had in subsequent decades in challenging the standard, official point of view on American history. The book begins, for instance, with Native Americans standing on a shoreline and witnessing the arrival of Columbus's Spanish ships. Immediately, one knows that one is reading a familiar story, but with a radically reframed point of view.

21. Following the TV interview, O'Reilly wrote on his online blog, "The peace people believe that our response should be contained, measured, that we should do various things to accommodate foreign governments that are aren't necessarily our friends. Now I respect that opinion, but I feel that it's wrong. And I believe many of the compromisers have hidden agendas. From all the interviews I've done on the topic, including the one last night with Woody Powell, the President of the Veterans for Peace Organization, a vivid picture emerges. Mr. Powell believes the United States has exploited the Third World economically, so they have a right to hate us. Others on the left embrace socialism in America, to create a world where everyone has a level playing field. Of course, that's impossible." Bill O'Reilly, "Hidden Agendas and Peace Protestors," *FoxNews.com* (blog), October 11, 2001, http://www.foxnews.com/story/2001/10/11/hidden-agendas-peace-protesters.html.

22. Michael McPherson is a widely respected leader in VFP. An Army field artillery officer during the Gulf War, McPherson, an African American, is also active in various antiracism organizations and efforts.

23. Wilson. M. Powell, ed., *The Democratization of Veterans for Peace, 1995–2007* (St. Louis, MO: VFP, 2008).

24. "The Man in Uniform" appears in *Long Ago and Yesterday: Poems of Wilson (Woody) Powell* (self-pub., 2007).

CHAPTER 4 — PAYING OFF MY KARMIC DEBT

1. "Fragging" is a term used to describe the deliberate killing or attempted killing of one's superior officer. See David Cortright, *Soldiers in Revolt: GI Resistance during the Vietnam War* (Chicago: Haymarket Books, 2005 [1975]). The impact of GI resistance to the war is summarized in Zinn, *People's History of the United States*, 492–497.

2. Nick Turse, *Kill Anything That Moves: The Real American War in Vietnam* (New York: Picador, 2013), 6, 27.

3. Adam J. Berinsky, *In Time of War: Understanding American Public Opinion from World War II to Iraq* (Chicago: University of Chicago Press, 2009), 21.

4. Messner, Greenberg, and Peretz, *Some Men*.

5. Tim O'Brien, *The Things They Carried* (New York: Mariner Books, 2009 [1990]).

6. Documentation of what some had suspected were government lies underlying the escalating war appeared most dramatically when Daniel Ellsberg released the Pentagon Papers. Sheehan and Smith, *Pentagon Papers*.

7. John Marciano, *The American War in Vietnam: Crime or Commemoration?* (New York: Monthly Review Press, 2016), 79.

8. J. William Fulbright, *The Arrogance of Power* (New York: Random House, 1973), 50–51.

9. See Gitlin, *Whole World Is Watching*.

10. Hamilton Gregory, *McNamara's Folly: The Use of Low-IQ Troops in the Vietnam War* (West Conshohocken, PA: Infinity Publishing, 2015), quotes from Kindle edition, locations 111, 116.

11. Hayden, *Hell No*, 94.

12. The number of Vietnamese casualties, including civilians, is still a matter of debate; I use here the most widely agreed upon estimates. For discussions of these numbers, see Tirman, *Deaths of Others*; Turse, *Kill Anything That Moves*.

13. Hunt, *Turning*, 163. For an informative oral history of VVAW, see Stacewicz, *Winter Soldiers*.

14. John Kerry, *New Soldier* (New York: Collier Books, 1971), 104.

15. Hunt, *Turning*, 149.

16. Lewis, *Hardhats, Hippies and Hawks*, 194.

17. Lewis cites *A Rich Man's War a Poor Man's Fight*, a book distributed by Labor for Peace in 1971—and also Martin Luther King, Malcolm X, and the Student Non-violent Coordinating Committee as taking leadership roles in opposing the war. Washington Labor for Peace, *A Rich Man's War a Poor Man's Fight: A Handbook for Trade Unionists on the Vietnam War* (Washington, DC: Washington Labor for Peace, 1971). Tom Hayden makes a similar point in *Hell No*.

18. Lembcke, *Spitting Image*.

19. W. D. Erhardt, "Viet Nam: Lessons Learned and Unlearned," in VFP, *Full Disclosure*, 8.

20. See Cortright, *Soldiers in Revolt*.

21. Grossman, *On Killing*, 287.

22. Maxine Hong Kingston, ed., *Veterans of War, Veterans of Peace* (Charlottesville, VA: Chiron Publications/Koa Books, 2006).

23. Some of Ross's poetry was included in a book compiled by the San Francisco and East Bay VFP chapters, and sold at the national convention. See Fred Norman, *Peace and Poetry* (Berkeley, CA: Veterans for Peace, 2006); copies can be obtained by emailing fnorman300@aol.com.

CHAPTER 5 — YOU CLOCK IN, YOU GO KILL PEOPLE

1. Andrew J. Bacevich, *America's War for the Greater Middle East: A Military History* (New York: Random House, 2016), 126.

2. PB (pyridostigmine bromide) pills were given to coalition troops in twenty-one-pill blister packs during the Gulf War to prevent death in the case of an enemy attack using the nerve gas soman. Many point to the pills as a source of chronic multisymptom illnesses Gulf War veterans commonly suffered from—often called Gulf War Syndrome—however the VA says that there is no proven association between ingesting PD pills and subsequent illnesses. See U.S. Department of Veterans Affairs, "Pyridostigmine Bromide and Gulf War Veterans," last modified March 28, 2017, https://www.publichealth.va.gov/exposures/gulfwar/sources/pyridostigmine-bromide.asp.

3. Craig's estimate of his hometown's population size and composition is correct. By the time he left Springer, New Mexico, for the Army in 1980 the town had hit its all-time population peak, at 1,657 people; his exodus corresponded with a gradual and continuing decline. The 2015 U.S. Census estimated the Springer population at 943, 70 percent of whom identified as Hispanic or Latino.

4. See Melissa L. Brown, *Enlisting Masculinity: The Construction of Gender in U.S. Military Recruiting Advertising during the All-Volunteer Force* (New York: Oxford University Press, 2012).

5. "To stay in business," Bacevich wrote, "U.S. Central Command needed to identify a new threat." See *America's War for the Greater Middle East*, 44–45.

6. Bacevich, *America's War for the Greater Middle East*, 117–118.

7. Bacevich, *America's War for the Greater Middle East*, 120.

8. U.S. Army, *Conduct of the Persian Gulf War: Final Report to Congress* (Washington, DC, 1992), 168.

9. Gray, *The Warriors*, 52.

10. Beth Osborne Daponte, "A Case Study in Estimating Casualties from War and Its Aftermath: The 1991 Persian Gulf War," *Medicine & Global Survival* 3, no. 1 (1993).

11. Bacevich, *America's War for the Greater Middle East*, 109, 113.

12. Glenn Kessler, "The Fact Checker: Cutting the Defense Budget," *Washington Post*, January 11, 2011, http://voices.washingtonpost.com/fact-checker/2011/01/cutting_the_defense_budget.html. This drawdown of U.S. forces would be reversed dramatically during the administration of George W. Bush.

13. Erin K. Dursa, Shannon K. Barth, Aaron Schneiderman, and Robert M. Bossarte, "Physical and Mental Health Status of Gulf War and Gulf Era Veterans: Results from a Large Population-Based Epidemiological Study," *Journal of Occupational and Environmental Medicine* 58 (2016): 444.

14. U. S. Department of Veterans Affairs, "Pyridostigmaine Bromide and Gulf War Veterans."

15. Research Advisory Committee on Gulf War Veterans' Illnesses, *Gulf War Illness and the Health of Gulf War Veterans: Scientific Findings and Recommendations* (Washington, DC: U.S. Government Printing Office, November 2008).

16. Daniel Quinn, *Ishmael: An Adventure of the Mind and Spirit* (New York: Bantam, 1992).

17. In an email, longtime Santa Fe VFP activist Ken Mayers described the two in this way: "Kip Corneli [was] a onetime Wisconsin farmer and longtime Quaker. Norm Budow was a former history professor in Illinois who always had a great story for any occasion. Norm and Kip both came to the corner for years and only gave up shortly before they each died."

18. Two Arlington West memorials are assembled every Sunday, from sunrise to sunset: near the pier in Santa Monica, CA, and at Stearns Wharf in Santa Barbara, CA. See http://www.arlingtonwestsantamonica.org.

CHAPTER 6 — LAYING THE TRACKS

1. A running month-by-month database on civilian casualties in Iraq since 2003 is kept on the Iraq Body Count website (https://www.iraqbodycount.org). Estimates of total civilian deaths in the Iraq War since 2003 vary widely. John Tir-

man observes that the official U.S. count in 2010 of 77,000 Iraqi dead is "well below every other account." Tirman, *Deaths of Others*, 317.

2. James Allen and John Lewis, *Without Sanctuary: Lynching Photography in America* (Santa Fe, NM: Twin Palms, 2000).

3. First published in 1975 to chronicle the GI antiwar movement during the American War in Vietnam, Cortright's book was republished in 2005 with a new introduction by historian Howard Zinn, and with an added focus on the current wars in the Middle East. Cortright, *Soldiers in Revolt*.

4. In terms of combat trauma, a key comparison point here is Gregory Ross, also a Navy veteran who also experienced his war (Vietnam) from the distance of a ship. However, Ross's was a gunship that was shelling the nearby coastline; Ross could hear and feel the guns firing, and could see the coastal areas they were shelling. By contrast, Hutto was aboard a carrier from which jets flew to more distant points of combat that remained, for Hutto, unseen and unheard.

5. Tomiko Brown-Nagin, *Courage to Dissent: Atlanta and the Long History of the Civil Rights Movement* (New York: Oxford University Press, 2012).

6. See James W. Loewen, *Sundown Towns: A Hidden Dimension of American Racism* (New York: Touchstone, 2006).

7. Karl Evanzz, *The Judas Factor: The Plot to Kill Malcolm X* (New York: Thunder's Mouth Press, 1992).

8. I wrote about the Million Man March in an earlier book that focused on men's movements of the 1970s through the 1990s; see Messner, *Politics of Masculinities*. In that book, I outlined how some feminists criticized the march's male-only emphasis, and its celebration of ideas of male leadership in families and communities. This was a tension amplified by the conservative gender politics of the Nation of Islam, which was at the center of the march's leadership. However, many black women supported the march, in part because they understood how it responded to the historical legacy of slavery, Jim Crow, and federal welfare policies that undermined or destroyed black families. The march also offered what many saw as a positive counterpoint to the wholesale destruction of solid working-class jobs held by African American men in the 1980s in a time of massive deindustrialization, coupled with the rise of the carceral state's escalating criminalization of young black men. See William Julius Wilson, *The Truly Disadvantaged* (Chicago: University of Chicago Press, 1987).

9. On Guyot's passing Hutto wrote a moving requiem in the *Washington Post*. Jonathan Hutto, "Remembering Lawrence Guyot," *Washington Post*, November 28, 2012. https://www.washingtonpost.com/blogs/therootdc/post/lawrence -guyot-soldier-of-the-people-mentor-for-the-youth/2012/11/28/aca397fc-396c -11e2-a263-foebffed2f15_blog.html?utm_term=.72e07cbdecdd.

10. Bacevich, *America's War for the Greater Middle East*, 249.

11. As quoted in Dower, *Violent American Century*, loc. 1382.

12. See Amy Lutz, "Who Joins the Military?: A Look at Race, Class, and Immigration Status," *Journal of Political and Military Sociology* 36 (2008): 167–188.

13. Gerald Astor, *The Right to Fight: A History of African Americans in the Military* (Cambridge, MA: Da Capo Press, 1998), 108.

14. Lutz, "Who Joins the Military?," 171. See also Sherie Mershon and Steven Schlossman, *Foxholes and Color Lines: Desegregating the U.S. Armed Forces* (Baltimore: Johns Hopkins University Press, 1998).

15. Douglas Walter Bristol Jr., "Terror, Anger and Patriotism: Understanding the Resistance of Black Soldiers during World War II," in *Integrating the U.S. Military: Race, Gender and Sexual Orientation since World War II*, ed. Douglas Walter Bristol Jr. and Heather Marie Stur (Baltimore: Johns Hopkins University Press, 2017), 10–35.

16. Lutz, "Who Joins the Military?," 172.

17. Lutz, "Who Joins the Military?," 173.

18. James E. Westheider, "African Americans, Civil Rights, and the Armed Forces during the Vietnam War," in Bristol and Stur, *Integrating the U.S.*, 96–121.

19. Mark Cooper, "About Face: Soldiers Call for Iraq Withdrawal," *The Nation*, December 16, 2006.

20. Berinsky, *In Time of War*, 1.

21. The devastating impact of the imposition of "stop-loss" on U.S. troops and their families was depicted in the 2008 film *Stop-Loss*, and in Phil Klay's highly acclaimed book *Redeployment* (New York: Penguin, 2014).

22. In 2008, IVAW organized "Winter Soldier: Iraq and Afghanistan," a four-day public hearing of testimony by more than 200 veterans, modeled on an earlier such effort by antiwar vets during the American War in Vietnam. Much of the 2008 testimony was gathered in Iraq Veterans Against the War and Glantz, *Winter Soldier*. In subsequent years, a rich history of Iraq veterans' antiwar activities emerged. See, for instance, Matthew Gutmann and Catherine Lutz, *Breaking Ranks: Iraq Veterans Speak Out against the War* (Berkeley: University of California Press, 2010); Lisa Leitz, *Fighting for Peace: Veterans and Military Families in the Anti-Iraq War Movement* (Minneapolis: University of Minnesota Press, 2014); Nan Levinson, *War Is Not a Game: The New Antiwar Soldiers and the Movement They Built* (New Brunswick, NJ: Rutgers University Press, 2014).

23. Jonathan W. Hutto, *Antiwar Soldier: How to Dissent within the Ranks of the Military* (New York: Nation Books, 2008).

24. See, for instance, Nate Terani, "Tehran, USA: Fighting Fundamentalism in America," *TomDispatch.com*, October 30, 2016, http://www.tomdispatch.com

/post/176204/tomgram%3A_nate_terani%2C_one_veteran%27s_war_on_islam ophobia.

25. See the "Veterans Challenge Islamophobia" statement and ancillary links at https://www.veteransforpeace.org/take-action/veterans-challenge-islama phobia.

CHAPTER 7 — THIS IS OUR SERVICE

1. Marine Corps veteran Camillo Mac Bica is among several VFP members who have written extensively about this issue. Camillo Mac Bica, *Worthy of Gratitude: Why Veterans May Not Want to Be Thanked for Their Service* (Commack, NY: Gnosis Press, 2015).

Bibliography

Abraham, Traci, Ann M. Cheney, and Geoffrey M. Curran. "A Bourdieusian Analysis of U.S. Military Culture in the Mental Health-Seeking Literature. *American Journal of Men's Health* 11, no. 5 (2015): 1358–1365.

Allen, James, and John Lewis. *Without Sanctuary: Lynching Photography in America*. Santa Fe, NM: Twin Palms, 2000.

Alvarez, Lizette, and Dan Frosch. "A Focus on Violence by Returning G.I.'s." *New York Times*, January 1, 2009.

Astor, Gerald. *The Right to Fight: A History of African Americans in the Military*. Cambridge, MA: De Capo Press, 1998.

Ayers, William. "Hearts and Minds: Military Recruitment and the High School Battlefield." *Phi Delta Kappan* (April 2006): 594–599.

Bacevich, Andrew J. *America's War for the Greater Middle East: A Military History*. New York: Random House, 2016.

Bakewell, Sarah. *At the Existentialist Café: Freedom, Being and Apricot Cocktails*. New York: Other Press, 2016.

Belasco, Amy. "The Cost of Iraq, Afghanistan and Other Global War on Terror Operations since 9/11." Congressional Research Service, 7-5700, RL33110, December 8, 2014.

Berinsky, Adam J. *In Time of War: Understanding American Public Opinion from World War II to Iraq*. Chicago: University of Chicago Press, 2009.

Bica, Camillo Mac. *Worthy of Gratitude: Why Veterans May Not Want to Be Thanked for Their Service*. Commack, NY: Gnosis Press, 2015.

Bird, Kai, and Martin J. Sherwin. *American Prometheus: The Triumph and Tragedy of J. Robert Oppenheimer*. New York: Vintage, 2006.

Bodnar, John. *The "Good War" in American Memory*. Baltimore: Johns Hopkins University Press, 2010.

Bourdieu, Pierre, and Loïc J. D. Wacquant. *An Invitation to Reflexive Sociology.* Chicago: University of Chicago Press, 1992.

Braudy, Leo. *From Chivalry to Terrorism: War and the Changing Nature of Masculinity.* New York: Vintage, 2003.

Bridges, Tristan, and C. J. Pascoe. "Hybrid Masculinities: New Directions in the Sociology of Men and Masculinities." *Sociology Compass* 8 (2014): 246–258.

Bristol, Douglas Walter, Jr. "Terror, Anger and Patriotism: Understanding the Resistance of Black Soldiers during World War II." In *Integrating the U.S. Military: Race, Gender and Sexual Orientation since World War II*, edited by Douglas Walter Bristol Jr. and Heather Marie Stur, 10–35. Baltimore: Johns Hopkins University Press, 2017.

Brown, Melissa L. *Enlisting Masculinity: The Construction of Gender in U.S. Military Recruiting Advertising during the All-Volunteer Force.* New York: Oxford University Press, 2012.

Brown-Nagin, Tomiko. *Courage to Dissent: Atlanta and the Long History of the Civil Rights Movement.* New York: Oxford University Press, 2012.

Brown University. "The Costs of War Project." Watson Institute, International and Public Affairs. http://watson.brown.edu/costsofwar/figures/2016/direct-war-death-toll-iraq-afghanistan-and-pakistan-2001-370000.

Bush, George H. W. "Remarks to the American Legislative Exchange Council." *The American Presidency Project*, March 1, 1991. http://www.presidency.ucsb.edu/ws/?pid=19351.

Butler, Smedley D. *War Is a Racket.* Port Townsend, WA: Feral House, 2003 (1935).

Canada, Geoffrey. *Fist, Stick, Knife, Gun: A Personal History of Violence in America.* Boston: Beacon Press, 1995.

Carmichael, Virginia. *Framing History: The Rosenberg Story and the Cold War.* Minneapolis: University of Minnesota Press, 1990.

Cave, Damien. "Growing Problem for Military Recruiters: Parents." *New York Times*, June 3, 2005, p. B-6.

Childers, Thomas. *Soldier from the War Returning: The Greatest Generation's Troubled Homecoming from World War II.* Boston: Houghton Mifflin Harcourt, 2009.

Cohen, Lizabeth. *A Consumer's Republic: The Politics of Mass Consumption in Postwar America.* New York: Vintage, 2003.

Collins, Patricia Hill. "Learning from the Outsider Within: The Sociological Significance of Black Feminist Thought." *Social Problems* 33 (1986): 14–32.

Connell, Raewyn. "Lives of Businessmen: Reflections on Life-History Method and Contemporary Hegemonic Masculinity." *Österreichische Zeitschrift für Soziologie* 35 (2010): 54–71.

———. *Masculinities*. Berkeley: University of California Press, 1995.

Cooper, Mark. "About Face: Soldiers Call for Iraq Withdrawal." *The Nation*, December 16, 2006.

Cortright, David. *Soldiers in Revolt: GI Resistance during the Vietnam War*. 2nd ed. Chicago: Haymarket Books, 2005 (1975).

———. "Why Dr. King Was Right to Oppose the Vietnam War." *David Cortright* (blog), April 3, 2017.

Courtenay, Will H. *Dying to Be Men: Psychosocial, Environmental, and Biobehavioral Directions in Promoting the Health of Men and Boys*. New York: Routledge, 2011.

Cumings, Bruce. *The Korean War: A History*. New York: Modern Library, 2010.

———. *Origins of the Korean War, I: Liberation and the Emergence of Separate Regimes, 1945–1947*. Princeton, NJ: Princeton University Press, 1981.

———. *Origins of the Korean War, II: The Roaring of the Cataract, 1947–1950*. Princeton, NJ: Princeton University Press, 1990.

Daponte, Beth Osborne. "A Case Study in Estimating Casualties from War and Its Aftermath: The 1991 Persian Gulf War." *Medicine & Global Survival* 3, no. 1 (1993).

De Beauvoir, Simone. *The Ethics of Ambiguity*. Translated by Bernard Frechtman. New York: Open Road, 1948.

DeBruyne, Nese F., and Anne Leland. "American War and Military Operations Casualties: Lists and Statistics." Congressional Research Service, 7-5700, RL32492, January 2, 2015.

Digby, Tom. *Love and War: How Militarism Shapes Sexuality and Romance*. New York: Columbia University Press, 2014.

Dower, John W. *The Violent American Century: War and Terror*. Chicago: Haymarket Books, 2017.

Dursa, Erin K., Shannon K. Barth, Aaron Schneiderman, and Robert M. Bossarte. "Physical and Mental Health Status of Gulf War and Gulf Era Veterans: Results from a Large Population-Based Epidemiological Study." *Journal of Occupational and Environmental Medicine* 58 (2016): 41–46.

El Akkad, Omar. *American War*. New York: Alfred A. Knopf, 2017.

Enloe, Cynthia. *Bananas, Beaches and Bases: Making Feminist Sense of International Politics*. Berkeley, University of California Press, 1989.

———. *Does Khaki Become You? The Militarization of Women's Lives*. London: Harper Collins, 1988.

———. *Maneuvers: The International Politics of Militarizing Women's Lives*. Berkeley: University of California Press, 2000.

Erhardt, W. D. "Viet Nam: Lessons Learned and Unlearned." In Veterans for Peace, *Full Disclosure: Truth about America's War in Viet Nam*, 1, 8–11. St. Louis, MO: Veterans for Peace, 2016.

Evanzz, Karl. *The Judas Factor: The Plot to Kill Malcolm X*. New York: Thunder's Mouth Press, 1992.

Fanning, Rory. "Why Doesn't the US Celebrate Armistice Day? We're More Comfortable with War Than Peace." *Guardian*, November 14, 2014. https:// www.theguardian.com/commentisfree/2014/nov/11/us-observe-armistice-day -more-comfortable-war-than-peace.

Ferguson, Ann Arnett. *Bad Boys: Public Schools and the Making of Black Masculinity*. Ann Arbor: University of Michigan Press, 2000.

Flores, David. "From Prowar Soldier to Antiwar Activist: Change and Continuity in the Narratives of Political Conversion among Iraq War Veterans." *Symbolic Interaction* 39, no. 2 (2016): 196–212.

Flores, Edward Orozco. *God's Gangs: Barrio Ministry, Masculinity, and Gang Recovery*. New York: New York University Press, 2013.

Fulbright, J. William. *The Arrogance of Power*. New York: Random House, 1973.

Fussell, Paul. *Wartime: Understanding and Behavior in the Second World War*. New York: Oxford University Press, 1989.

Garcia, Mario T. *The Chicano Generation: Testimonios of the Movement*. Berkeley: University of California Press, 2015.

Garza, Irene. "Advertising Patriotism: The 'Yo Soy El Army' Campaign and the Politics of Visibility for Latino/a Youth." *Latino Studies* 13 (2015): 245–268.

Gitlin, Todd. *The Whole World Is Watching: Mass Media in the Making and Unmaking of the New Left*. Berkeley: University of California Press, 1980.

Gray, J. Glenn. *The Warriors: Reflections on Men in Battle*. New York: Harper & Row, 1959.

Gregory, Hamilton. *McNamara's Folly: The Use of Low-IQ Troops in the Vietnam War*. West Conshohocken, PA: Infinity Publishing, 2015.

Grossman, Dave. *On Killing: The Psychological Cost of Learning to Kill in War and Society*. New York: Back Bay Books, 2009.

Gusterson, Hugh. *Drone: Remote Control Warfare*. Cambridge, MA: MIT Press, 2016.

———. "Understanding Mass Killings." *Sapiens: Anthropology/Everything Human* (blog), July 18, 2016, http://www.sapiens.org/blog/conflicted/mass-killers-military -service/.

Gutmann, Matthew, and Catherine Lutz. *Breaking Ranks: Iraq Veterans Speak Out against the War*. Berkeley: University of California Press, 2010.

Han, Kang K., Timothy A. Bullman, Derek J. Smolenski, Nancy A. Skopp, Gregory A. Gahm, and Mark A. Reger. "Suicide Risk among 1.3 Million Veterans Who Were on Active Duty during the Iraq and Afghanistan Wars." *Annals of Epidemiology* 25 (2015): 96–100.

Hanh, Thich Nhat. *Peace Is Every Step: The Path of Mindfulness in Everyday Life.* New York: Bantam, 1992.

Hastie, Mike. "My Gift at My Lai." In Veterans for Peace, *Full Disclosure: Truth about America's War in Viet Nam*, 28. St. Louis, MO: Veterans for Peace, 2017.

———. "My Lai Massacre, 49 Years Later." *Counterpunch*, March 21, 2017. https://www.counterpunch.org/2017/03/21/my-lai-massacre-49-years-later/.

Hathaway, Oona A., and Scott J. Shapiro. *The Internationalists: How a Radical Plan to Outlaw War Remade the World.* New York: Simon & Schuster, 2017.

Hayden, Tom. *Hell No: The Forgotten Power of the Vietnam Peace Movement.* New Haven, CT: Yale University Press, 2017.

Heller, Joseph. *Catch 22.* New York: Simon & Schuster, 1961.

Hochschild, Adam. *Spain in Our Hearts: Americans in the Spanish Civil War, 1936–1939.* Boston: Houghton Mifflin Harcourt, 2016.

Hong Kingston, Maxine, ed. *Veterans of War, Veterans of Peace.* Kihei, HI: Koa Books, 2006.

Hunt, Andrew E. *The Turning: A History of Vietnam Veterans Against the War.* New York: New York University Press, 1999.

Hutto, Jonathan W. *Antiwar Soldier: How to Dissent within the Ranks of the Military.* New York: Nation Books, 2008.

———. "Remembering Lawrence Guyot." *Washington Post*, November 28, 2012. https://www.washingtonpost.com/blogs/therootdc/post/lawrence-guyot-soldier-of-the-people-mentor-for-the-youth/2012/11/28/aca397fc-396c-11e2-a263-foebff ed2f15_blog.html?utm_term=.72e07cbdecdd.

Iraq Veterans Against the War and Aaron Glantz. *Winter Soldier Iraq and Afghanistan: Eyewitness Accounts of the Occupations.* Chicago: Haymarket Books, 2008.

Jeffords, Susan. *The Remasculinization of America: Gender and the Vietnam War.* Indianapolis: Indiana University Press, 1989.

Johnson, Chalmers. *Blowback: The Costs and Consequences of American Empire.* New York: Henry Holt, 2004.

Jones, James. *The Thin Red Line.* New York: Charles Scribner's Sons, 1962.

Kerry, John. *New Soldier.* New York: Collier Books, 1971.

Kessler, Glenn. "The Fact Checker: Cutting the Defense Budget." *Washington Post*, January 11, 2011. http://voices.washingtonpost.com/fact-checker/2011/01/cutting_the_defense_budget.html.

Kihlstrom, John F. "Trauma and Memory Revisited." In *Memory and Emotions: Interdisciplinary Perspectives*, edited by B. Uttl, N. Ohta, and A. L. Siegenthaler, 259–291. New York: Blackwell, 2006.

King, Martin Luther. "Beyond Vietnam." Address delivered at Riverside Church, New York City, April 4, 1967.

Klay, Phil. *Redeployment*. New York: Penguin, 2014.

Leitz, Lisa. *Fighting for Peace: Veterans and Military Families in the Anti-Iraq War Movement*. Minneapolis: University of Minnesota Press, 2014.

Lembcke, Jerry. *The Spitting Image: Myth, Memory, and the Legacy of Vietnam*. New York: New York University Press, 1998.

Levinson, Daniel J. *The Seasons of a Man's Life*. New York: Random House, 1978.

Levinson, Nan. *War Is Not a Game: The New Antiwar Soldiers and the Movement They Built*. New Brunswick, NJ: Rutgers University Press, 2014.

Lewis, Penny. *Hardhats, Hippies and Hawks: The Vietnam Antiwar Movement as Myth and Memory*. Ithaca, NY: ILR Press, 2013.

Litz, Brett T., Nathan Stein, Eileen Delaney, Leslie Lebowitz, William P. Nash, Caroline Silva, and Shira Maguen. "Moral Injury and Moral Repair in War Veterans: A Preliminary Model and Prevention Strategy." *Clinical Psychology Review* 29 (2007): 695–706.

Loewen, James W. *Sundown Towns: A Hidden Dimension of American Racism*. New York: Touchstone, 2006.

Lutz, Amy. "Who Joins the Military?: A Look at Race, Class, and Immigration Status." *Journal of Political and Military Sociology* 36 (2008): 167–188.

Marciano, John. *The American War in Vietnam: Crime or Commemoration?* New York: Monthly Review Press, 2016.

Martin, Patrick. "The Contradictions of Ken Burns and Lynn Novick's *The Vietnam War*." *WSWS.org*, October 22, 2017. http://www.wsws.org/en/articles/2017 /10/02/viet-002.html?view.

McCutchan, Phoebe K., Xian Liu, Cynthia A. LeardMann, Tyler C. Smith, Edward J. Boyko, Kristie L. Gore, Michael C. Freed, and Charles C. Engel. "Deployment, Combat and Risk of Multiple Physical Symptoms in the US Military: A Prospective Cohort Study." *Annals of Epidemiology* 26 (2016): 122–128.

Mershon, Sherie, and Steven Schlossman. *Foxholes and Color Lines: Desegregating the U.S. Armed Forces*. Baltimore: Johns Hopkins University Press, 1998.

Messner, Michael A. *King of the Wild Suburb: A Memoir of Fathers, Sons and Guns*. Austin, TX: Plain View Press, 2011.

———. "The Masculinity of the Governator: Muscle and Compassion in American Politics." *Gender & Society* 21 (2007): 461–481.

———. *Politics of Masculinities: Men in Movements*. Lanham, MD: Alta Mira Press, 1997.

Messner, Michael A., Max A. Greenberg, and Tal Peretz. *Some Men: Feminist Allies and the Movement to End Violence against Women*. New York: Oxford University Press, 2015.

Mills, C. Wright. *The Sociological Imagination*. New York: Oxford University Press, 1959.

Montez de Oca, Jeffrey. *Discipline and Indulgence: College Football, Media, and the American Way of Life during the Cold War*. New Brunswick, NJ: Rutgers University Press, 2013.

Morin, Raul. *Among the Valiant: Mexican Americans in WWII and Korea*. Alhambra, CA: Borden Publishing, 1966.

Mosse, George L. "Shell Shock as a Social Disease." *Journal of Contemporary History* 35 (2000): 101–108.

Nguyen, Viet Thanh. *Nothing Ever Dies: Vietnam and the Memory of War*. Cambridge, MA: Harvard University Press, 2016.

Norman, Fred. *Peace and Poetry*. Berkeley, CA: Veterans for Peace, 2016.

O'Brien, Tim. *The Things They Carried*. New York: Mariner Books, 2009 (1990).

Office of Public Health, Veterans Health Administration. *Report on VA Facilities Specific Operation Enduring Freedom (OEF), Operation Iraqi Freedom (OIF), and Operation New Dawn (OND) Veterans Diagnosed with Potential or Provisional PTSD (Cumulative from October 1, 2001, to September 30, 2014)*. Washington, DC: Department of Veterans Affairs, 2015.

O'Reilly, Bill. "Hidden Agendas and Peace Protestors." *FoxNews.com* (blog), October 11, 2001. http://www.foxnews.com/story/2001/10/11/hidden-agendas -peace-protesters.html.

Pollack, William. *Real Boys: Rescuing Our Sons from the Myths of Boyhood*. New York: Owl Books, 1999.

Powell, Wilson M., ed. 2008. *The Democratization of Veterans for Peace, 1995– 2007*. St. Louis, MO: Veterans for Peace.

———. "Kokan-Ri." *The Veteran: Vietnam Veterans Against the War* 30, no. 2 (Winter–Spring 2000): 15.

———. *Long Ago and Yesterday: Poems of Wilson (Woody) Powell*. Self-published, 2007.

Powell, Wilson M., and Zhou Ming-Fu. *Two Walk the Golden Road: Two Soldiers, Two Cultures, Their Histories Intertwined*. Mahoment, IL: Mayhaven Publishing, 2000.

Price, Jennifer L. 2003. "Findings from the National Vietnam Veterans Readjustment Study." National Center for PTSD, U.S. Department of Veterans Affairs.

http://www.ptsd.va.gov/professional/research-bio/research/vietnam-vets-study
.asp.

Quinn, Daniel. *Ishmael: An Adventure of the Mind and Spirit*. New York: Bantam, 1992.

Real, Terrence. *I Don't Want to Talk about It: Overcoming the Secret Legacy of Male Depression*. New York: Scribner, 1998.

Research Advisory Committee on Gulf War Veterans' Illnesses. *Gulf War Illness and the Health of Gulf War Veterans: Scientific Findings and Recommendations*. Washington, DC: U.S. Government Printing Office, November 2008.

Rivas Rodriguez, Maggie, Juliana Torres, Melissa Dipiero-D'Sa, and Lindsay Fitzpatrick, eds. *A Legacy Greater Than Words: Stories of U.S. Latinos and Latinas*. Austin, TX: U.S. Latino & Latina WWII Oral History Project, 2006.

Rotskoff, Lori. *Love on the Rocks: Men, Women, and Alcohol in Post-World War II America*. Chapel Hill: University of North Carolina Press, 2002.

Rubin, Lillian B. *Intimate Strangers: Men and Women Together*. New York: Harper & Row, 1984.

Rugg, Adam. "America's Game: The NFL's 'Salute to Service' Campaign, the Diffused Military Presence, and Corporate Responsibility." *Popular Communication* 14 (2016): 21–29.

Sabo, Donald, and David Frederick Gordon, eds. *Men's Health and Illness: Gender, Power, and the Body*. Thousand Oaks, CA: Sage, 1995.

Sanchez, George J. *Becoming Mexican American: Ethnicity, Culture and Identity in Chicano Los Angeles, 1900–1945*. New York: Oxford University Press, 1993.

Sartre, Jean Paul. *Search for a Method*. Translated by Hazel Barnes. New York: Vintage, 1963.

Schnurr, Paula P. "PTSD and Combat-Related Psychiatric Symptoms in Older Veterans." *PTSD Research Quarterly* 2 (Winter 1991): 1–6.

Schwab, Joseph R., Michael A. Addis, Christopher S. Reigeluth, and Joshua L. Berger. "Silence and (In)visibility in Men's Accounts of Coping with Stressful Life Events." *Gender & Society* 30 (2016): 289–311.

Sennett, Richard, and Jonathan Cobb. *The Hidden Injuries of Class*. New York: Random House, 1972.

Sheehan, Neil, and Herick Smith. *The Pentagon Papers: The Secret History of the Vietnam War*. New York: Bantam, 1971.

Spillar, Roger J. "Shellshock." *American Heritage* 41 (May–June 1990).

Stacewicz, Richard. *Winter Soldiers: An Oral History of the Vietnam Veterans Against the War*. Chicago: Haymarket Books, 1997.

Stough-Hunter, Anjel, and Julie Hart. "Understanding Masculine Identity among Antiwar Veterans." *NORMA: International Journal for Masculinity Studies* 10 (2015): 219–235.

Strayer, R., and L. Ellenhorn. "Vietnam Veterans: A Study Exploring Adjustment Patterns and Attitudes." *Journal of Social Issues* 3 (1975): 81–94.

Swanson, David. *When the World Outlawed War.* Self-published, eBookIt.com, 2011.

Terani, Nate. "Tehran, USA: Fighting Fundamentalism in America." *TomDispatch .com*, October 30, 2016. http://www.tomdispatch.com/post/176204/tomgram%3A _nate_terani%2C_one_veteran%27s_war_on_islamophobia/.

Theweleit, Klaus. *Male Fantasies, Volume 1: Women, Floods, Bodies, History.* Translated by Stephen Conway. Minneapolis: University of Minnesota Press, 1987.

Tirman, John. *The Deaths of Others: The Fate of Civilians in America's Wars.* New York: Oxford University Press, 2011.

Turse, Nick. *Kill Anything That Moves: The Real American War in Vietnam.* New York: Picador, 2013.

U.S. Army. *Conduct of the Persian Gulf War: Final Report to Congress.* Washington, DC: U.S. Department of Defense, 1992.

U.S. Department of Veteran Affairs. "Pyridostigmine Bromide and Gulf War Veterans." Last modified March 28, 2017. https://www.publichealth.va.gov /exposures/gulfwar/sources/pyridostigmine-bromide.asp.

Veterans for Peace. *Full Disclosure: Truth about America's War in Viet Nam.* St. Louis, MO: Veterans for Peace, 2017.

Washington Labor for Peace. *A Rich Man's War a Poor Man's Fight: A Handbook for Trade Unionists on the Vietnam War.* Washington, DC: Washington Labor for Peace, 1971.

Westheider, James E. "African Americans, Civil Rights, and the Armed Forces during the Vietnam War. In *Integrating the U.S. Military: Race, Gender and Sexual Orientation since World War II*, edited by Douglas Walter Bristol Jr. and Heather Marie Stur, 96–121. Baltimore: Johns Hopkins University Press, 2017.

Wilson, William Julius. *The Truly Disadvantaged.* Chicago: University of Chicago Press, 1987.

Wingfield, Adia Harvey. *No More Invisible Man: Race and Gender in Men's Work.* Philadelphia: Temple University Press, 2012.

Young, Allan. *The Harmony of Illusions: Inventing Post-Traumatic Stress Disorder.* Princeton, NJ: Princeton University Press, 1995.

Zinn, Howard. *A People's History of the United States.* New York: Harper Perennial, 2003.

Zucchino, David, and David S. Cloud. "U. S. Military and Civilians Are Increasingly Divided." *Angeles Times*, May 24, 2015.

Index

Note: Italic page locators indicate the presence of images.

About the Author

Michael A. Messner is professor of sociology and gender studies at the University of Southern California. His books include *Some Men: Feminist Allies and the Movement to End Violence against Women* (with Max A. Greenberg and Tal Peretz), *No Slam Dunk: Gender, Sport, and the Unevenness of Social Change* (with Cheryl Cooky), and *King of the Wild Suburb: A Memoir of Fathers, Sons and Guns*. He lives in South Pasadena, California.